THE KON-TIKI EXPEDITION

In preparation by the same author
THE AMERICAN ORIGINS OF THE POLYNESIANS

by Erik Hesselberg
KON-TIKI AND I

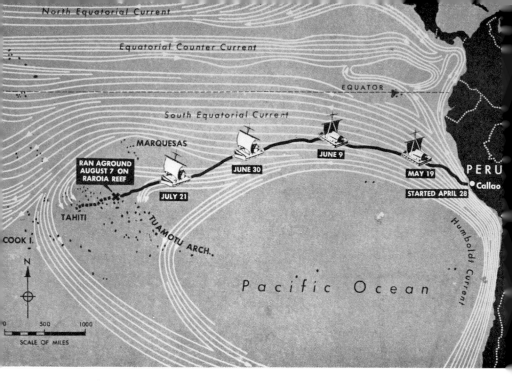

North Equatorial Current

Equatorial Counter Current

EQUATOR

South Equatorial Current

MARQUESAS

RAN AGROUND
AUGUST 7 ON
RAROIA REEF

JUNE 30

JUNE 9

MAY 19

PERU

Callao

JULY 21

STARTED APRIL 28

TAHITI

TUAMOTU ARCH.

COOK I.

N

Pacific Ocean

Humboldt Current

0   500   1000

SCALE OF MILES

Reproduced by permission of *Life*

Reproduced by permission of *Life* and *Pictorial Press*

SAIL
Canvas
15 x 18 Feet

FOREDECK
Bamboo Matting
12 Feet x 18 Feet

MAST
Mangrove Wood
29 Feet High

BOW
Pine

CABIN
Roof – Banana Leaves
Walls – Bamboo Plaits
8 Feet x 14 Feet

STEERING OAR
Mangrove Wood
19 Feet Long

MAIN LOGS
Balsa Wood
2 Feet x 45 Feet

CENTERBOARD
Pine

CROSS LOGS
Balsa Wood
1 Foot x 18 Feet

THE KON-TIKI EXPEDITION

BY RAFT ACROSS THE SOUTH SEAS

THOR HEYERDAHL

TRANSLATED BY F. H. LYON

GEORGE ALLEN & UNWIN LTD.
RUSKIN HOUSE MUSEUM STREET LONDON

FIRST PUBLISHED IN MARCH, 1950
SECOND IMPRESSION, APRIL, 1950
THIRD IMPRESSION, MAY, 1950
FOURTH IMPRESSION, JUNE, 1950
FIFTH IMPRESSION (100,000) JUNE, 1950
SIXTH IMPRESSION, JULY, 1950
SEVENTH IMPRESSION, SEPTEMBER 1950
EIGHTH IMPRESSION, NOVEMBER, 1950
NINTH IMPRESSION, DECEMBER, 1950
TENTH IMPRESSION, JANUARY, 1951
ELEVENTH IMPRESSION, FEBRUARY, 1951
TWELFTH IMPRESSION, APRIL, 1951
THIRTEENTH IMPRESSION, MAY, 1951

Translated from the Norwegian
KON-TIKI EKSPEDISJONEN
(Gyldendal Norsk Forlag, 1948)

PRINTED IN GREAT BRITAIN
in 12 point Bembo type
BY THE BLACKFRIARS PRESS LIMITED
LEICESTER

TO MY FATHER

CONTENTS

I. A Theory   *page* 11

II. An Expedition is Born   22

III. To South America   43

IV. Across the Pacific: I   73

V. Halfway   97

VI. Across the Pacific: II   129

VII. To the South Sea Islands   168

VIII. Among Polynesians   199

Appendix   230

Index   231

ILLUSTRATIONS

Facing Page

I. Members of the Kon-Tiki expedition (from left to   48
right): Knut Haugland, Bengt Danielsson, the
author, Erik Hesselberg, Torstein Raaby, Herman Watzinger

II. The Military Attaché's jeep in the Andes   49
Indian women spinning wool as they walk

III. Felling a balsa tree in the Ecuador jungle   64
Floating balsa logs down the Palenque to the Pacific

IV. Lashing the nine big logs together with hemp ropes   65

V. Ready to start in Callao harbour. The raft was an   80
exact copy of the old Indian vessels, with an
open bamboo cabin aft of a square-sail between
two masts lashed together

VI. Under full sail in the open sea. We had a hard   81
schooling in the Humboldt Current, for the last
instructors in raft sailing had been dead for
centuries

VII. Before our fresh fruit came to an end fish had   96
begun to come on board
We cooked over a Primus in a box, and had our
meals on the edge of the raft outside the cabin

VIII. In the bamboo cabin, sheltered from wind and sun.   97
(From left to right) Watzinger, Haugland,
Raaby, Danielsson, author
Raaby in the wireless corner, behind a cardboard
partition decorated by Danielsson. Raaby and
Haugland sent daily wireless reports to the
Meteorological Institute at Washington

IX. Hesselberg took our position daily   112

Facing Page

IX.—*contd.* The captain at the helm. We each in turn   112
      put in two hours at the steering oar
      Watzinger taking last wind measurement of the
      day
      Evening outside the cabin door

  X. Kon-Tiki's bearded face. The head was copied   113
      from a prehistoric carving of Kon-Tiki

 XI. Dolphins swam with the raft right across the Pacific   128
      —splendid eating and easily caught
      The gold-finned tunny provided excellent fishing.
      There was food enough in one fish for a whole
      flotilla of rafts

XII. Hauling a shark on board   129
      The shark once on deck, its captor kept out of the
      way till it had ceased to snap

XIII. Hesselberg singing and playing   144
      A good catch of tunnies, sharks and bonitos

XIV. A meal on deck   145

 XV. A whale at close quarters   160
      Top of whale shark's huge dorsal fin
      A whale shark, the world's largest fish
      Raaby with snake mackerel (*Gempylus*)

XVI. A faint breeze and tropical heat—things that   161
      troubled us little. On calm days we went for
      long trips in the rubber dinghy
      Halfway—over 2,000 sea miles from nearest land to
      east and west. Hesselberg, mounted on a box,
      taking the sun's altitude

XVII. Chaos on board after the stranding: the mast   176
      broken and the cabin knocked flat
      Kon-Tiki stranded on the Raroia coral reef. She
      lay there for several days

XVIII. Planting in Polynesia a cocoanut from Peru   177
      Teriieroo, the last chief on Tahiti. He had adopted
      the author as his son ten years before under
      the name Terai Mateata (Blue Sky)
      Vahine on Tahiti

CHAPTER I

A THEORY

Retrospect—The Old Man on Fatuhiva—Wind and Current—
Hunting for Tiki—Who peopled Polynesia?—Riddle of the South
Seas—Theories and Facts—Legend of Kon-Tiki and the White
Race—War comes.

JUST occasionally you find yourself in an odd situation. You get into it by degrees and in the most natural way but when you are right in the midst of it you are suddenly astonished and ask yourself how in the world it all came about.

If, for example, you put to sea on a wooden raft with a parrot and five companions, it is inevitable that sooner or later you will wake up one morning out at sea, perhaps a little better rested than ordinarily, and begin to think about it.

On one such morning I sat writing in a dew-drenched log-book :

"17th May. Norwegian Independence Day. Heavy sea. Fair wind. I am cook to-day and found 7 flying fish on deck, one squid on the cabin roof, and one unknown fish in Torstein's sleeping bag . . ."

Here the pencil stopped, and the same thought came sneaking out: this is really a queer Seventeenth of May; indeed, taken all round, a most peculiar existence. How did it all begin?

If I turned left, I had an unimpeded view of a vast blue sea with hissing waves, rolling by close at hand in an endless pursuit of an ever retreating horizon. If I turned right, I saw the inside of a shadowy cabin in which a bearded individual was lying on his back reading Goethe, with his bare toes carefully dug into the lattice-work in the low bamboo roof of the crazy little cabin that was our common home.

"Bengt," I said, pushing away the green parrot, which wanted to perch on the log-book. "Can you tell me how the hell we come to be doing this?"

Goethe sank down under the red-gold beard.

"The devil I do, you know best yourself. It was your damned idea, but I think it's grand."

He moved his toes three bars up and went on reading Goethe unperturbed. Outside the cabin three other fellows were working in the roasting sun on the bamboo deck. They were half-naked, brown-skinned and bearded, with stripes of salt down their backs and looking as if they had never done anything else than float wooden rafts westward across the Pacific. Eric came crawling in through the opening with his sextant and a pile of papers:

"Ninety-eight degrees forty-six minutes west by eight degrees two minutes south—a good last day's run, chaps!"

He took my pencil and drew a tiny circle on a chart which hung on the bamboo wall; a tiny circle at the end of a chain of nineteen circles that curved across from the port of Callao on the coast of Peru. Herman, Knut and Torstein too came eagerly crawling in to see the new little circle that placed us a good forty sea miles nearer the South Sea islands than the last in the chain.

"Do you see, boys?" said Herman proudly: "that means we're 850 sea miles from the coast of Peru."

"And we've another 3,500 to go to get to the nearest islands," Knut added cautiously.

"And to be quite precise," said Torstein, "we're 16,000 feet above the bottom of the sea and a few fathoms below the moon."

So now we all knew exactly where we were, and I could go on speculating as to why. The parrot did not care; he only wanted to tug at the log. And the sea was just as round, just as sky-encircled, blue upon blue.

Perhaps the whole thing had begun the winter before, in the office of a New York museum. Or perhaps it had already begun ten years earlier, on a little island in the Marquesas group in the middle of the Pacific. Perhaps we should land on the same island now, unless the north-east wind sent us farther south, in the direction of Tahiti and the Tuamotu group. I could see the little island clearly in my mind's eye, with its jagged rust-red mountains, the green jungle which flowed down their slopes towards the sea, and the slender palms that waited and waved along the shore. The island was called Fatuhiva, and there was no land between it and us where we lay drifting, but nevertheless it was thousands of sea miles away. I saw the narrow Ouia valley where it opened out towards the sea, and remembered so well how we sat there on the lonely beach and looked out over this same endless sea, evening after evening. I was accompanied by my wife then, not among bearded pirates as now. We were collecting all kinds of live creatures, and images and other relics of a dead culture. I remember very well one particular evening. The civilised world seemed so incomprehensibly remote and unreal. We had lived on the island for nearly a year, the only white people there; we had of our own will forsaken the good things of civilisation along with its evils. We lived in a hut we had built for ourselves on piles under the palms down by the shore, and ate what the tropical woods and the Pacific had to offer us.

In a hard, but practical school we gained insight into many of the curious problems of the Pacific. I think that both in body and mind we often followed in the traces of the first primitive men who had come to those islands from an unknown country, and whose Polynesian posterity ruled unchallenged over the island empire till men of our own race came with the Bible in one hand and powder and brandy in the other.

On that particular evening we sat, as so often before, down on the beach in the moonlight, with the sea in front of us. Wide awake and filled with the romance that surrounded us, we let no impression escape us. We filled our nostrils with an aroma of rank jungle and salt sea, and heard the wind's rustle in leaves and palm-tops. At regular intervals all other noises were drowned by the great breakers that rolled straight in from the sea and rushed in foaming over the land till they were broken up into circles of froth among the shore boulders. There was a roaring and rustling and rumbling among millions of glistening stones, till all grew quiet again when the sea-water had withdrawn to gather strength for a new attack on the invincible coast.

"It's queer," said my wife, "but there are never breakers like this on the other side of the island."

"No," said I, "but this is the windward side, there's always a sea running on this side."

We went on sitting there and admiring the sea which, it seemed, never wanted to give up demonstrating that here it came, rolling in from eastward, eastward, eastward. It was the eternal east wind, the trade wind, which had disturbed the sea's surface, dug it up and rolled it forward, up over the horizon to the east and over here to the islands. Here the unbroken advance of the sea was finally shattered against cliffs and reefs, while the east wind simply rose above coast and woods and mountains and continued westward unhindered, from island to island, towards the sunset.

So had the seas and the light cloud formations rolled up over the same eastern horizon since the morning of time. The first men who reached these islands knew well enough that this was so. Birds and insects knew it too, and the vegetation of the islands was completely dominated by this circumstance. And we knew ourselves that far, far below the horizon to eastward, where the clouds came up, lay the open coast of South America. It was 4,300 sea miles away, and there was nothing but sea between.

We gazed at the driving clouds and the heaving moonlit sea, and we listened to an old man who squatted half-naked before us and stared down into the dying glow from a little burnt-out fire.

"Tiki," the old man said quietly, "he was both god and chief. It was Tiki who brought my ancestors to these islands where we live now. Before that we lived in a big country beyond the sea."

He poked the coals with a stick to keep them from going out. The old man sat thinking. He lived for ancient times and was firmly fettered to them. He worshipped his forefathers and their deeds back to the time of the gods. And he looked forward to being reunited with them. Old Tei Tetua was the sole survivor of all the extinct tribes on the east coast of Fatuhiva. How old he was he did not know, but his wrinkled, bark-brown, leathery skin looked as if it had been dried in the sun and wind for a hundred years. He was certainly one of the few on these islands who still remembered and believed his father's and grandfather's legendary stories of the great Polynesian chief-god Tiki, son or the sun.

When we crept to bed that night in the little pile hut, old Tei Tetua's stories of Tiki and the islanders' old home beyond the sea continued to haunt my brain, accompanied by the muffled roar of the surf in the distance. It sounded like a voice from far-off times which, it seemed, had something it wanted to tell, out there in the night. I could not sleep. It was as though time no longer existed, and Tiki and his seafarers were just making their first landing in the surf on the beach below. A thought suddenly struck me, and I said to my wife:

"Say, have you noticed that the huge stone figures of Tiki up in the jungle are remarkably like the gigantic monoliths which are relics of extinct civilisations in South America?"

I felt sure that a roar of agreement came from the breakers. And then they slowly subsided, while I slept.

So, perhaps, the whole thing began. So began, in any case, a whole series of events which finally landed the six of us and a green parrot on board a raft off the coast of South America.

I remember how I scared my father and astonished my mother and my friends when I came back to Norway and handed over my glass jars of beetles and fish from Fatuhiva to the University Zoological Museum. I wanted to give up animal studies and tackle primitive peoples. The unsolved mysteries of the South Seas had fascinated me. There must be a rational solution of them, and I had made my objective the identification of the legendary hero Tiki.

In the years that followed breakers and jungle ruins were a kind of remote, unreal dream which formed the background and accompaniment to my studies of the Pacific peoples. Useless as it is to try to interpret the thoughts and actions of a primitive people by reading books and visiting museums, it is just as useless for an explorer in our time to try to reach the horizons which can be contained in a single bookshelf.

Scientific works, journals from the time of the earliest explorations, and endless collections in museums in Europe and America offered a wealth of material for use in the puzzle I wanted to try to put together. Since our own race first reached

the Pacific islands, after the discovery of America, investigators
in all branches of science have collected an almost bottomless
store of information about the inhabitants of the South Seas, and
all the peoples living round about them. But there has never been
any agreement as to the origin of this isolated island people, or
the reason why this type is only found scattered over all the
solitary islands in the eastern part of the Pacific.

When the first Europeans at last ventured to cross this greatest
of all oceans, they discovered to their amazement that right out
in the midst of it lay a number of small mountainous islands and
flat coral reefs, isolated from each other and from the world in
general by vast areas of sea. And every single one of these islands
was already inhabited by people who had come there before
them—tall handsome people who met them on the beach with
dogs and pigs and fowls. Where had they come from ? They
talked a language which no other people knew. And the men of
our race, who boldly called themselves the discoverers of the
islands, found cultivated fields, and villages with temples and huts,
on every single habitable island. On some islands, indeed, they
found old pyramids, paved roads and carved stone statues as high
as a four-storey house in Europe. But the explanation of the
whole mystery was lacking. Who were these people, and where
had they come from ?

One can safely say that the answers to these riddles have been
nearly as many in number as the works which have treated of
them. Specialists in different fields have put forward quite
different solutions, but have always had their affirmations dis-
proved later by logical arguments from experts who have worked
along other lines. Malaya, India, China, Japan, Arabia, Egypt,
the Caucasus, Atlantis, even Germany and Norway, have been
seriously championed as the Polynesians' homeland. But every
·time some "snag" of a decisive character has appeared and put
the whole affair into the melting-pot again.

And where science stopped imagination began. The mysterious
monoliths on Easter Island, and all the other relics of unknown
origin on this little exposed island, lying in complete solitude
halfway between the nearest islands and the coast of South

America, gave rise to all sorts of speculations. Many observed that the finds on Easter Island recalled in many ways the relics of the prehistoric civilisations of South America. Perhaps there had once been a bridge of land over the sea, and this had sunk? Perhaps Easter Island, and all the other South Sea islands which had monuments of the same kind, were remains which a sunken continent had left sticking up out of the sea?

This has been a popular theory and an acceptable explanation among laymen, but geologists and other investigators do not care for it. Zoologists, moreover, prove quite simply, from the study of insects and snails on the South Sea islands, that throughout the history of mankind these islands have been completely isolated from one another and from the continents round them, exactly as they are to-day.

We know, therefore, with absolute certainty that the original Polynesian race must at some time, willingly or unwillingly, have come drifting or sailing to these out-of-the-way islands. And a rather closer look at the inhabitants of the South Seas shows that it cannot have been very many centuries since they came. For even if the Polynesians live scattered over an area of sea four times as large as the whole of Europe, nevertheless they have not managed to develop different languages in the different islands. It is thousands of sea miles from Hawaii in the north to New Zealand in the south, from Samoa in the west to Easter Island in the east, but yet all these isolated tribes speak dialects of a common language which we have called Polynesian. Writing was unknown in all the islands, except for a few wooden tablets bearing incomprehensible hieroglyphs which the natives preserved on Easter Island, though neither they themselves nor anyone else could read them. But they had schools, and the poetical teaching of history was their most important branch, for in Polynesia history was the same as religion. They were ancestor-worshippers; they worshipped their dead chiefs right back to Tiki's time, and of Tiki himself it was said that he was son of the sun.

On almost every single island learned men could rattle off the names of all the island's chiefs right back to the time when it

B

was first peopled. And to assist their memories they often used a complicated system of knots on twisted strings, as the Inca Indians did in Peru. Modern investigators have collected all these local genealogies from the different islands, and found that they agree with one another with astonishing exactness, both in names and number of generations. It has been discovered in this way, by taking an average Polynesian generation to represent twenty-five years, that the South Sea islands were not peopled before about A.D. 500. A new cultural wave with a new string of chiefs shows that another and still later immigration reached the same islands as late as about A.D. 1100.

Where could such late immigrations have come from? Very few investigators seem to have taken into consideration the decisive factor that the people which came to the islands at so late a date was a pure Stone Age people. Despite their intelligence and in all other respects astonishingly high culture, these sea-farers brought with them a certain type of stone axe and a quantity of other characteristic Stone Age tools, and spread these over all the islands to which they came. We must not forget that, apart from single isolated peoples inhabiting primeval forest, and certain backward races, there were no cultures in the world of any reproductive capacity which were still at the Stone Age level in A.D. 500 or 1100, except in the New World. There even the highest Indian civilisations were totally ignorant of the uses of iron, and used stone axes and tools of the same type as those used in the South Sea islands right up to the time of the explorations.

These numerous Indian civilisations were the Polynesians' nearest relations to the east. To westward there lived only the black-skinned primitive peoples of Australia and Melanesia, distant relations of the negroes, and beyond them again were Indonesia and the coast of Asia, where the Stone Age lay farther back in time than, perhaps, anywhere else in the world.

Thus both my suspicions and my attention were turned more and more away from the Old World, where so many had searched and none had found, and over to the known and unknown Indian civilisations of America, which no one hitherto had taken into consideration. And on the nearest coast due east, where to-day the South American republic of Peru stretches from the Pacific up into the mountains, there was no lack of traces if one only looked for them. Here an unknown people had once lived and established one of the world's strangest civilisations, till suddenly, long ago, they had vanished as though swept away from the earth's surface. They left behind them enormous stone statues resembling human beings, which recalled those on Pitcairn, the Marquesas and Easter Islands, and huge pyramids built in steps like those on Tahiti and Samoa. They hewed out of the mountains with stone axes stone blocks as large as railway trucks and transported them for miles about the countryside, set them up on end or placed them on top of one another to form gateways, huge walls and terraces, exactly as we find them on some of the islands in the Pacific.

The Inca Indians had their great empire in this mountain country when the first Spaniards came to Peru. They told the Spaniards that the colossal monuments that stood deserted about the landscape were erected by a race of white gods which had lived there before the Incas themselves became rulers. These vanished architects were described as wise, peaceful instructors, who had originally come from the north long ago in the morning of time, and had taught the Incas' primitive forefathers architecture and agriculture, as well as manners and customs. They were unlike other Indians in having white skins and long beards; they were also taller than the Incas. Finally they left Peru as suddenly as they had come; the Incas themselves took over power in the country, and the white teachers vanished for ever from the coast of South America and fled westward across the Pacific.

Now it happened that when the Europeans came to the Pacific islands they were quite astonished to find that many of the natives had almost white skins and were bearded. On many of the islands there were whole families conspicuous for their remarkably pale skins, hair varying from reddish to blonde, blue-grey eyes, and almost Semitic, hook-nosed faces. The Polynesians, apart from these, had golden-brown skins, raven hair and flat pulpy noses. The red-haired individuals called themselves *urukehu* and said that they were directly descended from the first chiefs on the islands, who were white gods, such as Tangaroa, Kane and Tiki. Legends of mysterious white men, from whom the islanders were originally descended, were current all over Polynesia. When Roggeween discovered Easter Island in 1722 he noticed to his surprise "white men" among those on shore. And the people of Easter Island could themselves tot up those of their ancestors who were white-skinned, right back to the time of Tiki and Hotu Matua, when they first came sailing acros the sea "from a mountainous land in the east which was parched by the sun."

As I pursued my search, I found in Peru surprising traces in culture, mythology and language which impelled me to go on digging ever deeper and with greater concentration, to identify the place of origin of the Polynesian tribal god Tiki.

And I found what I hoped for. I was sitting reading the Inca legends of the sun-king Virakocha, who was the supreme head of the vanished white people in Peru. I read:

"Virakocha is an Inca (Ketchua) name and consequently of fairly recent date. The original name of the sun-god Virakocha, which seems to have been more used in Peru in old times, was Kon-Tiki or Illa-Tiki, which means Sun-Tiki or Fire-Tiki. Kon-Tiki was high priest and sun-king of the Incas' legendary 'white men' who had left the enormous ruins on the shores of Lake Titicaca. The legend runs that Kon-Tiki was attacked by a chief named Cari who came from the Coquimbo valley. In a battle on an island in Lake Titicaca the mysterious white men with beards were massacred, but Kon-Tiki himself and his closest companions escaped and later came down to the Pacific coast, whence they finally disappeared overseas to the westward."

I was no longer in doubt that the white chief-god Sun-Tiki, whom the Incas declared that their forefathers had driven out of Peru on to the Pacific, was identical with the white chief-god Tiki, son of the sun, whom the inhabitants of all the eastern Pacific islands hailed as the original founder of their race. And the details of Sun-Tiki's life in Peru, with the ancient names of places round Lake Titicaca, cropped up again in historic legends current among the natives of the Pacific islands.

But all over Polynesia I found indications that Kon-Tiki's

peaceable race had not been able to hold the islands alone for long. Indications that sea-going war canoes, as large as Viking ships, and lashed together two and two, had brought North-west Indians across the sea to Hawaii and farther south to all the other islands. They had mingled their blood with that of Kon-Tiki's race and brought a new civilisation to the island kingdom. This was the second Stone Age people that came to Polynesia, without metals, without the potter's art, without wheel or loom or cereal cultivation in A.D. 1100.

So it came about that I was excavating rock carvings in the ancient Polynesian style among the North-West Indians in British Columbia when the Germans burst into Norway.

Right turn, left turn, about turn. Washing barrack stairs, polishing boots, wireless school, parachute—and at last a Murmansk convoy to Finmark, where the war-god of technique reigned in the sun-god's absence all the dark winter through.

Peace came. And one day my theory was complete. I must go to America and put it forward.

CHAPTER II

AN EXPEDITION IS BORN

Among Specialists—The Turning Point—At the Sailors' Home—
Last Resource—Explorers Club—The New Equipment—I find a
Companion—A Triumvirate—One Painter and Two Saboteurs—
To Washington—Conference at the War Department—To Q.M.G.
with Desiderata—Money Problems—With Diplomatists at U.N.—
We fly to Ecuador.

SO it had begun, by a fire on a South Sea island, where an
old native sat telling legends and stories of his tribe. Many
years later I sat with another old man, this time in a dark
office on one of the upper floors of a big museum in New York.

Round us, in well-arranged glass cases, lay pottery fragments
from the known past, traces leading into the mists of antiquity.
The walls were lined with books too. Some of them one man
had written and hardly ten men had read. The old man, who
had read all these books and written some of them, sat behind
his work-table, white-haired and good-humoured. But now, for
sure, I had trodden on his toes, for he gripped the arms of his
chair uneasily and looked as if I had interrupted him in a game
of patience.

"No!" he said. "Never!"

Father Christmas would have looked as he did then if someone
had dared to affirm that next year Christmas would be on Mid-
summer Day.

"You're wrong, absolutely wrong," he repeated, and shook
his head indignantly to drive out the idea.

"But you haven't read my arguments yet," I urged, nodding
hopefully towards the manuscript which lay on the table.

"Arguments!" he said. "You can't treat ethnographic problems
as a sort of detective mystery!"

"Why not?" I said. "I've based all the conclusions on my own
observations and the facts that science has recorded."

22

"The task of science is investigation pure and simple," he said quietly. "Not to try to prove this or that."

He pushed the unopened manuscript carefully to one side and leaned over the table.

"It's quite true that South America was the home of some of the most curious civilisations of antiquity, and that we know neither who they were nor where they vanished to when the Incas came into power. But one thing we do know for certain—that none of the peoples of South America got over to the islands in the Pacific."

He looked at me searchingly, and continued:

"Do you know why? The answer's simple enough. They couldn't get there. They had no boats!"

"They had rafts," I objected hesitatingly. "You know, balsa-wood rafts."

The old man smiled and said quietly:

"Well, you can try a trip from Peru to the Pacific islands on a balsa-wood raft."

I could find nothing to say. It was getting late. We both rose. The old scientist patted me kindly on the shoulder as he saw me out, and said that if I wanted help I had only to come to him. But I must in future specialise on Polynesia *or* America, and not mix up two separate anthropological areas. He reached back over the table.

"You've forgotten this," he said, and handed back my manuscript. I glanced at the title "Polynesia and America; a Study of Prehistoric Relations." I stuck the manuscript under my arm and clattered down the stairs out into the crowds in the street.

That evening I went down and knocked on the door of an old flat in an out of the way corner of Greenwich Village. I liked taking my little problems down there when I felt they had made life a bit tangled.

A skinny little man with a long nose opened the door a chink before he threw it wide open with a broad smile and pulled me in. He took me straight into the little kitchen, where he set me to work carrying plates and forks while he himself doubled the quantity of the indefinable but savoury-smelling concoction he was heating over the gas.

"Nice of you to come," he said. "How goes it?"

"Rottenly," I said. "No one will read the manuscript."

He filled the plates and we attacked the contents.

"It's like this," he said; "all the people you've been to see think it's just a passing idea you've got. You know, here in America, people turn up with so many queer ideas."

"And there's another thing," I said.

"Yes," said he. "Your way of approaching the problem. They're specialists, the whole lot of them, and they don't believe in a method of work which cuts into every special branch from botany to archaeology. They limit their own scope to be able to dig in the depths for details with more concentration. Modern research demands that every special branch shall dig in its own hole. It's not usual for anyone to sort out what comes up out of the holes and try to put it together."

He rose and reached for a heavy manuscript.

"Look here," he said. "My last work on bird designs in Chinese peasant embroidery. Took me seven years, but it was accepted for publication at once. They want detailed work nowadays."

Carl was right. But to solve the problems of the Pacific without throwing light on them from all sides was, it seemed to me, like doing a puzzle and only using the pieces of one's own colour.

We cleared the table, and I helped him dry after washing up.

"Nothing fresh from the university in Chicago?"

"No."

"But what did your old friend at the museum say to-day?"

I drawled: "He wasn't interested either. He said that so long as the Indians had only open rafts, it was futile to consider the possibility of their having discovered the Pacific islands."

The little man suddenly began to dry his plate furiously.

"Yes," he said at last. "To tell the truth, to me too, that seems a practical objection to your theory."

I looked gloomily at the little ethnologist whom I had thought to be a sworn ally.

"But don't misunderstand me," he hastened to say. "In one way I think you're right, but in another way it's so incomprehensible. My work on designs supports your theory."

"Carl," I said. "I'm so sure that the Indians crossed the Pacific on their rafts that I'm willing to build a raft of the kind myself and cross the sea just to prove that it's possible."

"You're mad!"

My friend took it for a joke and laughed half-scared at the thought.

"You're mad! A raft?"

He did not know what to say, and only stared at me with a queer expression, as though waiting for a smile to show that I was joking.

He did not get one. I saw now that in practice no one would accept my theory, because of the apparently endless stretch of sea between Peru and Polynesia which I was trying to bridge with no other aid than a prehistoric raft.

Carl looked at me uncertainly.

"Now we'll go out and have a drink," he said.

We went out and had four.

My rent became due that week. At the same time a letter from the Bank of Norway informed me that I could have no more dollars. Currency restrictions. I picked up my trunk and took the underground out to Brooklyn. Here I was taken in at the Norwegian Sailors' Home, where the food was good and sustaining and the prices suited my wallet. I got a little room a floor or two up, but had my meals with all the seamen in a big dining-room downstairs.

Seamen came and seamen went. They varied in type, dimensions and degrees of sobriety, but they all had one thing in common—when they talked about the sea they knew what they were talking about. I learnt that waves and rough sea did not increase with the depth of the sea or distance from land. On the contrary, squalls were often more treacherous along the coast than in the open sea. And shoal water, backwash along the coast or ocean currents penned in close to the land could throw up a rougher sea than was usual far out. A vessel which could hold her own along an open coast could hold her own farther out. I also learnt that in a high sea big ships were inclined to plunge bow or stern into the seas, so that tons of water could rush on board and twist steel tubes like feathers, while a small boat in the same sea often made good weather, because she could find room between the lines of waves and dance freely over them like a gull. There were men who had got safely away in boats after the seas had made the ship herself founder.

But they knew little about rafts. A raft—that wasn't a ship, it had no keel or bulwarks. It was just something floating on which to save oneself in an emergency, until one was picked up by a boat of some kind. One of them, nevertheless, had great respect for rafts in the open sea; he had drifted about on one for three weeks when a German torpedo sank his ship in mid-Atlantic.

"But you can't navigate a raft," he added. "It goes sideways and backwards and round as the wind takes it."

In the library I dug out records left by the first Europeans who had reached the Pacific coast of South America. There was no lack of sketches or descriptions of the Indians' big balsa-wood rafts. They had square-sail and centreboard and a long steering oar astern. So they could be manoeuvred.

Weeks passed at the Sailors' Home. No reply from Chicago or the other cities to which I had sent copies of my theory. No one had read them.

Then, one Saturday, I pulled myself together and marched into a ship-chandler's shop down in Water Street. There I was politely addressed as "captain" when I bought a pilot chart of the Pacific. With the chart rolled up under my arm I took the suburban railway out to Ossining, where I was a regular week-end guest of a young Norwegian married couple who had a charming place in the country. He had been a sea captain and was now office manager for the Fred Olsen Line in New York.

After a refreshing plunge in the swimming pool city life was completely forgotten for the rest of the week-end, and when

Ambjörg brought the cocktail tray we sat down on the lawn in the hot sun. I could contain myself no longer, but spread the chart out on the grass and asked Wilhelm if he thought a raft could carry men alive from Peru to the South Sea islands.

He looked at me rather than at the chart, half taken aback, but replied at once in the affirmative. I felt as much lightened as if I had a balloon inside my shirt, for I knew that everything that had to do with navigation and sailing was to Wilhelm both job and hobby. He was initiated into my plans at once. To my astonishment he simply declared that it was sheer madness.

"But you said just now that you thought it was possible," I interrupted.

"Quite right," he admitted. "But the chances of its going wrong are just as great. You yourself have never been on a balsa raft, and you're imagining yourself all of a sudden across the Pacific on one. Perhaps it'll come off, perhaps it won't. The old Indians in Peru had generations of experience to build upon. Perhaps ten rafts went to the bottom for every one that got across—or perhaps hundreds in the course of centuries. As you say, the Incas navigated in the open sea with whole flotillas of these balsa rafts. Then, if anything went wrong, they could be picked up by the nearest raft. But who's going to pick you up, out in mid-ocean? Even if you take wireless for use in an emergency, don't think it's going to be easy to find a little raft down among the seas thousands of miles from land. In a storm you can be washed off the raft and drowned many times over before anyone gets to you. You'd better wait quietly here till someone has had time to read your manuscript. Write again and stir them up; it's no good if you don't."

"I can't wait any longer now; I shan't have a cent left soon."

"Then you can come and stay with us. For that matter, how can you think of starting an expedition from South America without money?"

"It's easier to interest people in an expedition than in an unread manuscript."

"But what can you gain by it?"

"Destroy one of the weightiest arguments against the theory, quite apart from the fact that science will pay some attention to the affair."

"But if things go wrong?"

"Then I shan't have proved anything."

"Then you'd ruin your own theory in the eyes of everyone, wouldn't you?"

"Perhaps, but all the same one in ten might have got through before us, as you said."

The children came out to play croquet, and we did not discuss the matter any more that day.

The next week-end I was back at Ossining with the chart under my arm. And when I left there was a long pencil line from the coast of Peru to the Tuamotu islands in the Pacific. My friend the captain had given up hope of making me drop the idea, and we had sat together for hours working out the raft's probable speed.

"Ninety-seven days," said Wilhelm, "but remember that's only in theoretically ideal conditions, with a fair wind all the time and assuming that the raft can really sail as you think it can. You must definitely allow at least four months for the trip, and be prepared for a good deal more."

"All right," I said optimistically, "let us allow at least four months, but do it in ninety-seven days."

The little room at the Sailors' Home seemed twice as cosy as usual when I came home that evening and sat down on the edge of the bed with the chart. I paced out the floor as exactly as the bed and chest of drawers gave me room to do. Oh yes, the raft would be much larger than this. I leaned out of the window to get a glimpse of the great city's remote starry sky, only visible right overhead, between the high yard walls. If there was little room on board the raft, anyhow there would be room for the sky and all its stars above us.

In West 72nd Street, near Central Park, is one of the most exclusive clubs in New York. There is nothing more than a brightly polished little brass plate with "Explorers Club" on it to tell passers-by that there is anything out of the way inside the doors. But once inside, one might have made a parachute jump into a strange world, thousands of miles from New York's lines of motor-cars flanked by skyscrapers. When the door to New York is shut behind one, one is swallowed up in an atmosphere of lion-hunting, mountaineering and polar life, combined with the feeling that one is sitting in the saloon of a comfortable yacht on a trip round the world. Trophies of hippopotamus and deer, big-game rifles, tusks, war drums and spears, Indian carpets, idols and model ships, flags, photographs and maps surround the members of the club when they assemble for a dinner or to hear lecturers from distant countries.

After my journey to the Marquesas Islands I had been elected an active member of the club, and as junior member I had seldom missed a meeting when I was in town. So when I now entered the club on a rainy November evening I was not a little surprised to find the place in an unusual state. In the middle of the floor lay an inflated rubber raft with boat rations and accessories, while parachutes, rubber overalls, safety jackets and polar equipment covered walls and tables, together with water distillation balloons and other curious inventions. A newly elected member of the club, Colonel Haskin, of the equipment laboratory of the Air Material Command, was to give a lecture and demonstrate a number of new military inventions which, he thought, would in the future be of use to scientific expeditions, in both north and south.

After the lecture there was a vigorous and cheerful discussion. The well-known Danish polar explorer Peter Freuchen, tall and bulky, rose with a sceptical shake of his huge beard. He had no faith in such new-fangled patents. He himself had once used a rubber boat and bag-tent on one of his Greenland expeditions instead of an Eskimo kayak and igloo, and it had all but cost him his life. First he had nearly been frozen to death in a snow-storm because the zip fastening of the tent had frozen up so that he could not even get in. And after that he had been out fishing when the hook caught in the inflated rubber boat, and the boat was punctured and sank under him like a bit of rag. He and an Eskimo friend had managed to get ashore that time in a kayak which came to their help. He was sure no clever modern inventor could sit in his laboratory and think out anything better than what the experience of thousands of years had taught the Eskimos to use in their own regions.

The discussion ended with a surprising offer from Colonel Haskin. Active members of the club could, on their next expeditions, select any they liked of the new inventions he had demonstrated, on the sole condition that they should let his laboratory know what they thought of the things when they came back.

That was that. I was the last to leave the club rooms that evening. I had to go over every minute detail of all this brand-new equipment which had so suddenly tumbled into my hands, and which was at my disposal for the asking. It was exactly what I wanted—equipment with which we could try to save our lives if, contrary to expectation, our wooden raft should show signs of breaking up and we had no other rafts near by.

All this equipment was still occupying my thoughts at the breakfast table in the Sailors' Home next morning when a well-dressed young man of athletic build came along with his breakfast tray and sat down at the same table as myself. We began to chat, and it appeared that he too was not a seaman, but a university-trained engineer from Trondheim who was in America to buy machinery parts and obtain experience in refrigerating technique. He was living not far away and often had his meals at the Sailors' Home because there was good Norwegian cooking there. He asked me what I was doing, and I gave him a short account of my plans. I said that if I did not get a definite answer about my manuscript before the end of the week, I should get under way with the starting of the raft expedition. My table companion did not say much, but listened with great interest.

Four days later we ran across one another again in the same dining-room.

"Have you decided whether you're going on your trip or not?" he asked.

"Yes," I said. "I'm going."

"When?"

"As soon as possible. If I hang about much longer now the

gales will be coming up from the Antarctic and it will be hurricane season in the islands too. I must leave Peru in a very few months, but I must get money first and get the whole business organised."

"How many men will there be?"

"I've thought of having six men in all; that'll give some change of society on board the raft and is the right number for four hours' steering in every twenty-four hours."

He stood for a moment or two as though chewing over a thought, then burst out emphatically:

"The devil, but how I'd like to be in it! I could undertake technical measurements and tests. Of course you'll have to support your experiment with accurate measurements of winds and currents and waves. Remember that you're going to cross vast spaces of sea which are practically unknown because they lie outside all shipping routes. An expedition like yours can make interesting hydrographic and meteorological investigations; I could make good use of my thermo-dynamics."

I knew nothing about the man beyond what an open face can say. It may say a good deal.

"All right," I said. "We'll go together."

His name was Herman Watzinger; he was as much of a landlubber as myself.

A few days later I took Herman as my guest to the Explorers Club. Here we ran straight into the polar explorer Peter Freuchen. Freuchen has the blessed quality of never disappearing in the crowd. As big as a barn door and bristling with beard, he looks like a messenger from the open tundra. A special atmosphere surrounds him—it is as though he were going about with a grizzly bear on a lead.

We took him over to a big map on the wall and told him about our plan of crossing the Pacific on an Indian raft. His boyish blue eyes grew as large as saucers, and he tugged at his beard as he listened. Then he stamped his wooden leg on the floor and tightened his belt several holes.

"Damn it, boys! I should like to go with you!"

The old Greenland traveller filled our beer-mugs and began to tell us of his belief in primitive peoples' vessels, and these peoples' ability to make their way by accommodating themselves to nature both on land and at sea. He himself had travelled by raft down the great rivers of Siberia and towed natives on rafts astern of his ship along the coast of the Arctic. And as he narrated he tugged at his beard and said we were certainly going to have a great time.

Through Freuchen's eager support of our plan the wheels began to turn at a dangerous speed, and they soon ran right into the printers' ink of the Scandinavian Press. The very next morning there came a violent knocking on my door in the Sailors' Home; I was wanted on the telephone in the passage downstairs. The result of the conversation was that Herman and I, the same evening, rang the door-bell of a flat in a fashionable quarter of the city. We were received by a well-dressed young man in patent leather slippers, wearing a silk dressing-gown over a blue suit. He made an impression almost of softness, and apologised for having a cold, with a scented handkerchief held under his nose. None the less we knew that this fellow had made a name in America by his exploits as an airman in the war. Besides our apparently sedate host, two energetic young journalists, simply bursting with activity and ideas, were present. We knew one of them as an able correspondent.

Our host explained over a bottle of good whisky that he was interested in our expedition. He offered to raise the necessary capital if we would undertake to write newspaper articles and go on lecture tours after our return. We came to an agreement at last, and drank to successful co-operation between the backers of the expedition and those taking part in it. From now on all our economic problems would be solved; they were taken over by our backers and would not trouble us. Herman and I were at once to set about raising a crew and equipment, build a raft, and get off before the hurricane season began.

Next day Herman resigned his post, and we set about our task seriously. I had already obtained a promise from the research laboratory of the Air Material Command to send everything I had asked for and more through the Explorers Club; they said that such an expedition as ours was admirably suited to test their equipment. This was a good start. Our most important tasks were now, first of all, to find four suitable men who were willing to go with us on the raft, and to obtain supplies for the journey.

A party of men who were to put to sea together on board a raft must be chosen with care. Otherwise there would be trouble and mutiny after a month's isolation at sea. I did not want to man the raft with sailors; they knew hardly any more about managing a raft than we did ourselves, and I did not want to have it argued afterwards, when we had brought the thing off, that it was perhaps because we were better seamen than the old raft-builders in Peru. Nevertheless we wanted one man on board who at any rate could use a sextant and mark our course on a chart as a basis for all our scientific reports.

"I know a painter," I said to Herman. "He's a big hefty chap who can play the guitar and is full of fun. He went through the navigation school and sailed round the world several times before he settled down at home with brush and palette. I've known him since we were boys and have often been on camping tours with him in the mountains at home. I'll write and ask him; I'm sure he'll come."

"He sounds all right," Herman nodded, "and then we want someone who can manage the wireless."

"Wireless!" I said, horrified, "what the hell do we want with that? It's out of place on a prehistoric raft."

"Not at all, it's a safety precaution which won't have any effect on your theory so long as we don't send out any SOS for help. And we shall need the wireless to send out weather observations and other reports. At the same time it'll be no use for us to receive gale warnings, because there are no reports for that part of the ocean, and even if there were, what good would they be to us on a raft?"

His arguments gradually swamped all my protests, the main ground for which was a lack of affection for push-buttons and turning knobs.

"Curiously enough," I admitted, "for getting into touch by wireless over great distances with tiny sets, I happen to have the
C

best connections. I was put into a wireless section in the war. Every man in the right place, you know. But I shall certainly write a line to Knut Haugland and Torstein Raaby."

"Do you know them?"

"Yes. I met Knut for the first time in England in 1944. He'd been decorated by the British for having taken part in the parachute action that held up the German efforts to get the atomic bomb; he was the wireless operator, you know, in the heavy water sabotage at Rjukan. When I met him he had just come back from another job in Norway; the Gestapo had caught him with a secret wireless set inside a chimney in the Maternity Clinic in Oslo. The Nazis had located him by DF, and the whole building was surrounded by German soldiers with machine-gun posts in front of every single door. Fehmer, the head of the Gestapo, was standing in the courtyard himself waiting for Knut to be carried down. But it was his own men who were carried down. Knut fought his way with his pistol from the attic down to the cellar, and from there out into the back yard, where he disappeared over the hospital wall with a hail of bullets after him. I met him at a secret station in an old English castle; he had come back to organise underground liaison between more than a hundred transmitting stations in occupied Norway.

"I myself had just finished my training as a parachutist, and our plan was to jump together in the Nordmark near Oslo. But just then the Russians marched into the Kirkenes region, and a small Norwegian detachment was sent from Scotland to F nmark to take over operations, so to speak, from the whole Russian army. I was sent up there instead. And there I met Torstein.

"It was real Arctic winter up in those parts, and the Northern Lights flickered up the starry sky which was arched over us, pitch-black, all day and all night. When we came into the ash-heaps of the burned area in Finmark, frozen blue and wearing furs, a cheery fellow with blue eyes and bristly fair hair crept out of a little hut up in the mountains. This was Torstein Raaby. He had first escaped to England and been on a course, and then he'd been smuggled into Norway somewhere near Tromsö. He'd been in hiding with a little transmitting set close to the battleship *Tirpitz*, and for ten months he had sent daily reports to England about all that happened on board. He sent his reports at night by connecting his secret transmitter to a receiving aerial put up by a German officer. It was his regular reports that guided the British bombers who at last finished off the *Tirpitz*.

"Torstein escaped to Sweden and from there over to England again, and then he made a parachute jump with a new wireless set behind the German lines up in the wilds of Finmark. When the Germans retreated, he found himself sitting behind our own lines, and came out of his hiding-place to help us with his little wireless set, as our main station had been destroyed by a mine. I'm ready to bet that both Knut and Torstein are fed up with hanging about at home now, and would be glad to go for a little trip on a wooden raft."

"Write and ask them," Herman proposed.

So I wrote a short letter, without any disingenuous persuasions, to Erik, Knut and Torstein:

"Am going to cross the Pacific on a wooden raft to support a theory that the South Sea islands were peopled from Peru. Will you come? I guarantee nothing but a free trip to Peru and the South Sea islands and back, and you will find good use for your technical abilities on the voyage. Reply at once."

Next day the following telegram arrived from Torstein:

"Coming. Torstein."

The other two also accepted.

As sixth member of the party we had in view now one man and now another, but each time some obstacle arose. In the meantime Herman and I had to attack the supply problem. We did not mean to eat aged llama flesh or dried kumara potatoes on our trip, for we were not making it to prove that we had once been Indians ourselves. Our intention was to test the performance and quality of the Inca raft, its seaworthiness and loading capacity, and see whether the elements would really propel it across the sea to Polynesia with its crew still on board. Our native forerunners could certainly have managed to live on dried meat and fish and dried kumara potatoes on board, as that was what they mainly lived on ashore. And we were going to try to find out, on the actual trip, whether they could have got fresh fish and rain-water while crossing the sea. As our own diet I had thought of simple field service rations, as we knew them from the war.

Just at that time a new assistant to the Norwegian Military Attaché in Washington had arrived. I had acted as second in command of his company in Finmark, and knew that he was a "ball of fire" who loved to attack and solve with savage energy any problem one set before him. Björn Rörholt was a man of that vital type which feels quite lost if it has fought its way out into the open without immediately sighting a new problem to tackle.

I wrote to him explaining the situation, and asked him to use his tracking sense to smell out a contact man in the supply department of the American Army. The chances were that the laboratory was experimenting with new field rations we could test, in the same way as we were testing equipment for the Air Force laboratory.

Two days later Björn rang us up from Washington. He had been in contact with the foreign liaison section of the American War Department, and they would like to know what it was all about.

Herman and I took the first train to Washington.

We found Björn in his room in the Military Attaché's office.

"I think it will be all right," he said. "We'll be received at the foreign liaison section tomorrow as long as we take a proper letter from the colonel."

"The Colonel" was Otto Munthe-Kaas, the Norwegian Military Attaché. He was well-disposed and more than willing to give us a proper letter of introduction when he heard what our business was.

When we came to fetch the document next morning he suddenly rose and said it would be best if he came with us himself. We drove out in the colonel's car to the Pentagon building, the largest in the world, where the offices of the War Department are. The colonel and Björn sat in front in their smartest military turn-out, while Herman and I sat behind and peered through the windscreen at the huge Pentagon building, which towered up on the plain before us. This gigantic building with thirty thousand clerks and sixteen miles of corridors was to form the frame of our impending "raft conference" with military "high-ups." Never, before or after, did the little raft seem to Herman and me so helplessly small.

After endless wanderings in ramps and corridors we reached the door of the foreign liaison section, and soon, surrounded by brand-new uniforms, we were sitting round a large mahogany table at which the head of the foreign liaison section himself presided.

The stern, broad-built West Point officer, who bulked big at the end of the table, had at first a certain difficulty in understanding what connection there might be between the American War Department and our wooden raft, but the colonel's well-considered words, and the favourable result of a hurricane-like examination by the officers round the table, slowly brought him over to our side, and he read with interest the letter from the equipment laboratory of the Air Material Command. Then he rose and gave his staff a concise order to help us through the proper channels, and, wishing us good luck for the present, marched out of the conference room. When the door had shut on him, a young staff captain whispered in my ear:

"I bet you'll get what you want. It sounds just like a little military operation, and brings a little change into our daily office peace-time routine; besides, it'll be a good opportunity of methodically testing equipment."

The liaison office at once arranged a meeting with Colonel Lewis at the Quartermaster-General's experimental laboratory, and Herman and I were taken over there by car.

Colonel Lewis was an affable giant of an officer with a sportsman's bearing. He at once called in the men in charge of experiments in the different sections. All were amicably disposed and immediately suggested quantities of equipment they would like us to test thoroughly. They exceeded our wildest hopes as they rattled off the names of nearly everything we could want, from field rations to sunburn ointment and splash-proof sleeping-bags. Then they took us on a round tour to look at the things. We tasted special rations in smart packings; we tested matches which struck as well if they had been dipped in water, new Primus stoves and water kegs, rubber bags and special boots, kitchen utensils and knives which would float, and all that an expedition could want.

I glanced at Herman. He looked like a good, expectant little boy walking through a chocolate shop with a rich aunt. The tall colonel walked in front demonstrating all these delights, and when the round was completed staff clerks had made notes of the kinds of goods and the quantities we required. I thought the battle was won, and felt only an urge to rush home to the hotel in order to assume a horizontal position and think things over in peace and quiet. Then the tall, friendly colonel suddenly said:

"Well, now we must go in and have a talk with the boss; it's he who'll decide whether we can give you these things."

I felt my heart sink down into my boots. So we were to start our eloquence right from the beginning again, and heaven alone knew what kind of type the "boss" was.

We found that the boss was a little officer with an intensely earnest manner. He sat behind his writing-table and examined us with keen blue eyes as we came into the office. He asked us to sit down.

"Well, what do these gentlemen want?" he asked Colonel Lewis sharply, without taking his eyes off mine.

"Oh, a few little things," Lewis hastened to reply. He explained the whole of our errand in outline, while the chief listened patiently without moving a finger.

"And what can they give us in return?" he asked, quite unimpressed.

"Well," said Lewis in a conciliatory tone, "we hoped that perhaps the expedition would be able to write reports on the new provisions and some of the equipment in the severe conditions in which they will be using it."

The intensely earnest officer behind the writing-table leant back in his chair with unaffected slowness, with his eyes still fixed on mine, and I felt myself sinking to the bottom of the deep leather chair as he said coolly:

"I don't see at all how they can give us anything in return."

There was dead silence in the room. Colonel Lewis fingered his collar, and neither of us said a word.

"But," the chief suddenly broke out, and now a gleam had come into the corner of his eye:

"Courage and enterprise count too. Colonel Lewis, let them have the things!"

I was still sitting, half intoxicated with delight, in the cab which was taking us home to the hotel, when Herman began to laugh and giggle to himself at my side.

"Are you tight?" I asked anxiously.

"No," he laughed shamelessly, "but I've been calculating that the provisions we got include 684 boxes of pineapple, and that's my favourite dish."

There are a thousand things to be done, and mostly at the same time, when six men and a wooden raft and its cargo are to assemble at a place down the coast of Peru. And we had three months and no Aladdin's lamp at our disposal.

We flew to New York with an introduction from the liaison office and met Professor Behre at Columbia University. He was head of the War Department's Geographical Research Committee, and it was he who pressed the buttons which at last brought Herman all his valuable instruments and apparatus for scientific measurements.

Then we flew to Washington to meet Admiral Glover at the Naval Hydrographic Institute. The good-natured old sea-dog called in all his officers and pointed to the chart of the Pacific on the wall as he introduced Herman and me:

"These young gentlemen want to check up on our current maps. Help them!"

When the wheels had rolled a bit further the English Colonel Lumsden called a conference at the British Military Mission in Washington to discuss our future problems and the chances of a favourable outcome. We received plenty of good advice and a selection of British equipment which was flown over from England to be tried out on the raft expedition. The British medical officer was an enthusiastic advocate of a mysterious "shark powder." We were to sprinkle a few pinches of the powder on the water if a shark became too impudent, and the shark would vanish immediately.

"Sir," I said politely, "can we rely on this powder?"

"Well," said the Englishman, smiling, "that's just what we want to find out ourselves!"

When time is short, and plane replaces train while car replaces legs, one's wallet crumples up like a withered herbarium. When we had spent the cost of my return ticket to Norway, we went and knocked up our friends and backers in New York to get our finances straight. There we encountered surprising and discouraging problems. The financial manager was ill in bed with fever, and his two colleagues were powerless till he was in action again. They stood firmly by our economic agreement, but they could do nothing for the time being. We were asked to postpone the business, a useless request, for we could not stop the numerous wheels which were now revolving vigorously. We could only hold on now; it was too late to stop or brake. Our friends the backers agreed to dissolve the whole syndicate in order to give us a free hand to act quickly and independently without them.

So there we were in the street with our hands in our trousers pockets.

"December, January, February," said Herman.

"And at a pinch March," said I, "but then we simply must start!"

If all else seemed obscure, one thing was clear to us. Ours was a journey with an objective, and we did not want to be classed with acrobats who roll down Niagara in empty barrels or sit on the knobs of flag-staffs for seventeen days.

"No chewing-gum or coca-cola backing," Herman said.

On this point we were in profound agreement.

We could get Norwegian kroner. But that did not solve the problems on our side of the Atlantic. We could apply for a grant, but could scarcely get one for a disputed theory; after all, that was just why we were going on the raft expedition. We soon found that neither Press nor private promoters dared to put money into what they themselves and all the insurance companies regarded as a suicide voyage; but if we came back safe and sound it would be another matter.

Things looked pretty gloomy, and for many days we could see no land. It was then that Colonel Munthe-Kaas came into the picture again.

"You're in a fix, boys," he said. "Here's a cheque to begin with, I can have it when you come back from the South Sea islands."

Several other people followed his example, and the private loan was soon big enough to tide us over without help from agents or others. We were to fly to South America and start building the raft.

The old Peruvian rafts were built of balsa wood, which in a dry state is lighter than cork. The balsa tree grows in Peru, but only beyond the mountains in the Andes range, so the seafarers in Inca times went up along the coast to Ecuador, where they felled their huge balsa trees right down on the edge of the Pacific. We meant to do the same.

To-day's travel problems are different from those of Inca times. We can find cars and planes and travel bureaux, but, so as not to make things altogether too easy, we have also got things called frontiers, with brass-buttoned chuckers-out who doubt one's alibi, maltreat one's luggage and weigh one down with stamped forms if one is lucky enough to get in at all. It was the fear of these men with brass buttons that decided us that we could not land in South America with packing-cases and trunks full of strange objects, raise our hats and ask politely in broken Spanish to be allowed to come in and sail away on a raft. We should be clapped into gaol. "No," said Herman. "We must have an official introduction."

One of our friends in the dissolved triumvirate was a correspondent at the United Nations, and took us out there by car. We were greatly impressed when we came into the great hall of the Assembly where men of all nations sat on benches side by side listening silently to the flow of speech from a black-haired Russian in front of the gigantic map of the world that decorated the back wall.

Our friend the correspondent managed in a quiet moment to get hold of one of the delegates from Peru, and later one of Ecuador's representatives. On a deep leather sofa in an ante-chamber they listened eagerly to our plan of crossing the sea to support a theory that men of an ancient civilisation from their own country had been the first to reach the Pacific islands. Both promised to inform their governments, and guaranteed us support when we came to their respective countries. Trygve Lie, passing through the ante-room, came over to us when he heard we were countrymen of his, and someone proposed that he should come with us on the raft. But there were billows enough for him on land. An assistant secretary of the United Nations, Dr. Benjamin Cohen from Chile, was himself a well-known amateur archaeologist, and he gave me a letter to the President of Peru, who was a personal friend of his. We also met in the hall the Norwegian Ambassador, Wilhelm von Munthe of Morgenstierne, who from now on gave the expedition invaluable support.

So we bought two tickets and flew to South America. When the four heavy engines began to roar one after another, we sank back into the deep armchairs, worn out. We had an unspeakable feeling of relief that the first stage of the programme was over, and that we were now going straight ahead to the adventure.

CHAPTER III

TO SOUTH AMERICA

*We Land on the Equator—Balsa Problems—By Air to Quito—
Head-hunters and Bandidos—Over the Andes by Jeep—Into the
Depths of the Jungle—At Quivedo—We Fell Balsa Trees—Down
the Palenque by Raft—The Alluring Naval Harbour—At the
Ministry of Marine in Lima—With the President of Peru—
Danielsson Comes—Back to Washington—Twenty-six Pounds of
Paper—Herman's Baptism of Fire—We build the Raft in the Naval
Harbour—Warnings—Before the Start—Naming of the Kon-Tiki
—Farewell to South America.*

A S the aircraft crossed the equator it began a slanting
descent through the milk-white clouds which till then
had lain beneath us like a blinding waste of snow in the
burning sun. The fleecy vapour clung to the windows till it
dissolved and remained hanging over us like clouds, and the
bright green roof of a rolling, billowy jungle appeared. We flew
in over the South American republic of Ecuador and landed at
the tropical port of Guayaquil.

With yesterday's jackets, waistcoats, and overcoats over our
arms, we crawled out into the atmosphere of a hothouse to
meet chattering Southerners in tropical kit, and felt our shirts
sticking to our backs like wet paper. We were embraced by
Customs and immigration officials and almost carried shoulder-
high to a cab, which took us to the best hotel in the town, the
only good one. Here we quickly found our way to our respective
baths and lay down flat under the cold water tap.

We had reached the country where the balsa tree grows, and
were to buy timber to build the raft.

The first day we spent in learning the monetary system and
enough Spanish to find our way back to the hotel.

On the second day we ventured away from our baths in
steadily widening circles, and when Herman had satisfied his
childhood's longing to touch a proper palm tree, and I was a

walking bowl of fruit salad, we decided to go and negotiate for balsa.

Unfortunately this was easier said than done. We could certainly buy balsa in quantities, but not in the form of whole logs, as we wanted it. The days when balsa trees were accessible down on the coast were past. The last war had put an end to them; they had been felled in thousands and shipped to the aircraft factories, because the wood was so gaseous and light. We were told that the only place where large balsa trees grew was in the jungle in the interior of the country.

"Then we must go inland and fell them ourselves," we said.

"Impossible," said the authorities. "The rains have just begun, and all the roads into the jungle are impassable because of flood water and deep mud. If you want balsa wood, you must come back to Ecuador in six months; the rains will be over then and the roads up country will have dried."

In our extremity we called on Don Gustavo von Buchwald, the balsa king of Ecuador, and Herman unrolled his sketch of the raft with the lengths of timber we required. The skinny little balsa king seized the telephone eagerly and set his agents to work searching. They found planks and light boards and separate short blocks in every single saw-mill, but they could not find one single serviceable log. There were two big logs, as dry as tinder, at Don Gustavo's own dump, but they would not take us far. It was clear that the search was useless.

"A brother of mine has a big balsa plantation," said Don Gustavo. "His name is Don Federico and he lives at Quivedo, a little jungle town right up country. He can get you all you want as soon as we can get hold of him after the rains. It's no use now because of the jungle rain up country."

If Don Gustavo said a thing was no use, all the balsa experts in Ecuador would say it was no use. So here we were in Guayaquil with no timber for the raft, and with no possibility of going in and felling the trees ourselves until several months later, when it would be too late anyhow.

"Time's short," said Herman.

"And balsa we must have," said I. "The raft must be an exact copy, or we shall have no guarantee of coming through alive."

A little school map we found in the hotel, with green jungle, brown mountains, and inhabited places ringed round in red, told us that the jungle stretched unbroken from the Pacific right to the foot of the towering Andes. I had an idea. It was clearly impracticable now to get from the coastal area through the jungle to the balsa trees at Quivedo, but suppose we could get to the trees from the inland side, by coming straight down into the interior of the jungle from the bare snow mountains of the Andes range? Here was a possibility, the only one we saw.

Out on the airfield was a little cargo plane which was willing to take us up to Quito, the capital of this queer country, high up on the Andes plateau, 9,000 feet above sea level. Between packing cases and furniture we caught occasional glimpses of green jungle and shining rivers before we disappeared into the clouds. When we came out again the lowlands were hidden under an endless sea of rolling vapour, but ahead of us dry mountain-sides and bare cliffs rose from the sea of mist right up to a brilliant blue sky.

The aircraft climbed straight up the mountain-side as in an invisible funicular railway, and although the equator itself was in sight, at last we had shining snowfields alongside us. Then we glided between the mountains and over a rich alpine plateau clad in spring green, on which we landed close to the world's most peculiar capital.

Most of Quito's 150,000 inhabitants are pure or half-breed mountain Indians, for it was their forefathers' own capital long before Columbus and our own race knew America. The city receives its stamp from ancient monasteries containing art treasures of immeasurable value and other magnificent buildings dating from Spanish times, towering over the roofs of low Indian houses built of bricks of sun-dried clay. A labyrinth of alleys winds between the clay walls, and these alleys we found swarming with mountain Indians in red-speckled cloaks and big home-made hats. Some were going to market with pack donkeys, while others sat hunched up along the adobe walls dozing in the hot sun. A few motor-cars containing aristocrats of Spanish origin in tropical kit succeeded, going at half-speed and hooting ceaselessly, in finding a path along the one-way alleys among children and donkeys and bare-legged Indians. The air up here on the high plateau was of such brilliant crystalline clearness that the mountains round us seemed to come into the street picture and contribute to its other-world atmosphere.

Our friend from the cargo plane, Jorge, nicknamed "the crazy flyer," belonged to one of the old Spanish families in Quito. He installed us in an antiquated, amusing hotel, and then went round, sometimes with and sometimes without us, trying to get us transport over the mountains and down into the jungle to Quivedo. We met in the evening in an old Spanish café, and Jorge was full of bad news; we must just put the idea of going to Quivedo out of our heads. Neither men nor vehicle were to be obtained to take us over the mountains, and certainly not down into the jungle where the rains had begun, and where there was danger of attack if one stuck fast in the mud. Only last year a party of ten American oil engineers had been found killed by poisoned arrows in the eastern part of Ecuador, where there were still great numbers of forest Indians who went about in the jungle stark naked and hunted with poisoned arrows.

"Some of them are head-hunters," Jorge said in a hollow voice, seeing that Herman, quite unperturbed, was helping himself to more beef and red wine.

"You think I exaggerate," he continued in a low voice. "But although it is strictly forbidden, there are still people in this country who make a living by selling shrunken human heads. It's impossible to control it, so to this very day the jungle Indians cut off the heads of their enemies among other nomad tribes. They smash up and remove the skull itself and fill the empty skin of the head with hot sand, so that the whole head shrinks till it's hardly bigger than a cat's head, without losing its shape or its features. These shrunken heads of enemies were once valuable trophies, now they're rare black market goods. Half-breed middle-men see that they get down to the buyers on the coast, who sell them to tourists for fabulous prices."

Jorge looked at us triumphantly. He little knew that Herman and I that same day had been dragged into a porter's lodge and offered two of these heads at 1,000 sucres apiece. These heads nowadays are often fakes, made up from monkeys' heads, but these two were genuine enough, pure Indians, and so true to life that every single tiny feature was preserved. They were the heads of a man and a woman, both the size of oranges; the woman was actually pretty, though only the eyelashes and long black hair had preserved their natural size. I shuddered at the thought, but expressed my doubts whether there were head-hunters west of the mountains.

"One can never know," said Jorge gloomily. "And what would you say if your friend disappeared and his head came into the market in miniature? That happened to a friend of mine once," he added, staring at me stubbornly.

"Tell us about it," said Herman, chewing his beef slowly and with only moderate enjoyment.

I laid my fork carefully aside, and Jorge told his story. He was once living with his wife on an outpost in the jungle, washing gold and buying up the take of the other gold-washers. The family had at that time a native friend who brought his gold regularly and sold it for goods. One day this friend was killed in the jungle. Jorge tracked down the murderer and threatened to shoot him. Now the murderer was one of those who were suspected of selling shrunken human heads, and Jorge promised to spare his life if he handed over the head at once. The murderer at once produced the head of Jorge's friend, now as small as a man's fist. Jorge was quite upset when he saw his friend again, for he was quite unchanged, except that he had become so very small. Much moved, he took the little head home to his wife. She fainted when she saw it, and Jorge had to hide his friend in a trunk. But it was so damp in the jungle that clusters of green mould formed on the head, so that Jorge had to take it out now and then and dry it in the sun. It hung very nicely by the hair on a clothesline, and Jorge's wife fainted every time she caught sight of it. But one day a mouse gnawed its way into the trunk and made a horrid mess of his friend. Jorge was much distressed and buried his friend with full ceremonies in a tiny little hole up on the airfield. For after all he was a human being, Jorge concluded.

"Nice dinner," I said, to change the subject.

As we went home in the dark I had a disagreeable feeling that Herman's hat had sunk far down over his ears. But he had only pulled it down to protect himself from the cold night wind from the mountains.

Next day we were sitting with our own Consul-General Bryhn and his wife under the eucalyptus trees at their big country place outside the town. Bryhn hardly thought our planned jungle trip to Quivedo would lead to any drastic change in our hat sizes, but—! There were robbers about in just those regions we had thought of visiting. He produced cuttings from local papers announcing that soldiers were to be sent out when the dry season came to extirpate the *bandidos* who infested the regions around Quivedo. To go there now was the sheerest madness, and we should never get guides or transport. While we were talking to him we saw a jeep from the American Military Attaché's office tear past along the road, and this gave us an idea. We went up to the American Embassy accompanied by the Consul-General, and were able to see the Military Attaché himself. He was a trim, buoyant young man in khaki and riding-boots, and asked laughingly why we had strayed to the top of the Andes when the local papers said we were to go to sea on a wooden raft.

We explained that the wood was still standing upright in the Quivedo jungle. And we were up here on the roof of the continent and could not get at it. We asked the Military Attaché either (a) to lend us a plane and two parachutes or (b) a jeep with a driver who knew the country.

The Military Attaché at first sat speechless at our assurance; then he shook his head despairingly and said with a smile: all right, as we gave him no third choice, he preferred the second!

At a quarter past five the next morning a jeep rolled up to the hotel entrance, and an Ecuadorian captain of engineers jumped out and reported himself at our service. His orders were to drive us to Quivedo, mud or no mud. The jeep was packed full of petrol cans, for there were no petrol pumps or wheel-tracks along the route we were to take. Our new friend, Captain Agurto Alexis Alvarez, was armed to the teeth with knives and fire-arms

Plate I

Members of the Kon-Tiki expedition (from left to right): Knut Haugland, Bengt Danielsson, the author, Erik Hesselberg, Torstein Raaby, Herman Watzinger.

PLATE II

The Military At-
taché's jeep 13,000
ft. above sea level
in the Andes.

Indian women
the Andes spi
ning wool as th
walk.

on account of the reports of *bandidos*. We had come to the country peacefully in jackets and ties to buy timber for ready money down on the coast, and the whole of our equipment on board the jeep consisted of a bag of tinned food, except that we had hurriedly acquired a second-hand camera and a pair of tear-proof khaki breeches for each of us. Further, the Consul-General had pressed upon us his big parabellum revolver with an ample supply of ammunition to exterminate everything that crossed our path. The jeep whizzed away through the empty alleys where the moon shone ghostly pale on whitewashed adobe walls, till we came out into the country, and raced at a giddy speed along a good sand road southward through the mountain region.

It was good going all along the range as far as the mountain village of Latakunga, where windowless Indian houses clustered blindly round a whitewashed country church with palms in a square. Here we turned off along a mule track which undulated and twisted westward over hill and valley into the Andes. We came into a world we had never dreamt of. It was the mountain Indians' own world—east of the sun and west of the moon—outside time and beyond space. On the whole drive we saw not a carriage or a wheel. The traffic consisted of bare-legged goat-herds in gaily-coloured ponchos driving forward disorderly herds of stiff-legged dignified llamas, and now and then whole families of Indians came along the road. The husband usually rode ahead on a mule, while his little wife trotted behind with her entire collection of hats on her head and the youngest child in a bag on her back. And all the time she ran she span wool with her fingers. Donkeys and mules jogged behind at leisure, loaded with boughs and rushes and pottery.

The farther we went the fewer the Indians who spoke Spanish, and soon Agurto's linguistic capacities were as useless as our own. A cluster of huts lay here and there up in the mountains; fewer and fewer were built of clay, while more and more were made of twigs and dry grass. Both the huts and the sun-browned wrinkle-faced people seemed to have grown up out of the earth itself, from the baking effect of the mountain sun on the Andes' rock walls. They belonged to cliff and scree and upland pasture
D

as naturally as the mountain grass itself. Poor in possessions and
small in stature, the mountain Indians had the wiry hardiness of
wild animals and the child-like alertness of a primitive people,
and the less they could talk the more they could laugh. Radiant
faces with snow-white teeth shone upon us from all we saw.
There was nothing to say that the white man had lost or earned
a shilling in these regions. There were no advertisement posters
or road-signs here, and if a tin box or a scrap of paper was flung
down by the roadside, it would be picked up at once as a useful
household article.

We went on up over sun-smitten slopes without a bush or tree
and down into valleys of desert sand and cactus, till we climbed
right up and reached the topmost crest, with snowfields round
the peak and a wind so bitingly cold that we had to slacken speed
in order not to freeze to bits as we sat in our shirts longing for
jungle heat. For long stretches we had to drive across country
between the mountains, over scree and grassy ridges, searching
for the next bit of road. But when we reached the west wall,
where the Andes range falls precipitously to the lowlands, the
mule track was cut along shelves in the loose rock, and sheer
cliffs and gorges were all about us. We put all our trust in friend
Agurto as he sat crouched over the steering-wheel and always
swung out when we came to a precipice. Suddenly a violent gust
of wind met us; we had reached the outermost crest of the Andes
chain, where the mountain fell away sharply in a series of
precipices to the jungle far down in a bottomless abyss 12,000
feet beneath us. But we were cheated of the dizzy view over the
sea of jungle, for as soon as we reached the edge thick cloud-
banks rolled about us like steam from a witches' cauldron. But
now our road ran down unhindered into the depths. Always
down, in steep loops along gorges and bluffs and ridges, while
the air grew damper and warmer and ever fuller of the heavy
deadening hothouse air which rose from the jungle world
below.

And then the rain began. First gently, then it began to pour
and beat upon the jeep like drumsticks, and soon the chocolate-
coloured water was flowing down the rocks on every side of us.

We almost flowed down too, away from the dry mountain plateaux behind us and into another world, where stick and stone and clay slope were soft and lush with moss and turf. Leaves shot up; soon they became giant leaves hanging like green umbrellas and dripping over the hillside. Then came the first feeble advanced posts of the jungle trees, with heavy fringes and beards of moss, and climbing plants, hanging from them. There was a gurgling and splashing everywhere. As the slopes grew gentler, the jungle rolled up swiftly like an army of green giant growths that swallowed up the little jeep as it splashed along the waterlogged clay road. We were in the jungle. The air was moist and warm and heavy with the smell of vegetation.

Darkness had fallen when we reached a cluster of palm-roofed huts on a ridge. Dripping with warm water we left the jeep for a night under a dry roof. The horde of fleas that attacked us in the hut were drowned in next day's rain. With the jeep full of bananas and other southern fruit we went on downhill through the jungle, down and down, though we thought we had reached bottom long ago. The mud grew worse, but it did not stop us, and the robbers kept at an unknown distance.

Not till the road was barred by a broad river of muddy water rolling down through the jungle did the jeep give up. We stood stuck fast, unable to move either up or down along the river bank. In an open clearing stood a hut where a few half-breed Indians were stretching out a jaguar-skin on a sunny wall, while dogs and fowls were splashing about and enjoying themselves on top of some cocoa beans spread out to dry in the sun. When the jeep came bumping along the place came to life, and people who spoke Spanish declared that this was the river Palenque, and that Quivedo was just on the other side. There was no bridge there, and the river was swift and deep, but they were willing to float us and the jeep over by raft. This queer contraption lay down by the bank. Curved logs as thick as arms and legs were fastened together with vegetable fibres and bamboos to form a flimsy raft, twice the length and breadth of the jeep. With a plank under each wheel and our hearts in our mouths we drove the jeep out on to the logs, and if most of them were submerged under the muddy water, they did bear the jeep and us and four half-naked chocolate-coloured men who pushed us off with long poles.

"Balsa?" Herman and I asked in the same breath.

"Balsa," one of the fellows nodded, with a disrespectful kick at the logs.

The current seized us and we whirled down the river, while the men pushed in their poles at the right places and kept the raft on an even diagonal course across the current and into quieter water on the other side. This was our first meeting with the balsa tree and our first trip on a balsa raft. We brought the raft safely to land at the farther bank and motored triumphantly into Quivedo. Two rows of tarred wooden houses with motionless vultures on the palm roofs formed a kind of street, and this was the whole place. The inhabitants dropped whatever they might be carrying, and black and brown, young and old appeared to be swarming out of both doors and windows. They rushed to meet the jeep, a menacing, chattering tide of humanity. They scrambled on to it and under it and round it. We kept a tight hold on our worldly possessions while Agurto attempted desperate ma- noeuvres at the steering-wheel. Then the jeep had a puncture and went down on one knee. We had arrived at Quivedo and had to endure the embrace of welcome.

Don Federico's plantation lay a bit farther down the river. When the jeep came bumping into the yard along a path between the mango trees with Agurto, Herman and me, the lean old jungle-dweller came to meet us at a trot with his nephew Angelo, a small boy who lived with him out in the wilds. We gave messages from Don Gustavo, and soon the jeep was standing alone in the yard while a fresh tropical shower streamed down over the jungle. There was a festive meal in Don Federico's bungalow; sucking pigs and chickens crackled over an open fire, while we sat round a dish loaded with southern fruit and explained what we had come for. The jungle rain pouring down on the ground outside sent a warm sweet gust of scented blossoms and clay in through the window-netting.

Don Federico had become as brisk as a boy. Why, yes, he had known balsa rafts since he was a child. Fifty years ago, when he lived down by the sea, the Indians from Peru still used to come sailing up along the coast on big balsa rafts to sell fish in Guayaquil. They could bring a couple of tons of dried fish in a bamboo cabin in the middle of the raft, or they might have wives and children and dogs and fowls on board. Such big balsa trees as they had used for their rafts it would be hard to find now in the rains, for flood water and mud had already made it impossible to get to the balsa plantation up in the forest, even on horseback. But Don Federico would do his best; there might still be some single trees growing wild in the forest nearer the bungalow, and we did not need many.

Late in the evening the rain stopped for a time, and we went for a turn under the mango trees round the bungalow. Here Don Federico had every kind of wild orchid in the world hanging down from the branches, with half-cocoanuts as flower-pots. Unlike cultivated orchids, these rare plants gave out a wonderful scent, and Herman was bending down to stick his nose into one of them, when something like a long thin glittering eel emerged from the leaves above him. A lightning blow from Angelo's whip, and a wriggling snake fell to the ground. A second later it was held fast to the earth with a forked stick over its neck, and then its head was crushed.

"Mortal," said Angelo, and exposed two curved poison-fangs to show what he meant.

We thought we saw poisonous snakes lurking in the foliage everywhere, and slipped into the house with Angelo's trophy hanging lifeless across a stick. Herman sat down to skin the green monster, and Don Federico was telling fantastic stories about poisonous snakes and boa constrictors as thick as plates, when we suddenly noticed the shadows of two enormous scorpions on the wall, the size of lobsters. They rushed at one another and engaged in a life and death battle with their pincers, with their hinderparts turned up and the curved poisonous sting at the tail ready for the deathblow. It was a horrible sight, and not till we moved the oil lamp did we see that it had cast a supernaturally gigantic shadow of two quite ordinary scorpions of the size of one's finger, which were fighting on the edge of the bureau.

"Let them be," Don Federico laughed. "One'll kill the other, and we want the survivor in the house to keep the cockroaches away. Just keep your mosquito net tight round the bed and shake your clothes before you put them on, and you'll be all right. I've often been bitten by scorpions and I'm not dead yet," said the old man, laughing.

I slept well, except that I woke up thinking of poisonous creatures every time a lizard or bat squeaked and scrabbled too noisily near my pillow.

Next morning we got up early to go and search for balsa trees.

"Better shake our clothes," said Agurto, and as he spoke a scorpion fell out of his shirt-sleeve and shot down into a crack in the floor.

Soon after sunrise Don Federico sent his men out on horseback in all directions to look for accessible balsa trees along the paths. Our own party consisted of Don Federico, Herman and myself, and we soon found our way to an open place where there was a gigantic old tree of which Don Federico knew. It towered high above the trees round about, and the trunk was three feet thick. In Polynesian style we christened the tree before we touched it; we gave it the name Ku, after a Polynesian deity of American origin. Then we swung the axe and drove it into the balsa trunk till the forest echoed our blows. But cutting a sappy balsa was like cutting cork with a blunt axe; it simply rebounded, and I had not delivered many strokes of the axe before Herman had to relieve me. The axe changed hands time after time, while the splinters flew and the sweat trickled in the heat of the jungle.

Late in the day Ku was standing like a cock on one leg, quivering under our blows; soon he tottered and crashed down heavily over the surrounding forest, big branches and small trees being pulled down by the giant's fall. We had torn the branches from the trunk and were beginning to rip off the bark in zigzags in the Indian style when Herman suddenly dropped the axe and leapt into the air as if doing a Polynesian war dance, with his hand pressed to his leg. Out of his trouser leg fell a shining ant as big as a scorpion and with a long sting at its tail. It must have had a skull like a lobster's claw, for it was almost impossible to stamp it under one's heel on the ground.

"A kongo," Don Federico explained with regret. "The little brute's worse than a scorpion, but it isn't dangerous to a healthy man."

Herman was tender and sore for several days, but this did not prevent his galloping with us on horseback along the jungle paths, looking for more giant balsas in the forest. From time to time we heard creaking and crashing and a heavy thud somewhere in the virgin forest. Don Federico nodded with a satisfied air. It meant that his half-bred Indians had felled a new giant balsa for the raft. In a week Ku had been followed by Kane, Kama, Ilo, Mauri, Ra, Rangi, Papa, Taranga, Kura, Kukara and Hiti, twelve mighty balsas, all christened in honour of Polynesian legendary figures whose names had once been borne with Tiki over the sea from Peru. The logs, glistening with sap, were dragged down through the jungle first by horses and for the last bit by Don Federico's tractor, which brought them to the river bank in front of the bungalow.

The logs, full of sap, were far from being as light as corks. They certainly weighed a ton apiece, and we waited with great anxiety to see how they floated in the water. We rolled them out to the edge of the bank one by one; there we made fast a rope of tough climbing plants to the end of the log, that they might not vanish down stream when we let them enter the water. Then we rolled them in turn down the bank and into the river. There was a mighty splash. They swung round and floated, about as much above as below the surface of the water, and if we went out along them they remained steady. We bound the timbers together with tough lianas that hung down from the tops of the jungle trees, so as to make two temporary rafts, one towing the other. Then we loaded the rafts with all the bamboos and lianas we should need later, and Herman and I went on board with two men of a mysterious mixed race, with whom we had no common language.

When we cut our moorings we were caught by the whirling masses of water and went off downstream at a good pace. The last glimpse we had in the drizzle, as we rounded the first head-land, was of our excellent friends standing on the end of the point in front of the bungalow, waving. Then we crept under a little shelter of green banana leaves and left steering problems to the two brown experts who had stationed themselves one in the bows and one astern, each holding a huge oar. They kept the raft in the swiftest current with nonchalant ease, and we danced downstream on a winding course between sunken trees and sandbanks.

The jungle stood like a solid wall along the banks on both sides, and parrots and other bright-coloured birds fluttered out of the dense foliage as we passed. Once or twice an alligator hurled itself into the river and became invisible in the muddy water. But we soon caught sight of a much more remarkable monster. This was an iguana, or giant lizard, as big as a crocodile, but with a large throat and fringed back. It lay dozing on the clay bank as if it had overslept from prehistoric times, and did not move as we glided past. The oarsmen made signs to us not to shoot. Soon afterwards we saw a smaller specimen about three feet long. It was running away along a thick branch which hung out over the raft. It only ran till it was in safety, and then it sat shining in blue and green and stared at us with cold snake's eyes as we passed. Later we passed a fern-clad hillock, and on the top of it lay the biggest iguana of all. It was like the silhouette of a fringed Chinese dragon carved in stone as it stood out motionless against the sky with chest and head raised. It did not as much as turn its head as we curved round it under the hillock and vanished into the jungle.

Farther down we smelt smoke, and passed several huts with straw roofs which lay in clearings along the bank. We on the raft were the objects of close attention from sinister-looking individuals on land, an unpleasant mixture of Indian, negro and Spaniard. Their boats, great dug-out canoes, lay drawn up on to the bank.

When meal-times came we relieved our friends at the steering oars while they fried fish and bread-fruit over a little fire regulated with wet clay. Roast chicken, eggs and southern fruits were also part of the menu on board, while the logs transported themselves and us at a fine speed down through the jungle towards the sea. What did it matter now if the water swept and splashed round us? The more it rained, the swifter the current ran.

When darkness fell over the river an ear-splitting orchestra struck up on the bank. Toads and frogs, crickets and mosquitoes croaked or chirped or hummed in a prolonged chorus of many voices. Now and again the shrill scream of a wild cat rang through the darkness, and soon another, and yet another, from birds scared into flight by the night prowlers of the jungle. Once or twice we saw the gleam of a fire in a native hut, and heard bawling voices and the barking of dogs as we slid past in the night. But for the most part we sat alone with the jungle orchestra under the stars, till drowsiness and rain drove us into the cabin of leaves, where we went to sleep with our pistols loose in their holsters.

The farther down stream we drifted, the thicker became the huts and native plantations, and soon there were regular villages on the banks. The traffic here consisted of dug-out canoes punted along with long poles, and now and then we saw a little balsa raft loaded with heaps of green bananas.

Where the Palenque joined the Rio Guayas the water had risen so high that the paddle steamer was plying busily between Vinces and Guayaquil down on the coast. To save valuable time Herman and I each got a hammock on board the paddle steamer, and steamed off across the thickly populated flat country to the coast. Our brown friends were to follow, drifting down alone with the timber.

At Guayaquil Herman and I parted. He remained at the mouth of the Guayas to stop the balsa logs as they came drifting down. Thence he was to take them on, as cargo in a coasting steamer, to Peru, where he was to direct the building of the raft and make a faithful copy of the Indians' old-time vessels. I myself took the regular plane southward to Lima, the capital of Peru, to find a suitable place for building the raft.

The aircraft ascended to a great height along the shore of the Pacific, with the desert mountains of Peru on one side and a

glittering ocean far below us on the other. It was here we were
to put to sea on board the raft. The sea seemed endless when
seen from an aircraft high up. Sky and sea melted into one
another along an indefinable horizon far, far away to the westward, and I could not rid myself of the thought that even beyond
that horizon many hundred similar sea plains curved round a
fifth of the earth before there was any more land, in Polynesia.
I tried to project my thoughts a few weeks ahead, when we should
be drifting on a speck of a raft on that blue expanse below, but
quickly dismissed the thought again, for it gave me the same
unpleasant feeling inside as sitting in readiness to jump with a
parachute.

On my arrival in Lima I took the tram down to the port of
Callao to find a place where we could build the raft. I saw at
once that the whole harbour was chock-full of ships and cranes
and warehouses, with Customs sheds and harbour offices and all
the rest. And if there was any open beach farther out, it swarmed
with bathers to such a degree that inquisitive people would pull
the raft and fittings to pieces as soon as our backs were turned.
Callao was now the most important port in a country of seven
millions, white and brown. Times had changed for raft-builders
in Peru even more than in Ecuador, and I saw only one possibility
—to get inside the high concrete walls round the naval harbour,
where armed men stood on guard behind the iron gate and cast
menacing and suspicious looks on me and other unauthorised
persons who loafed past the walls. If one could only get in there
one would be safe.

I had met the Peruvian Naval Attaché in Washington and had
a letter from him to support me. I went to the Ministry of Marine
next day with the letter and sought an audience of the Minister
of Marine, Manuel Nieto. He received in the morning in the
elegant Empire drawing-room of the Ministry, gleaming with
mirrors and gilding. After a time he himself came in in full
uniform, a short broadly-built officer, as stern as Napoleon,
straightforward and concise in his manner of speech. He asked
why and I said why. I asked to be allowed to build a wooden
raft in the naval dockyard.

"Young man," said the Minister, drumming uneasily with his fingers. "You've come in by the window instead of the door. I'll be glad to help you, but the order must come from the Foreign Minister to me; I can't let foreigners into the naval area and give them the use of the dockyard as a matter of course. Apply to the Foreign Ministry in writing, and good luck."

I thought apprehensively of papers circulating and disappearing into the blue. Happy were the rude days of Kon-Tiki, when applications were an unknown hindrance.

To see the Foreign Minister in person was considerably harder. Norway had no local legation in Peru, and our helpful Consul-General Bahr could, therefore, take me no further than the counsellors of the Foreign Ministry. I was afraid things would get no further. Dr. Cohen's letter to the President of the Republic might come in useful now. And I sought through his adjutant an audience of His Excellency Don Jose Bustamante y Rivero, President of Peru. A day or two later I was told to be at the Palace at twelve o'clock.

Lima is a modern city with half a million inhabitants, and lies spread over a green plain at the foot of the desert mountains. Architecturally, and thanks not least to its gardens and plantations, it is surely one of the most beautiful capitals in the world —a bit of modern Riviera or California variegated with old Spanish architecture. The President's palace lies in the middle of the city and is strongly guarded by armed sentries in gaily coloured costumes. An audience in Peru is a serious business, and few people have seen the President except on the screen. Soldiers in shining bandoliers escorted me upstairs and to the end of a long corridor; here my name was taken and registered by three civilians and I was shown through a colossal oak door into a room with a long table and rows of chairs. A man dressed in white received me, asked me to sit down, and himself disappeared. A moment later a large door opened and I was shown into a much handsomer room, where an imposing person in a spotless uniform advanced towards me.

"The President," I thought, drawing myself up. But no. The man in the gold-edged uniform offered me an antique straight-backed chair and disappeared. I had sat on the edge of my chair for barely a minute when yet another door opened and a servant bowed me into a large gilded room with gilded furniture and splendidly decorated. The fellow vanished as quickly as he had appeared, and I sat quite alone on an antique sofa with a view of a string of empty rooms whose doors stood open. It was so silent that I could hear someone coughing cautiously several rooms away. Then steady steps approached, and I jumped up and hesitatingly greeted an imposing gentleman in uniform. But no, this too was not he. But I understood enough of what he said to gather that the President sent me his greetings, and would be free very soon when a Meeting of Ministers was over.

Ten minutes later steady steps once more broke the silence, and this time a man with gold lace and epaulettes came in. I sprang briskly from the sofa and bowed deeply. The man bowed still more deeply, and led me through several rooms and up a staircase with thick carpets. Then he left me in a tiny little room with one leather-covered chair and one sofa. In came a little man in a white suit, and I waited resignedly to see where he intended to take me. But he took me nowhere, only greeted me amiably and remained standing. This was President Bustamante Rivero.

The President had twice as much English as I had Spanish, so when we had greeted one another and he had begged me with a gesture to sit down, our common vocabulary was exhausted. Signs and gesticulations will do a lot, but they will not get one permission to build a raft in a naval harbour in Peru. The only thing I perceived was that the President did not understand what I was saying, and he grasped that still more clearly himself, for in a little while he disappeared and came back with the Air Minister. The Air Minister, General Reveredo, was a vigorous athletic man in an Air Force uniform with wings on his chest. He spoke English splendidly with an American accent.

I apologised for the misunderstanding and said it was not to the airfield that I had been trying to ask for admission, but to the naval harbour. The general laughed and explained that he had only been called in as interpreter. Bit by bit the theory was translated to the President, who listened closely and put sharp questions through General Reveredo. At last he said:

"If it is possible that the Pacific islands were first discovered from Peru, Peru has an interest in this expedition. If we can do anything for you, tell us."

I asked for a place where we could build the raft within the walls of the naval area, access to the naval workshops, a place for the storage of equipment and facilities for bringing it into the country, the use of the dry dock and of naval personnel to help us in the work, and a vessel to tow us out from the coast when we started.

"What is he asking for?" the President asked eagerly, so that I too understood.

"Nothing much," Reveredo answered, looking at me with a twinkle in his eye. And the President, satisfied, nodded as a sign of approval.

Before the meeting broke up Reveredo promised that the Foreign Minister should receive orders from the President personally, and that the Minister of Marine Nieto should be given a free hand to give us all the help we had asked for.

"God preserve you all!" said the general, laughing and shaking his head. The adjutant came in and escorted me out to a waiting messenger.

That day the Lima papers published a paragraph about the Norwegian raft expedition which was to start from Peru; at the same time they announced that a Swedish-Finnish scientific expedition had finished its studies among the jungle Indians in the Amazon regions. Two of the Swedish members of the Amazon expedition had come on up the river by canoe to Peru, and had just arrived in Lima. One was Bengt Danielsson, from Uppsala University, who was now going to study the mountain Indians in Peru.

I cut out the paragraph, and was sitting in my hotel writing to Herman about the site for building the raft, when I was interrupted by a knock on the door. In came a tall sun-burnt fellow in tropical kit, and when he took off his white helmet it looked as if his flaming red beard had burned his face and scorched his hair thin. That fellow came from the wilds, but his place was clearly a lecture-room.

"Bengt Danielsson," I thought.

"Bengt Danielsson," said the man, introducing himself.

"He's heard about the raft," I thought, and asked him to sit down.

" I've just heard about the raft plans," said the Swede.

"And now he's come to knock down the theory, because he's an ethnologist," I thought.

"And now I've come to ask if I may come with you on the raft," the Swede said peaceably. "I'm interested in the migration theory."

I knew nothing about the man except that he was a scientist and that he had come straight out of the depths of the jungle. But if a solitary Swede had the pluck to go out on a raft with five Norwegians, he could not be squeamish. And not even that imposing beard could hide his placid nature and gay humour.

Bengt became the sixth member of the crew, for the place was still vacant. And he was the only one who spoke Spanish.

When the passenger aircraft droned northward along the coast a few days later, I again looked down with respect on to the endless blue sea beneath us. It seemed to hang and float loose in the firmament itself. Soon we six were to be packed together like microbes on a mere speck, down there where there was so much water that it looked as if it overflowed all along the western horizon. We were to acquire a desolate world without being able to get more than a few steps away from each other. For the time being, at any rate, there was elbow-room enough between us. Herman was in Ecuador waiting for the timber. Knut Haugland and Torstein Raaby had just arrived in New York by air. Erik Hesselberg was on board ship from Oslo, bound for Panama. I myself was en route for Washington by air, and Bengt was in the hotel at Lima ready to start, waiting to meet the others.

No two of these fellows had met before, and they were all of entirely different types. That being so, we should have been on the raft for some weeks before we got tired of each other's stories. No storm-clouds with low pressure and dirty weather held greater menace for us than the danger of psychological cloudburst among six men shut up together for months on a drifting raft. In such circumstances a good joke was often as valuable as a life-belt.

Up in Washington there was still bitter winter weather, cold and snowy. It was February when I came back. Björn had tackled the wireless problem and had interested the Radio Amateur League of America in listening in for reports from the raft, and Knut and Torstein were busy preparing the transmission, which was to be done partly with short wave transmitters specially constructed for our purpose and partly with secret sabotage sets used during the war. There were a thousand things to prepare, big and small, if we were to overcome what we planned to do on the voyage.

And the piles of paper in the files grew. Military and civilian documents, white, yellow and blue, in English, Spanish, French and Norwegian. Even a raft trip had to cost the paper industry half a fir-tree in our practical age. Laws and regulations tied our hands everywhere, and knot after knot had to be loosened in turn.

"I'll swear this correspondence weighs twenty pounds," said Knut one day despairingly as he bent over his typewriter.

"Twenty-six," said Torstein drily. "I've weighed it."

My mother must have had a clear idea of the conditions in these days of dramatic preparation, when she wrote: "And I only wish I knew you were all six safe on board the raft!"

Then one day an express telegram came from Lima. Herman had been caught in the backwash of a breaker and flung ashore, badly injured, with his neck dislocated. He was under treatment in Lima hospital.

Torstein Raaby was sent down by air at once with Gerd Vold, the popular London secretary of the Norwegian parachute saboteurs in the war, who was now helping us in Washington. They found him better; he had been hung up by a strap round his head for half an hour while the doctors twisted the atlas vertebra in his neck back into position. The X-ray picture showed that the highest bone in his neck was cracked and had been turned right round. Herman's splendid condition had saved his life, and he was soon back, blue and green and stiff and rheumatic, in the naval dockyard, where he had assembled the balsa wood and started the work. He had to remain in the doctors' hands for several weeks, and it was doubtful whether he would be able to make the voyage with us. He himself never doubted it for a moment, despite his initial rough handling in the embrace of the Pacific.

Then Erik arrived by air from Panama and Knut and I from Washington, and so we were all assembled at the starting point in Lima.

Down in the naval dockyard lay the big balsa logs from the Quivedo forest. It was really a pathetic sight. Fresh-cut round logs, yellow bamboos, reeds and green banana leaves lay in a heap, our building materials, in between rows of threatening grey submarines and destroyers. Six fair-skinned Northerners and two brown naval ratings with Inca blood in their veins swung axes and long machete knives, and tugged at ropes and knots. Trim naval officers in blue and gold walked over and stared in bewilderment at these pale strangers and these vegetable materials which had suddenly appeared in their midst, in the dockyard of all places.

For the first time for hundreds of years a balsa raft was being built in Callao bay. In these coastal waters where Inca legends hold that their ancestors first learnt to sail such rafts from Kon-Tiki's vanished clan, there history records that modern Indians were forbidden to use such rafts by men of our own race. Sailing on an open raft can cost human lives. The descendants of the Incas have moved with the times; like us, they have creases in their trousers and are safely protected by the guns of their naval craft. Bamboos and balsa belong to the primitive past; here too things are marching on—to armour and steel.

The ultra-modern dockyard gave us wonderful support. With Bengt as interpreter and Herman as chief constructor we had the run of the carpenter's and sail-maker's shops, as well as half the storage space as a dump for our equipment, and a small floating

PLATE III
Felling a balsa tree in the Ecuador jungle.

loating balsa logs
own the Palen-
ue to the Pacific.

PLATE IV

Lashing the nine big logs together with hemp ropes. No nails or other metal were used on the raft.

pier where the timber was put into the water when the building began.

Nine of the thickest logs were chosen as sufficient to form the actual raft. Deep grooves were cut in the wood to prevent the ropes which were to fasten them and the whole raft together from slipping. Not a single spike, nail or wire rope was used in the whole construction. The nine great logs were first laid loose side by side in the water so that they might all fall freely into their natural floating position before they were lashed securely together. The longest log, 45 feet long, was laid in the middle and projected a long way at both ends. Shorter and shorter logs were laid symmetrically on both sides of this, so that the sides of the raft were 30 feet long, and the bow stuck out like a blunt plough. Astern the raft was cut off straight across, except that the three middle logs projected and supported a short thick block of balsa wood which lay athwart ship and held tholepins for the long steering oar. When the nine balsa logs were lashed securely together with separate lengths of inch and a quarter inch hemp rope, the thin balsa logs were made fast crossways over them at intervals of about three feet. The raft itself was now complete, laboriously fastened together with about three hundred different lengths of rope, each firmly knotted. A deck of split bamboos was laid upon it, fastened to it in the form of separate strips, and covered with loose mats of plaited bamboo reeds. In the middle of the raft, but nearer the stern, we erected a small open cabin of bamboo canes, with walls of plaited bamboo reeds and a roof of bamboo slats with leathery banana leaves overlapping one another like tiles. Forward of the cabin we set up two masts side by side. They were cut from mangrove wood as hard as iron, and leaned towards one another, so that they were lashed together crosswise at the top. The big rectangular square-sail was hauled up on a yard made of two bamboo stems bound together to secure double strength.

The nine big logs of timber which were to carry us over the sea were pointed at their forward ends in native fashion, that they might glide more easily through the water, and quite low splash-boards were fastened to the bow above the surface of the water.

E

At various places where there were large chinks between the logs we pushed down in all five solid fir planks which stood on their edges right down in the water under the raft. They were scattered about without system and went down five feet into the water, an inch thick and two feet wide. They were kept in place with wedges and ropes, and served as tiny parallel keels or centreboards. Centreboards of this kind were used on all the balsa rafts of Inca times long before the time of the discoveries, and were meant to prevent the flat wooden rafts from drifting sideways with wind and sea. We did not make any rail or protection round the raft, but we had a long slim balsa log which afforded foothold along each side.

The whole construction was a faithful copy of the old vessels in Peru and Ecuador except for the low splashboards in the bows, which later proved to be entirely unnecessary. After that, of course, we could arrange the details on board as we liked, so long as this had no influence on the vessel. We knew that this raft was to be our whole world in the time that lay before us, and that consequently the smallest detail on board would increase in dimensions and importance as the weeks passed.

Therefore we gave the little deck as much variation as possible. The bamboo strips did not deck in the whole raft, but formed a floor forward of the bamboo cabin and along the starboard side of it where the wall was open. The port side of the cabin was a kind of back-yard full of boxes and gear made fast, with a narrow edge left to walk along. Forward in the bows, and in the stern as far as the after wall of the cabin, the nine gigantic logs were not decked in at all. So when we moved round the bamboo cabin, we stepped from yellow bamboos and wicker-work down on to the round grey logs astern, and up again on to piles of cargo on the other side. It was not many steps, but the psychological effect of the irregularity gave us variation, and compensated us for our limited freedom of movement. Right up at the masthead we placed a wooden platform, not so much in order to have a look-out post when at last we came to land, as to be able to clamber up while en route and look at the sea from another angle.

When the raft began to take shape and lay there among the warships, golden and fresh with ripe bamboos and green leaves, the Minister of Marine himself came to inspect us. We were immensely proud of our vessel as she lay there, a fresh little reminder of Inca times among the uncanny big warships. But the Minister of Marine was utterly horrified by what he saw. I was summoned to the naval office to sign a paper freeing the Navy from all responsibility for what we had built in its harbour, and to the harbour-master to sign a paper saying that if I left the harbour with men and cargo on board it was entirely on my own responsibility and at my own risk.

Later a number of foreign naval experts and diplomatists were admitted to the dockyard to see the raft. They were no more encouraging, and a few days afterwards I was sent for by the ambassador of one of the Great Powers.

"Are your parents living?" he said. And when I replied in the affirmative, he looked me straight in the eyes and said in a hollow voice, full of ill-boding:

"Your mother and father will be very grieved when they hear of your death."

As a private individual he begged me to give up the voyage while there was yet time. An admiral who had inspected the raft had told him that we should never get across alive. In the first place, the raft's dimensions were wrong. It was so small that it would founder in a big sea, and at the same time it was just long enough to be lifted up by two lines of waves at the same time, and with the raft filled with men and cargo the fragile balsa logs would break under the strain. And, what was worse, the biggest balsa exporter in the country had told him that the porous balsa logs would float only a quarter of the distance across the sea before they became so completely water-logged that they would sink under us.

This sounded bad, but as we stuck to our guns, we were given a Bible as a present to take with us on our voyage. Taken all round there was little encouragement to be had from the experts who looked at the raft. Gales and perhaps hurricanes would wash us overboard and destroy the low and open craft, which would

simply lie helpless and drift in circles about the ocean before wind
and sea. Even in an ordinary choppy sea we should be continually
drenched with salt water which would take the skin off our legs
and ruin everything on board. And if we totted up all that the
different experts, each in turn, had pointed out as the vital flaw
in the construction itself, there was not a length of rope, not a
knot, not a measurement, not a piece of wood in the whole raft
which would not cause us to founder at sea. High wagers were
made as to how many days the raft would last, and a flippant
naval attaché bet all the whisky the members of the expedition
could drink in the rest of their lives if they reached a South Sea
island alive.

Worst of all was when a Norwegian ship came into port and
we took the skipper and one or two of his most experienced
seadogs into the dockyard. We were eager to hear their practical
reactions. And our disappointment was great when they all agreed
that the blunt-bowed, clumsy craft would never get any help
from the sail, while the skipper maintained that, if we kept afloat,
the raft would take a year or two to drift across with the Humboldt Current. The boatswain looked at our lashings and shook
his head. We need not worry. The raft would not hold together
for a fortnight before every single rope was worn through, for
when at sea the big logs would be continually moving up and
down and rubbing against one another. Unless we used wire
ropes or chains we might as well pack up.

These were difficult arguments to stifle. If only one of them
proved to be right, we had not a chance. I am afraid I asked
myself many times if we knew what we were doing. I could not
myself counter the warnings one by one, because I was not a
seaman. But I had in reserve one single trump in my hand, on
which the whole voyage was founded. I knew all the time in my
heart that a prehistoric civilisation had been spread from Peru
and across to the islands at a time when rafts like ours were the
only vessels on that coast. And I drew the general conclusion that
if balsa wood had floated and lashings held for Kon-Tiki in
A.D. 500, they would do the same for us now if we just blindly
made our raft an exact copy of his. Bengt and Herman had gone

into the theory most thoroughly, and while the experts lamented, all the boys took the thing quite calmly and had a royal time in Lima. There was just one evening when Torstein asked anxiously if I was sure the ocean currents went the right way. We had been to the cinema and seen Dorothy Lamour dancing about in a straw skirt among palms and hula girls on a lovely South Sea island.

"That's where we must go," said Torstein. "And I'm sorry for you if the currents don't go as you say they do!"

When the day of our departure was approaching we went to the ordinary passport control office to get permission to leave the country. Bengt stood first in the queue as interpreter.

"What is your name?" asked a ceremonious little clerk, looking suspiciously over his spectacles at Bengt's huge beard.

"Bengt Emmerik Danielsson," Bengt answered respectfully.

The man put a long form into his typewriter.

"By what boat did you come to Peru?"

"Well, you see," Bengt explained, bending over the scared little man, "I didn't come by boat, I came to Peru by canoe."

The man looked at Bengt dumb with astonishment and tapped out "canoe" in an open space on the form.

"And by what boat are you leaving Peru?"

"Well, you see, again," said Bengt politely, "I'm not leaving Peru by boat, I'm leaving by raft."

"So likely, so likely!" the clerk cried angrily, and tore the paper out of the machine. "Will you please answer my questions properly?"

A few days before we sailed, provisions and water and all our equipment were stowed on board the raft. We took provisions for six men for four months, in the form of solid little cardboard cartons containing military rations. Herman had the idea of boiling asphalt and pouring it so as to make a level layer round each separate carton. Then we strewed sand on them to prevent the cartons from sticking together, and stowed them, packed close, under the bamboo deck, where they filled the space between the nine low cross-beams which supported the deck.

At a crystal-clear spring high up in the mountains we filled

56 small water cans with in all 250 gallons of drinking water. These too we made fast in between the cross-beams so that the sea might always splash round them. On the bamboo deck we lashed fast the rest of the equipment and large wicker baskets full of fruit and cocoanuts.

Knut and Torstein took one corner of the bamboo cabin for the wireless, and inside the hut, down between the cross-beams, we made fast eight boxes. Two were reserved for scientific instruments and films; the other six were allotted to each of us, with an intimation that each man could take with him as much private property as he could find room for in his own box. As Erik had brought several rolls of drawing-paper and a guitar, his box was so full that he had to put his stockings in Torstein's. Then four naval ratings came along carrying Bengt's box. He brought nothing but books, but he had managed to cram in 73 sociological and ethnological works. We laid on top of the boxes plaited reed mats and our straw mattresses, and then we were ready to start.

First the raft was towed out of the naval area and paddled round in the harbour for a while to see if the cargo was stowed evenly, and then she was towed across to the Callao Yacht Club, where invited guests and other persons interested were to be present at the naming of the raft the day before we sailed.

On April 27 the Norwegian flag was hoisted, and along a yard at the masthead waved the flags of the foreign countries which had given the expedition practical support. The quay was black with people who wanted to see the strange craft christened. Both colour and lineaments betrayed that many of them had remote ancestors who had sailed along the coast on balsa rafts. But there were also descendants of the old Spaniards, headed by representatives of the Navy and the Government, besides the ambassadors of the United States, Great Britain, France, China, Argentina and Cuba, the ex-governor of the British colonies in the Pacific, the Swedish and Belgian Ministers, and our friends from the little Norwegian colony with Consul-General Bahr at their head. There were swarms of journalists and a clicking of cinema cameras; indeed, the only things that were lacking were

a brass band and a big drum. One thing was quite clear to us all
—that if the raft went to pieces outside the bay we would paddle
to Polynesia, each of us on a log, rather than dare come back
there again.

Gerd Vold, the expedition's secretary and contact on the main-
land, was to christen the raft with milk from a cocoanut, partly
to be in harmony with the Stone Age, and partly because, owing
to a misunderstanding, the champagne had been put at the bottom
of Torstein's private box. When our friends had been told in
English and Spanish that the raft was named after the Incas' great
forerunner—the sun-king who had vanished westward over the
sea from Peru and appeared in Polynesia 1500 years ago—Gerd
Vold christened the raft *Kon-Tiki*. She smashed the cocoanut
(cracked) so hard against the stem that milk and bits of kernel
filled the hair of all those who stood reverently around.

Then the bamboo yard was hauled up and the sail shaken out,
with Kon-Tiki's bearded head, painted in red by the artist Erik,
in its centre. It was a faithful copy of the sun-king's head cut in
red stone on a statue in the ruined city of Tiahuanaco.

"Ah! Señor Danielsson," the foreman of our dockyard workers
cried in delight when he saw the bearded face on the sail.

He had called Bengt Señor Kon-Tiki for two months, since we
had shown him the bearded face of Kon-Tiki on a piece of paper.
But now he had at last realised that Danielsson was Bengt's right
name.

Before we sailed we all had a farewell audience of the President,
and then we went for a trip far up into the black mountains to
look our fill on rock and scree before we drifted out into the
endless ocean. While we were working on the raft down on the
coast we had stayed in a pension in a palm grove outside Lima,
and driven to and from Callao in an Air Ministry car with a
private chauffeur whom Gerd had contrived to borrow for the
expedition. Now we asked the chauffeur to drive us straight to
the mountains, and as far in as he could get in a day; and so we
drove up over desert roads, along old irrigation canals from Inca
times, till we came to the dizzy height of 12,000 feet above the
raft's mast. Here we simply devoured rocks and mountain peaks

and green grass with our eyes, and tried to surfeit ourselves with
the tranquil mountain mass of the Andes range that lay before us.
We tried to convince ourselves that we were thoroughly tired of
stone and solid earth, and wanted to sail out and get to know
the sea.

CHAPTER IV

ACROSS THE PACIFIC: I

*A Dramatic Start—We are Towed Out to Sea—A Wind Springs
Up—Fighting the Waves—Life in the Humboldt Current—Plane
Fails to Find Us—The Logs Absorb Water—Wood against Ropes—
Flying Fish for Meals—An Unusual Bedfellow—Snake Fish
Makes a Blunder—Eyes in the Sea—A Marine Ghost Story—We
Meet the World's Biggest Fish—A Sea Turtle Hunt.*

THERE was a bustle in Callao harbour the day the *Kon-Tiki* was to be towed out to sea. The Minister of Marine
had ordered the naval tug *Guardian Rios* to tow us out
of the bay and cast us off clear of the coastal traffic, out where
in times gone by the Indians used to lie fishing from their rafts.
The papers had published the news under both red and black
headlines, and there was a crowd of people down on the quays
from early in the morning of April 28.

We six who were to assemble on board all had little things to
do at the eleventh hour, and when I came down to the quay
only Herman was there keeping guard over the raft. I intentionally stopped the car a long way off and walked the whole
length of the mole to stretch my legs thoroughly for the last
time for no one knew how long. I jumped on board the raft,
which looked an utter chaos of banana clusters, fruit baskets and
sacks which had been hurled on board at the very last moment
and were to be stowed and made fast as soon as we got into some
kind of order. In the middle of the heap Herman sat resignedly
holding on to a cage with a green parrot in it, a farewell present
from a friendly soul in Lima.

"Look after the parrot a minute," said Herman; "I must go
ashore and have a last glass of beer. The tug won't be here for
hours."

He had hardly disappeared among the swarm on the quay
when people began to point and wave. And round the point at

full speed came the tug *Guardian Rios*. She dropped anchor on the farther side of a waving forest of masts which blocked the way in to the *Kon-Tiki*, and sent in a large motor-boat to tow us out between the sailing craft. She was packed full of naval ratings, officers and cinema photographers, and while orders rang out and cameras clicked, a stout tow-rope was made fast to the raft's bow.

"*Un momento*," I shouted in despair from where I sat with the parrot. "It's too early, we must wait for the others—*los expedicionarios*," I explained, and pointed towards the city.

But nobody understood. The officers only smiled politely, and the knot at our bows was made fast in more than exemplary manner. I cast off the rope and flung it overboard with all manner of signs and gesticulations. The parrot utilised the opportunity afforded by all the confusion to stick its beak out of the cage and turn the knob of the door, and when I turned round it was strutting cheerfully about the bamboo deck. I tried to catch it, but it shrieked rudely in Spanish and fluttered away over the banana clusters. With one eye on the sailors who were trying to cast a rope over the bows, I started a wild chase after the parrot. It fled shrieking into the bamboo cabin, where I got it into a corner and caught it by one leg as it tried to flutter over me. When I came out again and stuffed my flapping trophy into its cage, the sailors on land had cast off the raft's moorings, and we were dancing helplessly in and out with the backwash of the long swell that came rolling in over the mole. In despair I seized a paddle and vainly tried to parry a violent bump as the raft was flung against the wooden piles of the quay. Then the motor-boat started, and with one jerk the *Kon-Tiki* began her long voyage. My only companion was a Spanish-speaking parrot which sat glaring sulkily in a cage. People on shore cheered and waved, and the swarthy cinema photographers in the motor-boat almost jumped into the sea in their eagerness to catch every detail of the expedition's dramatic start from Peru. Despairing and alone I stood on the raft looking out for my lost companions, but no one came. So we came out to the *Guardian Rios*, which was lying with steam up ready to lift anchor and start. I was up the rope-ladder in a twinkling and made so much row on board that the start was postponed and a boat sent back to the quay. It was away a good while, and then it came back full of pretty *señoritas*, but without a single one of the *Kon-Tiki*'s missing men. This was all very well, but it did not solve my problems, and while the raft swarmed with charming *señoritas*, the boat went back on a fresh search for *los expedicionarios noruegos*.

Meanwhile Erik and Bengt came sauntering down to the quay with their arms full of reading matter and oddments. They met the whole stream of people on its way home, and were finally stopped at a police barrier by a kindly official who told them there was nothing more to see. Bengt told the constable, with an airy gesture with his cigar, that they had not come to see anything; they themselves were going with the raft.

"It's no use," the constable said indulgently. "The *Kon-Tiki* sailed an hour ago."

"Impossible," said Erik, producing a parcel; "here's the lantern!"

"And there's the navigator," said Bengt, "and I'm the steward."

They forced their way past, but the raft had gone. They trotted desperately to and fro along the mole, where they met the rest of the party, who also were searching eagerly for the vanished raft. Then they caught sight of the boat coming in, and so we were all six united and the water was foaming round the raft as the *Guardian Rios* towed us out to sea.

It had been late in the afternoon when at last we started, and the *Guardian Rios* would not cast us off till we were clear of the coastal traffic next morning. Directly we were clear of the mole we met a bit of a head sea, and all the small boats which were accompanying us turned back one by one. Only a few big yachts came with us right out to the entrance to the bay to see how things would go out there.

The *Kon-Tiki* followed the tug like an angry billy-goat on a rope, and she butted her bows into the head sea so that the water rushed on board. This did not look very promising, for this was a calm sea compared with what we had to expect. In the middle of the bay the tow-rope broke, and our end of it sank peacefully to the bottom while the tug steamed ahead. We flung ourselves down along the side of the raft to fish for the end of the tow-rope, while the yachts went on and tried to stop the tug. Stinging jelly-fish as thick as wash-tubs splashed up and down with the seas alongside the raft, and covered all the ropes with a slippery stinging coating of jelly. When the raft rolled one way, we hung flat over the side waving our arms down towards the surface of the water, until our fingers just touched the slimy rope. Then the raft rolled back again and we all stuck our heads deep down into the sea, while salt water and giant jelly-fish poured over our backs. We spat and cursed and pulled jelly-fish fibres out of our hair, but when the tug came back the rope-end was up and ready for splicing. When we were about to throw it on board the tug we suddenly drifted in under the vessel's overhanging stern and were in danger of being crushed against her by the pressure of the water. We dropped everything we had and tried to push ourselves clear with bamboo sticks and paddles before it was too late. But we never got a proper purchase, for when we were in the trough of the sea we could not reach the iron roof above us, and when the water rose again the *Guardian Rios* dropped her whole stern down into the water and would have crushed us flat if the suction had carried us underneath. Up on the tug's deck people were running about and shouting; at last the propeller began to turn just alongside us, and it helped us clear of the backwash under the *Guardian Rios* in the last second. The bows of the raft had had a few hard knocks and had become a little crooked in the lashings, but this rectified itself by degrees.

"When a thing starts so damnably it's bound to end well," said Herman. "If only this towing could stop; it'll shake the raft to bits."

The towing went on all night at a slow speed and with only one or two small hitches. The yachts had bidden us farewell long ago, and the last coast light had disappeared astern. Only a few ships' lights passed us in the darkness. We divided the night into watches to keep an eye on the tow-rope, and we all had a good snatch of sleep. When it grew light next morning, a thick mist lay over the coast of Peru, while we had a brilliant blue sky ahead of us to westward. The sea was running in a long quiet swell covered with little white crests, and clothes and logs and everything we took hold of were soaking wet with dew. It was chilly, and the green water round us was astonishingly cold for 12° south. This was the Humboldt Current, which carried its cold masses of water up from the Antarctic and swept them north all along the coast of Peru till they swung west and out across the sea just below the equator. It was out here that Pizarro, Zarate and the other early Spaniards came for the first time upon the Inca Indians' big sailing rafts, which used to go out for 50–60 sea miles to catch tunnies and dolphins in the very Humboldt Current. All day long there was an off-shore wind out here, but in the evening the on-shore wind reached as far out as this and helped them home if they wished it.

The tug was lying close by, and we took care that the raft lay to well away from her bows while we launched our little inflated rubber dinghy. It floated on the waves like a football and danced away with Erik, Bengt and myself till we got hold of the *Guardian Rios's* rope-ladder and clambered on board. With Bengt as interpreter we had the exact position shown us on our chart. We were 50 sea miles from land in a north-westerly direction from Callao, and we must carry lights the first few nights so as not to be sunk by coasting ships. Farther out there was not a single ship, for no shipping route ran through that part of the Pacific.

We took a ceremonious farewell of all on board, and many strange looks followed us as we climbed down into the dinghy and went tumbling back over the waves to the *Kon-Tiki*. Then the tow-rope was cast off and the raft was alone again. Thirty-five men on board the *Guardian Rios* stood at the rail waving for as long as we could distinguish outlines. And six men sat on the boxes on board the raft and followed the tug with their eyes as long as they could see her. Not till the black column of smoke had dissolved and vanished over the horizon did we shake our heads and look at one another.

"Good-bye, good-bye," said Torstein. "Now we'll have to start the engine, boys!"

We laughed, and felt the wind. There was a rather light breeze, which had veered from south to south-east. We hoisted the bamboo yard with the big square-sail. It only hung down slack, giving Kon-Tiki's face a wrinkled, discontented appearance.

"The old man doesn't like it," said Erik, "there were fresher breezes when he was young."

"It looks as if we were losing way," said Herman, and threw a piece of balsa wood overboard at the bows.

"One—two—three . . . thirty-nine, forty, forty-one."

The piece of balsa wood still lay quietly in the water alongside the raft; it had not yet got halfway along our side.

"We'll have to go over with it," said Torstein optimistically.

"Hope we don't drift astern with the evening breeze," said Bengt. "It was great fun saying good-bye at Callao, but I'd just as soon miss our welcome back again!"

Now the piece of wood had reached the end of the raft. We shouted hurrah and began to stow and make fast all the things that had been flung on board at the last moment. Bengt set up a Primus stove at the bottom of an empty box, and soon after we were regaling ourselves on hot cocoa and biscuits and making a hole in a fresh cocoanut. The bananas were not quite ripe yet.

"We're well off now in one way," Erik chuckled. He was rolling about in wide sheepskin trousers under a huge Indian hat, with the parrot on his shoulder.

"There's only one thing I don't like," he added, "and that's all the little-known cross-currents which can fling us right upon the rocks along the coast, if we go on lying here like this."

We considered the possibility of paddling, but agreed to wait for a wind.

And the wind came. It blew up from the south-east quietly and steadily. Soon the sail filled and bent forward like a swelling breast, with Kon-Tiki's head bursting with pugnacity. And the *Kon-Tiki* began to move. We shouted westward ho! and hauled on sheets and ropes. The steering oar was put into the water and the watch roster began to operate. We threw balls of paper and chips overboard at the bows and stood aft with our watches.

"One, two, three . . . eighteen, nineteen—now!"

Paper and chips of wood passed the steering oar, and soon lay like pearls on a thread, dipping up and down in the trough of the waves astern. We went forward, yard by yard. The *Kon-Tiki* did not plough through the sea like a sharp-prowed racing craft. Blunt and broad, heavy and solid she splashed sedately forward over the waves. She did not hurry, but when she had once got going she pushed ahead with unshakeable energy.

At the moment the steering arrangements were our greatest problem. The raft was built exactly as the Spaniards described it, but there was no one living in our time who could give us a practical advance course in sailing an Indian raft. The problem had been thoroughly discussed among the experts on shore, but with meagre results. They knew just as little about it as we did. As the south-easterly wind increased in strength it was necessary to keep the raft on such a course that the sail was filled from astern. If the raft turned her side too much to the wind, the sail suddenly swung round and banged against cargo and men and bamboo cabin, while the whole raft turned round and continued on the same course stern first. It was a hard struggle, three men fighting with the sail and three others rowing with the long steering oar to get the nose of the wooden raft round and away from the wind. And as soon as we got her round, the steersman had to take good care that the same thing did not happen again the next minute.

The steering oar, nineteen feet long, rested loose between two thole-pins on a huge block astern. It was the same steering oar our native friends had used when we floated the timber down the Palenque in Ecuador. The long mangrove-wood pole was as tough as steel, but so heavy that it would sink if it fell overboard. At the end of the pole was a large oar-blade of fir-wood lashed on with ropes. It took all our strength to hold this long steering oar steady when the seas drove against it, and our fingers were tired out by the convulsive grip which was necessary to turn the pole so that the oar-blade stood straight up in the water. This last problem was solved by our lashing a cross-piece to the handle of the steering oar, so that we had a sort of lever to turn. And meanwhile the wind increased.

By the late afternoon the trade wind was already blowing at full strength. It quickly stirred up the ocean into roaring seas which swept against us from astern. Now we fully realised for the first time that here was the sea itself come to meet us; it was bitter earnest now, our communications were cut. Whether things went well now would depend entirely on the balsa raft's good qualities in the open sea. We knew that from now onwards we should never get another on-shore wind or chance of turning back. We had got into the real trade wind, and every day would carry us farther and farther out to sea. The only thing to do was to go ahead under full sail; if we tried to turn homewards we should only drift farther out to sea stern first. There was only one possible course, to sail before the wind with our bows towards the sunset. And, after all, that was just the object of our voyage, to follow the sun in its path, as we thought Kon-Tiki and the old sun-worshippers must have done when they were chased out to sea from Peru.

We noted with triumph and relief how the wooden raft rose up over the first threatening wave-crests that came foaming towards us. But it was impossible for the steersman to hold the oar steady when the roaring seas rolled towards him and lifted the oar out of the thole-pins, or swept it to one side so that the steersman was swung round like a helpless acrobat. Not even two men at once could hold the oar steady when the seas rose against us and poured down over the steersman aft. We hit on the idea of running ropes from the oar-blade to each side of the raft, and, with other ropes holding the oar in place in the thole-pins, it obtained a limited freedom of movement and could defy the worst seas if only we ourselves could hold on.

As the troughs of the sea gradually grew deeper it became clear that we had got into the swiftest part of the Humboldt Current. This sea was obviously caused by a current and not simply raised by the wind. The water was green and cold and everywhere about us; the jagged mountains of Peru had vanished into the dense cloud-banks astern. When darkness crept over the sea our first duel with the elements began. We were still not sure of the sea; it was still uncertain whether it would show itself a

PLATE V

Ready to start in Callao harbour. The raft was an exact
copy of the old Indian vessels, with an open bamboo cabin
aft of a square-sail between two masts lashed together.

PLATE VI
Under full sail in the open sea. We had a hard schooling in the Humboldt
Current, for the last instructors in raft sailing had been dead for centuries.

friend or an enemy in the intimate proximity we ourselves had sought. When, swallowed up by the darkness, we heard the general noise from the sea around us suddenly deafened by the hiss of a roller close by, and saw a white crest come groping towards us on a level with the cabin roof, we held on tight and waited uneasily to feel the masses of water smash down over us and the raft. But every time there was the same surprise and relief. The *Kon-Tiki* calmly swung up her stern and rose skyward unperturbed, while the masses of water rolled along her sides. Then we sank down again into the trough of the waves and waited for the next big sea. The biggest seas often came two or three in succession, with a long series of smaller seas in between. It was when two big seas followed one another too closely that the second broke on board aft, because the first was still holding our bows in the air. It was, therefore, an unbreakable law that the steering watch must have ropes round their waists, the other ends of which were made fast to the raft. For there were no bulwarks here. Their task was to keep the sail filled by holding our stern to sea and wind. We had made an old boat's compass fast to a box aft so that Erik could check our course and calculate our position and speed. For the time being it was uncertain where we were, for the sky was overclouded and the horizon one single chaos of rollers. Two men at a time took turns as steering watch, and, side by side, they had to put all their strength into the fight with the leaping oar, whilst the others tried to snatch a little sleep inside the open bamboo cabin. When a really big sea came, the men at the helm left the steering to the ropes and jumped up and hung on to a bamboo pole from the cabin roof, while the masses of water thundered in over them from astern and disappeared between the logs or over the side of the raft. Then they had to fling themselves at the oar again before the raft could turn round and the sail thrash about. For if the raft took the seas at an angle the waves could easily pour right into the bamboo cabin. When they came on board from astern they disappeared between the projecting logs at once, and seldom came so far forward as the cabin wall. The round logs astern let the water pass as if through the prongs of a fork. The advantage of a raft was

F

obviously this: the more leaks the better—through the gaps in our floor the water ran out, but never in.

About midnight a ship's light passed in a northerly direction. At three another passed, on the same course. We waved our little paraffin lamp and called them up with flashes from an electric torch, but they did not see us, and the lights passed slowly northwards into the darkness and disappeared. Little did those on board guess that a real live Inca raft lay close to them tumbling among the waves. And just as little did we on board the raft guess that this was our last ship and the last trace of men we should see till we had reached the other side of the ocean.

We clung like flies, two and two, to the steering oar in the darkness, and felt the fresh sea water pouring off our hair while the oar hit us till we were tender both behind and before, and our hands grew stiff with the exertion of hanging on. We had a good schooling those first days and nights; it turned landlubbers into seamen. For the first twenty-four hours every man, in unbroken succession, had two hours at the helm and three hours' rest. We arranged that every hour a fresh man should relieve the one of the two steersmen who had been at the helm for two hours. Every single muscle in the body was strained to the uttermost throughout the watch to cope with the steering. When we were tired out with pushing the oar we went over to the other side and pulled, and when arms and chest were sore with pressing, we turned our backs, while the oar kneaded us green and blue in front and behind. When at last the relief came, we crept half dazed into the bamboo cabin, tied a rope round our legs, and fell asleep with our salty clothes on before we could get into our sleeping bags. Almost at the same moment there came a brutal tug at the rope; three hours had passed, and one had to go out again and relieve one of the two men at the steering oar.

The next night was still worse; the seas grew higher instead of going down. Two hours on end of struggling with the steering oar was too long; a man was not much use in the second half of his watch, and the seas got the better of us and hurled us round and sideways, while the water poured on board. Then we changed over to one hour at the helm and an hour and a half's rest. So the first sixty hours passed, in one continuous struggle against a chaos of waves that rushed upon us, one after another, without cessation. High waves and low waves, pointed waves and round waves, slanting waves and waves on the top of other waves. The one of us who suffered the worst was Knut. He was let off steering watch, but to compensate for this he had to sacrifice to Neptune and suffered silent agonies in a corner of the cabin. The parrot sat sulkily in its cage and hung on with its beak and flapped its wings every time the raft gave an unexpected pitch and the sea splashed against the wall from astern. The *Kon-Tiki* did not roll so excessively. She took the seas more steadily than any boat of the same dimensions, but it was impossible to predict which way the deck would lean next time, and we never learned the art of moving about the raft easily, for she pitched as much as she rolled.

On the third night the sea went down a bit, although it was still blowing hard. About four o'clock an unexpected pursuer came foaming through the darkness and knocked the raft right round before the steersmen realised what was happening. The sail thrashed against the bamboo cabin and threatened to tear both the cabin and itself to pieces. All hands had to go on deck and secure the cargo and haul on sheets and stays in the hope of getting the raft on her right course again, so that the sail might fill and curve forward peacefully. But the raft would not right herself. She would go stern foremost, and that was all. The only result of all our hauling and pushing and rowing was that two men nearly went overboard in a sea when the sail caught them in the dark. The sea had clearly become calmer. Stiff and sore, with skinned palms and sleepy eyes, we were not worth many rows of beans. Better to save our strength in case the weather should call us out to a worse passage of arms. One could never know. So we furled the sail and rolled it round the bamboo yard. The *Kon-Tiki* lay sideways on to the seas and took them like a cork. Everything on board was lashed fast, and all six of us crawled into the little bamboo cabin, huddled together and slept like mummies in a sardine tin.

We little guessed that we had struggled through the hardest

steering of the voyage. Not till we were far out on the ocean did we discover the Incas' simple and ingenious way of steering a raft.

We did not wake till well on in the day, when the parrot began to whistle and halloo, and dance to and fro on its perch. Outside the sea was still running high, but in long even ridges and not so wild and confused as the day before. The first thing we saw was that the sun was beating down on the yellow bamboo deck and giving the sea all round us a bright and friendly aspect. What did it matter if the seas foamed and rose high so long as they only left us in peace on the raft? What did it matter if they rose straight up in front of our noses when we knew that in a second the raft would go over the top and flatten out the foaming ridge like a steam-roller, while the heavy threatening mountain of water only lifted us up in the air and rolled groaning and gurgling under the floor? The old masters from Peru knew what they were doing when they avoided a hollow hull which could fill with water, or a vessel so long that it would not take the waves one by one. A cork steam-roller, that was what the balsa raft amounted to.

Erik took our position at noon, and found that in addition to our run under sail we had made a big deviation northward along the coast. We still lay in the Humboldt Current just 100 sea miles from land. The great question was whether we should get into the treacherous eddies south of the Galapagos. This could have fatal consequences, for up there we might be swept in all directions by strong ocean currents making towards the coast of Central America. But if things went as we calculated, we should swing west across the sea with the main current before we got as far north as the Galapagos. The wind was still blowing straight from south-east. We hoisted the sail, turned the raft stern to sea, and continued our steering watches.

Knut had now recovered from the torments of sea-sickness, and he and Torstein clambered up to the swaying masthead, where they experimented with mysterious wireless aerials which they sent up both by balloon and by kite. Suddenly one of them shouted from the wireless corner of the cabin that he could hear

the naval station at Lima calling us. They told us that the American
Ambassador's plane was on its way out from the coast to bid us
a last good-bye and see what we looked like at sea. Soon after we
obtained direct contact with the operator in the aircraft, and
then an undeniably unexpected chat with the secretary to the
expedition, Gerd Vold, who was on board. We gave our position
as exactly as we could and sent direction-finding signals for hours.
And the voice in the ether grew stronger and weaker as ARMY-
119 circled round near and far and searched. But we did not hear
the drone of the engines and never saw the plane. It was not so
easy to find the low raft down in the trough of the seas, and our
view was strictly limited. At last the aircraft had to give it up
and returned to the coast. It was the last time anyone tried to
search for us.

The sea ran high in the days that followed, but the waves came
hissing along from the south-east with even spaces between them,
and the steering went more easily. We took the sea and wind on
the port quarter, so that the steersman got fewer seas over him
and the raft went more steadily and did not swing round. We
noted anxiously that the south-east trade wind and the Humboldt
Current were day after day sending us straight across on a course
leading to the counter currents round the Galapagos Islands.
And we were going due north-west so quickly that our daily
average in those days was 55–60 sea miles, with a record of 71
sea miles.

"Is it all right on the Galapagos?" Knut asked cautiously one
day and looked at our chart, where a string of pearls indicating
our positions was marked and resembled a finger pointing bale-
fully towards the accursed Galapagos Islands.

"Hardly," I said. "The Inca Tupac Yupanqui is said to have
sailed from Ecuador to the Galapagos just before the time of
Columbus, but neither he nor any other native settled there
because there was no water."

"O.K.," said Knut. "Then we damned well won't go there. I
hope we don't anyhow."

We were now so accustomed to having the sea dancing round
us that we took no account of it. What did it matter if we danced

round a bit with a thousand fathoms of water under us, so long as we and the raft were always on top? It was only that here the next question arose—how long could we count on keeping on top? It was easy to see that the balsa logs absorbed water. The aft cross-beam was worse than the others; on it we could press the whole finger-tip into the soaked wood till the water squelched. Without saying anything I broke off a piece of the sodden wood and threw it overboard. It sank quietly beneath the surface and slowly vanished down into the depths. Later I saw two or three of the other fellows do exactly the same thing when they thought no one was looking. They stood looking reverently at the water-logged piece of wood sinking quietly into the green water. We had noted the waterline on the raft when we started, but in the rough sea it was impossible to see how deep we lay, for one moment the logs were lifted out of the water and the next they went deep down into it. But if we drove a knife into the timber we saw to our joy that the wood was dry an inch or so below the surface. We calculated that if the water continued to force its way in at the same pace, the raft would be lying and floating just under the surface of the water by the time we could expect to be approaching land. But we hoped that the sap further in would act as an impregnation and check the absorption.

Then there was another menace which troubled our minds a little during the first weeks. The ropes. In the daytime we were so busy that we thought little about it, but when darkness had fallen and we had crept into bed on the cabin floor, we had more time to think, feel and listen. As we lay there, each man on his straw mattress, we could feel the reed matting under us heaving in time with the wooden logs. In addition to the movements of the raft itself, all nine logs moved reciprocally. When one came up, another went down with a gentle heaving movement. They did not move much, but it was enough to make one feel as if one was lying on the back of a large breathing animal, and we preferred to lie on a log lengthways. The first two nights were the worst, but then we were too tired to bother about it. Later the ropes swelled a little in the water and kept the nine logs quieter. But all the same there was never a flat surface on board which kept quite still in relation to its surroundings. As the foundation moved up and down and round at every joint, everything else moved with it. The bamboo deck, the double mast, the four plaited walls of the cabin, and the roof of slats with the leaves on it—all were just made fast with ropes, and twisted about and lifted themselves in opposite directions. It was almost unnoticeable, but it was clear enough. If one corner went up, the other corner went down, and if one half of the roof dragged all its laths forward, the other half dragged its laths astern. And if we looked out through the open wall there was still more life and movement, for there the sky moved quietly round in a circle while the sea leapt high towards it.

The ropes took the whole pressure. All night we could hear them creaking and groaning, chafing and squeaking. It was like one single complaining chorus round us in the dark, each rope having its own note according to its thickness and tautness. Every morning we made a thorough inspection of the ropes. We were even let down with our heads in the water over the edge of the raft, while two men held us tight by the ankles, to see if the ropes on the bottom of the raft were all right.

But the ropes held. A fortnight, the seamen had said. Then all the ropes would be worn out. But in spite of this consensus of opinion we had not so far found the smallest sign of wear. Not till we were far out to sea did we find the solution. The balsa wood was so soft that the ropes wore their way slowly into the wood and were protected, instead of the logs wearing the ropes.

After a week or so the sea grew calmer, and we noticed that it became blue instead of green. We began to go west-north-west instead of due north-west, and took this as the first faint sign that we had got out of the coastal current and had some hope of being carried out to sea.

The very first day we were left alone on the sea we had noticed fish round the raft, but were too much occupied with the steering to think of fishing. The second day we went right into a thick shoal of sardines, and soon afterwards an eight-foot blue shark came along and rolled over with its white belly uppermost as it rubbed against the raft's stern, where Herman and

Bengt stood barelegged in the seas, steering. It played round us for a while, but disappeared when we got the hand harpoon ready for action.

Next day we were visited by tunnies, bonitos and dolphins, and when a big flying fish thudded on board we used it as bait and at once pulled in two large dolphins (dorados) weighing from 20 to 35 lbs. each. This was food for several days. On steering watch we could see many fish we did not even know, and one day we came into a school of porpoises which seemed quite endless. The black backs tumbled about, packed close together, right in to the side of the raft, and sprang up here and there all over the sea as far as we could see from the masthead. And the nearer we came to the equator, and the farther from the coast, the commoner flying fish became. When at last we came out into the blue water where the sea rolled by majestically, sunlit and sedate, ruffled by gusts of wind, we could see them glittering like a rain of projectiles, shooting from the water and flying in a straight line till their power of flight was exhausted and they vanished beneath the surface.

If we set the little paraffin lamp out at night flying fish were attracted by the light and, large and small, shot over the raft. They often struck the bamboo cabin or the sail and tumbled helpless on the deck. For, unable to get a take-off by swimming through the water, they just remained lying and kicking help-lessly, like large-eyed herrings with long breast fins. It sometimes happened that we heard an outburst of strong language from a man on deck when a cold flying fish came unexpectedly at a good speed slap into his face. They always came at a good pace and snout first, and if they caught one full in the face they made it burn and tingle. But the unprovoked attack was quickly for-given by the injured party, for this, with all its drawbacks, was a maritime land of enchantment where delicious fish dishes came hurtling through the air. We used to fry them for breakfast, and whether it was the fish, the cook, or our appetites, they reminded us of fried troutlings once we had scraped the scales off.

The cook's first duty when he got up in the morning was to go out on deck and collect all the flying fish that had landed on board in the course of the night. There were usually half a dozen or more, and one morning we found twenty-six fat flying fish on the raft. Knut was much upset one morning because, when he was standing operating with the frying pan, a flying fish struck him on the hand instead of landing right in the cooking fat.

Our neighbourly intimacy with the sea was not fully realised by Torstein till he woke one morning and found a sardine on his pillow. There was so little room in the cabin that Torstein was lying with his head in the doorway and, if anyone inadvertently trod on his face when going out at night, he bit him in the leg. He grasped the sardine by the tail and confided to it under-standingly that all sardines had his entire sympathy. We con-scientiously drew in our legs so that Torstein should have more room the next night, but then something happened which caused Torstein to find himself a sleeping-place on the top of all the kitchen utensils in the wireless corner.

It was a few nights later. It was overcast and pitch dark, and Torstein had placed the paraffin lamp just by his head, so that the night watches should see where they were treading when they crept in and out over his head. . . . About four o'clock Torstein was woken by the lamp tumbling over and something cold and wet flapping about his ears. "Flying fish," he thought, and felt for it in the darkness to throw it away. He caught hold of some-thing long and wet that wriggled like a snake, and let go as if he had burned himself. The unseen visitor twisted itself away and over to Herman, while Torstein tried to get the lamp alight. Herman started up too, and this made me wake thinking of the octopus which came up at night in these waters. When we got the lamp alight, Herman was sitting in triumph with his hand gripping the neck of a long thin fish which wriggled in his hands like an eel. The fish was over three feet long, as slender as a snake, with dull black eyes and a long snout with a greedy jaw full of long sharp teeth. The teeth were as sharp as knives and could be folded back into the roof of the mouth to make way for what it swallowed. Under Herman's grip a large-eyed white fish, about eight inches long, was suddenly thrown up from the stomach and out of the mouth of the predatory fish, and soon after up came another like it. These were clearly two deep water fish, much torn by the snake-fish's teeth. The snake-fish's thin skin was bluish violet on the back and steel blue underneath, and it came loose in flakes when we took hold of it.

Bengt too was woken at last by all the noise, and we held the lamp and the long fish under his nose. He sat up drowsily in his sleeping bag and said solemnly:

"No, fish like that don't exist."

With which he turned over quietly and fell asleep again.

Bengt was not far wrong. It appeared later that we six sitting round the lamp in the bamboo cabin were the first men to have seen this fish alive. Only the skeleton of a fish like this one had been found a few times on the coast of South America and the Galapagos Islands; ichthyologists called it *Gempylus*, or snake mackerel, and thought it lived at the bottom of the sea at a great depth, because no one had ever seen it alive. But if it lived at a great depth, this must at any rate be by day, when the sun blinded the big eyes. For on dark nights *Gempylus* was abroad high over the surface of the seas; we on the raft had experience of that.

A week after the rare fish had landed in Torstein's sleeping bag, we had another visit. Again it was four in the morning, and the new moon had set so that it was dark, but the stars were shining. The raft was steering easily, and when my watch was over I took a turn along the edge of the raft to see if everything was shipshape for the new watch. I had a rope round my waist, as the watch always had, and, with the paraffin lamp in my hand, I was walking carefully along the outermost log to get round the mast. The log was wet and slippery, and I was furious when someone quite unexpectedly caught hold of the rope behind me and jerked till I nearly lost my balance. I turned round wrathfully with the lantern, but not a soul was to be seen. There came a new tug at the rope, and I saw something shiny lying writhing on the deck. It was a fresh *Gempylus*, and this time it had got its teeth so deep into the rope that several of them broke before I got the rope loose. Presumably the light of the lantern had flashed along the curving white rope, and our visitor from the depths of the sea had caught hold in the hope of jumping up and snatching an extra long and tasty tit-bit. It ended its days in a jar of formalin.

The sea contains many surprises for him who has his floor on a level with the surface, and drifts along slowly and noiselessly. A sportsman who breaks his way through the woods may come back and say that no wild life is to be seen. Another may sit down on a stump and wait, and often rustlings and cracklings will begin, and curious eyes peer out. So it is on the sea too. We usually plough across it with roaring engines and piston strokes, with the water foaming round our bows. Then we come back and say that there is nothing to see far out on the ocean.

Not a day passed but we, as we sat floating on the surface of the sea, were visited by inquisitive guests which wriggled and waggled about us, and a few of them, such as dolphins and pilot fish, grew so familiar that they accompanied the raft across the sea and kept round us day and night.

When night had fallen, and the stars were twinkling in the dark tropical sky, the phosphorescence flashed around us in rivalry with the stars, and single glowing plankton resembled round live coals so vividly that we involuntarily drew in our bare legs when the glowing pellets were washed up round our feet at the raft's stern. When we caught them we saw that they were little brightly shining species of shrimp. On such nights we were sometimes scared when two round shining eyes suddenly rose out of the sea right alongside the raft and glared at us with an unblinking hypnotic stare—it might have been the Old Man of the Sea himself. These were often big squids which came up and floated on the surface with their devilish green eyes shining in the dark like phosphorus. But sometimes they were the shining eyes of deep water fish which only came up at night and lay staring, fascinated by the glimmer of light before them. Several times, when the sea was calm, the black water round the raft was suddenly full of round heads two or three feet in diameter, lying motionless and staring at us with great glowing eyes. On other nights balls of light three feet and more in diameter would be visible down in the water, flashing at irregular intervals like electric lights turned on for a moment.

We gradually grew accustomed to having these subterranean or submarine creatures under the floor, but nevertheless we were just as surprised every time a new version appeared. About two o'clock on a cloudy night, on which the man at the helm had difficulty in distinguishing black water from black sky, he caught sight of a faint illumination down in the water which slowly took the shape of a large animal. It was impossible to say whether it was plankton shining on its body, or if the animal itself had a phosphorescent surface, but the glimmer down in the black water gave the ghostly creature obscure, wavering outlines. Sometimes it was roundish, sometimes oval or triangular, and suddenly it split into two parts which swam to and fro under the raft independently of one another. Finally there were three of these large shining phantoms wandering round in slow circles under us. They were real monsters, for the visible parts alone were some five fathoms long, and we all quickly collected on deck and followed the ghost dance. It went on for hour after hour, following the course of the raft. Mysterious and noiseless, our shining companions kept a good way beneath the surface, mostly on the starboard side, where the light was, but often they were right under the raft or appeared on the port side. The glimmer of light on their backs revealed that the beasts were bigger than elephants, but they were not whales, for they never came up to breathe. Were they giant ray-fish which changed shape when they turned over on their sides? They took no notice at all if we held the light right down on the surface to lure them up, so that we might see what kind of creatures they were. And like all proper goblins and ghosts, they had sunk into the depths when the dawn began to break.

We never got a proper explanation of this nocturnal visit from the three shining monsters, unless the solution was afforded by another visit we received a day and a half later in the full midday sunshine. It was May 24, and we were lying drifting on a leisurely swell in exactly 95° west by 7° south. It was about noon, and we had thrown overboard the guts of two big dolphins we had caught early in the morning. I was having a refreshing plunge overboard at the bows, lying in the water, keeping a good look out and hanging on to a rope-end, when I caught sight of a thick brown fish, six feet long, which came swimming inquisitively towards me through the crystal-clear sea water. I hopped quickly up on to the edge of the raft and sat in the hot sun looking at the fish as it passed quietly, when I heard a wild war-whoop from Knut, who was sitting aft behind the bamboo cabin. He bellowed "Shark!" till his voice cracked in a falsetto, and as we had sharks swimming alongside the raft almost daily without creating such excitement, we all realised that this must be something extra special, and flocked astern to Knut's assistance.

Knut had been squatting there, washing his pants in the swell, and when he looked up for a moment he was staring straight into the biggest and ugliest face any of us had ever seen in the whole of our lives. It was the head of a veritable sea monster, so huge and so hideous that if the Old Man of the Sea himself had come up he could not have made such an impression on us. The head was broad and flat like a frog's, with two small eyes right at the sides, and a toadlike jaw which was four or five feet wide and had long fringes hanging drooping from the corners of the mouth. Behind the head was an enormous body ending in a long thin tail with a pointed tail fin which stood straight up and showed that this sea monster was not any kind of whale. The body looked brownish under the water, but both head and body were thickly covered with small white spots. The monster came quietly, lazily swimming after us from astern. It grinned like a bulldog and lashed gently with its tail. The large round dorsal fin projected clear of the water and sometimes the tail fin as well, and when the creature was in the trough of the swell the water flowed about the broad back as though washing round a submerged reef. In front of the broad jaws swam a whole crowd of zebra-striped pilot fish in fan formation, and large remora fish and other parasites sat firmly attached to the huge body and travelled with it through the water, so that the whole thing looked like a curious zoological collection crowded round something that resembled a floating deep water reef.

A 25 lbs. dolphin, attached to six of our largest fish-hooks, was hanging behind the raft as bait for sharks, and a swarm of pilot fish shot straight off, nosed the dolphin without touching it, and then hurried back to their lord and master, the sea king. Like a mechanical monster it set its machinery going and came gliding at leisure towards the dolphin which lay, a beggarly trifle, before its jaws. We tried to pull the dolphin in, and the sea monster followed slowly, right up to the side of the raft. It did not open its mouth, but just let the dolphin bump against it, as if to throw open the whole door for such an insignificant scrap was not worth while. When the giant came right up to the raft, it rubbed its back against the heavy steering oar, which was just lifted up out of the water, and now we had ample opportunity of studying the monster at the closest quarters—at such close quarters that I thought we had all gone mad, for we roared stupidly with laughter and shouted over-excitedly at the completely fantastic sight we saw. Walt Disney himself, with all his powers of imagination, could not have created a more hair-raising sea monster than that which thus suddenly lay with its terrific jaws along the raft's side.

The monster was a whale shark, the largest shark and the largest fish known in the world to-day. It is exceedingly rare, but scattered specimens are observed here and there in the tropical oceans. The whale shark has an average length of 50 feet, and according to zoologists it weighs 15 tons. It is said that large specimens can attain a length of 65 feet, and a harpooned baby had a liver weighing 600 lbs., and a collection of three thousand teeth in each of its broad jaws.

The monster was so large that when it began to swim in circles round us and under the raft its head was visible on one side while the whole of its tail stuck out on the other. And so incredibly grotesque, inert and stupid did it appear when seen full-face that we could not help shouting with laughter, although we realised that it had strength enough in its tail to smash both balsa logs and ropes to pieces if it attacked us. Again and again it described narrower and narrower circles just under the raft, while all we could do was to wait and see what might happen. When out on the other side it glided amiably under the steering oar and lifted it up in the air, while the oar-blade slid along the creature's back.

We stood round the raft with hand harpoons ready for action, but they seemed to us like toothpicks in relation to the heavy beast we had to deal with. There was no indication that the whale shark ever thought of leaving us again; it circled round us and followed like a faithful dog, close to the raft. None of us had ever experienced or thought we should experience anything like it; the whole adventure, with the sea monster swimming behind and under the raft, seemed to us so completely unnatural that we could not really take it seriously.

In reality the whale shark went on encircling us for barely an hour, but to us the visit seemed to last a whole day. At last it became too exciting for Erik, who was standing at a corner of the raft with an eight-foot hand harpoon, and encouraged by ill-considered shouts, he raised the harpoon above his head. As the whale shark came gliding slowly towards him, and had got its broad head right under the corner of the raft, Erik thrust the harpoon with all his giant strength down between his legs and deep into the whale shark's gristly head. It was a second or two before the giant understood properly what was happening. Then in a flash the placid half-wit was transformed into a mountain of steel muscles. We heard a swishing noise as the harpoon line rushed over the edge of the raft, and saw a cascade of water as the giant stood on its head and plunged down into the depths. The three men who were standing nearest were flung about the place head over heels and two of them were flayed and burnt by the line as it rushed through the air. The thick line, strong enough to hold a boat, was caught up on the side of the raft but snapped at once like a piece of twine, and a few seconds later a broken-off harpoon shaft came up to the surface two hundred yards away. A shoal of frightened pilot fish shot off through the water in a desperate attempt to keep up with their old lord and master, and we waited a long time for the monster to come racing back like an infuriated submarine; but we never saw anything more of the whale shark.

We were now in the South Equatorial Current and moving in a westerly direction just 400 sea miles south of the Galapagos. There was no longer any danger of drifting into the Galapagos currents, and the only contacts we had with this group of islands were greetings from big sea turtles which no doubt had strayed far out to sea from the islands. One day we saw a thumping big sea turtle lying struggling with its head and one great fin above the surface of the water. As the swell rose we saw a shimmer of green and blue and gold in the water under the turtle, and we discovered that it was engaged in a life and death struggle with dolphins. The fight was apparently quite one-sided; it consisted in twelve to fifteen big-headed, brilliantly coloured dolphins attacking the turtle's neck and fins and apparently trying to tire it out, for the turtle could not lie for days on end with its head and paddles drawn inside its shell.

When the turtle caught sight of the raft, it dived and made straight for us, pursued by the glittering fish. It came close up to the side of the raft and was showing signs of wanting to climb up on to the timber when it caught sight of us already standing there. If we had been more practised we could have captured it with ropes without difficulty as the huge carapace paddled quietly along the side of the raft. But we spent the time that mattered in staring, and when we had the lasso ready the giant turtle had already passed our bows. We flung the little rubber dinghy into the water, and Herman, Bengt and Torstein went in pursuit of the sea turtle in the round nutshell, which was not a great deal bigger than what swam ahead of them. Bengt as steward saw in his mind's eye endless meat dishes and the most delicious turtle soup. But the faster they rowed, the faster the turtle slipped through the water just below the surface, and they were not more than a hundred yards from the raft when the turtle suddenly disappeared without trace. But they had done one good deed at any rate. For when the little yellow rubber dinghy came dancing back over the water, it had the whole glittering school of dolphins after it. They circled round the new turtle, and the boldest snapped at the oar-blades which dipped in the water like fins; meanwhile the peaceful turtle escaped successfully from all its ignoble persecutors.

fore our fresh
it came to an
d fish had begun
come on board.

We cooked over a
Primus in a box,
and had our meals
on the edge of the
raft outside the
cabin.

Raaby in the wire-
less corner, behind
a cardboard parti-
tion decorated by
Danielsson. Raaby
and Haugland sent
daily wireless re-
ports to the Meteor-
ological Institute at
Washington.

CHAPTER V

HALFWAY

Daily Life and Experiments—Drinking Water for Raftsmen—Potato and Gourd Betray a Secret—Cocoanuts and Crabs—Johannes—We Sail through Fish Soup—Plankton—Edible Phosphorescence—Intercourse with Whales—Ants and Barnacles—Swimming Pets—The Dolphin as a Companion—Catching Sharks—The Kon-Tiki Becomes a Sea Monster—Pilot Fish and Remora Left us by Sharks—Flying Squids—Unknown Visitors—The Diving Basket—With Tunny and Bonito in their own Element—The Spurious Reef—Centreboard Solves a Riddle—Halfway.

THE weeks passed. We saw no sign either of a ship or of drifting remains to show that there were other people in the world. The whole sea was ours, and with all the gates of the horizon open real peace and freedom were wafted down from the firmament itself.

It was as though the fresh salt tang in the air, and all the blue purity that surrounded us, had washed and cleansed both body and soul. To us on the raft the great problems of civilised man appeared false and illusory, mere perverted products of the human mind. Only the elements mattered. And the elements seemed to ignore the little raft. Or perhaps they accepted it as a natural object which did not break the harmony of the sea, but which adapted itself to current and sea like bird and fish. Instead of being a fearsome enemy, flinging itself at us in foam, the elements had become a reliable friend which steadily and surely helped us onward. While wind and waves pushed and propelled, the ocean current lay under us and pulled, straight towards our goal.

If a boat had cruised our way on any average day out at sea, it would have found us bobbing quietly up and down over a long rolling swell covered with little white-crested waves, while the trade winds held the orange sail bent towards Polynesia.

Those on board would have seen, at the stern of the raft, a

brown bearded man with no clothes on, either struggling desperately with a long steering oar while he hauled on a tangled rope, or, in calm weather, just sitting on a box dozing in the hot sun and keeping a leisurely hold on the steering oar with his toes.

If this man happened not to be Bengt, the latter would have been found lying on his stomach in the cabin door with one of his seventy-three sociological books. Bengt had further been appointed steward and was responsible for fixing the daily rations. Herman might have been found just anywhere at all times of the day—at the masthead with meteorological instruments, underneath the raft with diving-goggles on, checking a centreboard, or in tow in the rubber dinghy, busy with balloons and curious measuring apparatus. He was our technical chief and responsible for meteorological and hydrographical observations.

Knut and Torstein were always doing something with their wet dry batteries, soldering irons and circuits. All their war-time training was required to keep the little wireless station going in spray and dew a foot above the surface of the water. Every night they took turns to send our reports and weather observations out into the ether, where they were picked up by casual radio amateurs who passed the reports on to the Meteorological Institute in Washington and other destinations. Erik was usually sitting patching sails and splicing ropes, or carving in wood and drawing sketches of bearded men and odd fish. And at noon every day he took the sextant and mounted a box to look at the sun and find out how far we had moved since the day before. I myself had enough to do with the log-book and reports, and the collecting of plankton, fishing and filming. Every man had his sphere of responsibility, and no one interfered with the others' work. All dirty jobs, like steering watch and cooking, were divided equally. Every man had two hours each day and two hours each night at the steering oar. And duty as cook was in accordance with a daily roster. There were few laws and regulations on board, except that the night watch must have a rope round his waist, that the life-saving rope had its regular place, that all meals were consumed outside the cabin wall, and that the "right place" was only at the farthest end of the logs astern. If an important decision was to be taken on board, we called a pow-wow in Indian style and discussed the matter before anything was settled.

An ordinary day on board the *Kon-Tiki* began with the last night watch shaking some life into the cook, who crawled out sleepily on to the dewy deck in the morning sun and began to gather flying fish. Instead of eating the fish raw, according to both Polynesian and Peruvian recipes, we fried them over a small Primus stove at the bottom of a box which stood lashed fast to the deck outside the cabin door. This box was our kitchen. Here there was usually shelter from the south-east trade wind which regularly blew on to our other quarter. Only when wind and sea juggled too much with the Primus flame did this set fire to the wooden box, and once when the cook had fallen asleep the whole box became a mass of flames which spread to the very wall of the bamboo cabin. But the fire on the wall was quickly put out when the smoke poured into the hut, for, after all, we had never far to go for water on board the *Kon-Tiki*.

The smell of fried fish seldom managed to wake the snorers inside the bamboo cabin, so the cook usually had to stick a fork into them or sing "Breakfast's ready!" so out of tune that no one could bear to listen to him any longer. If there were no sharks' fins alongside the raft, the day began with a quick plunge in the Pacific, followed by a breakfast in the open air on the edge of the raft.

The food on board was above reproach. The cuisine was divided into two experiments, one dedicated to the quartermaster in the twentieth century, one to Kon-Tiki and the fifth century. Torstein and Bengt were the subjects of the first experiment, and restricted their diet to the slim little packages of special provisions which we had squeezed down into the hole between the logs and the bamboo deck. Fish and marine food, however, had never been their strong side. Every few weeks we untied the lashings which held down the bamboo deck and took out fresh supplies, which we lashed fast forward of the bamboo cabin. The tough layer of asphalt outside the cardboard proved resistant, while the hermetically sealed tins lying loose beside it were penetrated and ruined by the sea water which continually washed round our provisions.

Kon-Tiki, on his original voyage across the sea, had no asphalt or hermetically sealed tins; nevertheless he had no serious food problems. In those days too supplies consisted of what the men took with them from land and what they got for themselves on the voyage. We may assume that when Kon-Tiki sailed from the coast of Peru after his defeat by Lake Titicaca he had one of these two objects. As the spiritual representative of the sun among an entirely sun-worshipping people, it is very probable that he ventured right out to sea to follow the sun itself on its journey in the hope of finding a new and more peaceful country. An alternative possibility for him was to sail his rafts up the coast of South America in order to land higher up and found a new kingdom out of reach of his persecutors. Clear of the dangerous rocky coast and the hostile tribes along the shore, he would, like ourselves, fall an easy prey to the south-east trade wind and the Humboldt Current, and, in the power of the elements, he would drift in exactly the same large semi-circle right towards the sunset.

Whatever these sun-worshippers' plans were when they fled from their homeland, they certainly provided themselves with supplies for the voyage. Dried meat and fish and sweet potatoes were the most important part of their primitive diet. When the raftsmen of that time put to sea along the desert coast of Peru, they had ample supplies of water on board. Instead of clay vessels they generally used the skin of giant bottle gourds, which was resistant to bumps and blows, while even more adapted to raft use were thick canes of giant bamboos; they bored through all the knots and poured water in through a little hole at the end, which they stopped with a plug or with pitch or resin. Thirty or forty of these thick bamboo canes could be lashed fast along the raft under the bamboo deck, where they lay shaded and cool, with fresh sea water—about 79° Fahrenheit in the Equatorial Current—washing about them. A store of this kind would contain twice as much water as we ourselves used on our whole voyage, and still more could be taken simply by lashing on more bamboo canes in the water underneath the raft, where they weighed nothing and occupied no space.

We found that after two months fresh water began to grow

stale and have a bad taste. But by then one is well through the
first ocean area in which there is little rain, and has long ago
arrived in regions where heavy rain-showers can maintain the
water supply. We served out a good quart of water per man
daily, and it was by no means always that the ration was consumed.

Even if our predecessors had started from land with inadequate
supplies, they would have managed well enough as long as they
drifted across the sea with the current, in which fish abounded.
There was not a day on our whole voyage on which fish were
not swimming round the raft and could not easily be caught.
Scarcely a day passed without at any rate flying fish coming on
board of their own accord. It even happened that large bonitos,
delicious eating, swam on board with the masses of water that
came from astern, and lay kicking on the raft when the water
had vanished down between the logs as in a sieve. To starve to
death was impossible.

The old natives knew well the device which many shipwrecked
men hit upon during the war—chewing thirst-quenching mois-
ture out of raw fish. One can also press the juices out by twisting
pieces of fish in a cloth, or, if the fish is large, it is a fairly simple
matter to cut holes in its side, which soon become filled with
ooze from the fish's lymphatic glands. It does not taste good if
one has anything better to drink, but the percentage of salt is so
low that one's thirst is quenched.

The necessity for drinking water was greatly reduced if we
bathed regularly and lay down wet in a shady cabin. If a shark
was patrolling majestically round about us and preventing a real
plunge from the side of the raft, one had only to lie down on the
logs aft and get a good grip of the ropes with one's fingers and
toes. Then we got several bathfuls of crystal clear Pacific pouring
over us every few seconds.

When tormented by thirst in heat one generally assumes that
the body needs water, and this may often lead to immoderate
inroads on the water ration without any benefit whatever. On
really hot days in the tropics you can pour tepid water down
your throat till you taste it at the back of your mouth, and you

are just as thirsty. It is not liquid the body needs then, but, curiously enough, salt. The special rations we had on board included salt tablets to be taken regularly on particularly hot days, because perspiration drains the body of salt. We experienced days like this when the wind died away and the sun blazed down on the raft without mitigation. Our water ration could be ladled into us till it squelched in our stomachs, but our throats malignantly demanded much more. On such days we added from 20 to 40 per cent of bitter salt sea water to our fresh water ration, and found to our surprise that this brackish water quenched our thirst. We had the taste of sea water in our mouths for a long time afterwards, but never felt unwell, and moreover had our water ration considerably increased.

One morning as we sat at breakfast an unexpected sea splashed into our gruel and taught us quite gratuitously that the taste of oats removed the greater part of the sickening taste of sea water.

The old Polynesians had preserved some curious traditions, according to which their earliest forefathers, when they came sailing across the sea, had with them leaves of a certain plant which they chewed, with the result that their thirst disappeared. Another effect of the plant was that at a pinch they could drink sea water neat without being sick. No such plants grew in the South Sea islands; they must therefore have originated in their ancestors' homeland. The Polynesian historians persisted so obstinately in these statements that modern investigators looked into the matter and came to the conclusion that the only known plant with such an effect was the coca plant, which grew only in Peru. And in prehistoric Peru this very coca plant, which contains cocaine, was regularly used both by the Incas and by their vanished forerunners, as is shown by discoveries in pre-Inca graves. On exhausting mountain journeys and sea voyages they took with them piles of these leaves and chewed them for days on end to remove the feelings of thirst and weariness. And over a fairly short period the chewing of coca leaves will even allow one to drink sea water with a certain immunity.

We did not test coca leaves on board the *Kon-Tiki*, but we had on the foredeck large wicker baskets full of other plants which had left a deeper impression in the South Sea islands. The baskets stood lashed fast in the lee of the cabin wall, and as time passed yellow shoots and green leaves shot up higher and higher from the wickerwork. It was like a little tropical garden on board the wooden raft. When the first Europeans came to the Pacific islands, they found large plantings of sweet potatoes on Easter Island and in Hawaii and New Zealand, and the same potato was also cultivated on the other islands, but only within the Polynesian area. It was quite unknown in the part of the world which lay farther west. The sweet potato was one of the most important cultivated plants in these remote islands where the people other-wise lived mainly on fish, and many of the Polynesians' legends centred round this plant. According to tradition it had been brought by no less a personage than Tiki himself, when he came with his wife Pani from their ancestors' original homeland, where the sweet potato had been an important article of food. New Zealand legends declare that the sweet potato was brought over the sea in vessels which were not canoes, but consisted of "wood bound together with ropes."

Now, as is known, America is the only place in the rest of the world where the potato grew before the time of the Europeans. And the sweet potato Tiki brought with him to the islands, *Ipomœa batatas,* is exactly the same as that which the Indians have cultivated in Peru from the oldest times. Dried sweet potatoes were the most important travel provisions both for the seafarers of Polynesia and for the natives in old Peru. In the South Sea islands the potato will only grow if carefully tended by man, and as it cannot bear sea water it is idle to explain its wide distribution over these scattered islands by declaring that it can have drifted over 4,000 sea miles with ocean currents from Peru. This attempt to explain away so important a clue is particularly futile seeing that philologists have pointed out that on all the widely scattered South Sea islands the name of the sweet potato is *kumara,* and that *kumara* is just what the sweet potato was called among the old Indians in Peru. The name followed the potato across the sea.

Another very important Polynesian cultivated plant we had with us on board the *Kon-Tiki* was the bottle gourd, *Lagenaria*

vulgaris. As important as the fruit itself was the skin, which the
Polynesians dried over a fire and used to hold water. This typical
garden plant also, which again cannot propagate itself in a wild
state by drifting across the sea alone, the old Polynesians had in
common with the original population of Peru. These bottle
gourds, converted into water containers, are found in prehistoric
desert graves on the coast of Peru, and were used by the fishing
population there centuries before the first men came to the islands
in the Pacific. The Polynesian name for the bottle gourd, *kimi*, is
found again among the Indians in Central America, where the
civilisation of Peru has its deepest roots.

In addition to a few chance southern fruits which we ate up in
a few weeks before they went rotten, we had on board a third
plant which, along with the sweet potato, has played the greatest
part in the history of the Pacific. We had two hundred cocoanuts,
and they gave us exercise for our teeth and refreshing drinks.
Several of the nuts soon began to sprout, and when we had been
just ten weeks at sea we had half a dozen baby palms a foot high,
which had already opened their shoots and formed thick green
leaves. The cocoanut grew before Columbus' time both on the
isthmus of Panama and in South America. The chronicler Oviedo
writes that the cocoanut palm occurred in great numbers along
the Pacific coast of Peru when the Spaniards arrived. At that
time it had long existed on all the islands in the Pacific. Botanists
have still no certain proof in which direction it spread over the
Pacific. But one thing has now been discovered. Not even the
cocoanut, with its famous shell, can spread over the ocean without
men's help. The nuts we had in baskets on deck remained eatable
and capable of germinating the whole way to Polynesia. But we
had laid about half among the special provisions below deck,
with the waves washing round them. Every single one of these
was ruined by the sea water. And no cocoanut can float over the
sea faster than a balsa raft moves with the wind behind it. It was
the eyes of the cocoanut which sucked in the water and grew
soft so that the sea water got through. Or else it was the refuse
collectors all over the ocean who took care that no edible thing
that floated should get across from one world to the other.

Sometimes, on quiet days far out on the blue sea, we sailed close
to a white floating bird's feather. Single petrels and other sea
birds which can sleep on the sea we met thousands of sea miles
from the nearest land. If, on approaching the little feather, we
looked at it closely, we saw that there were two or three
passengers on board it, sailing along at their ease before the wind.
When the *Kon-Tiki* was about to pass like another Goliath, the
passengers noticed that a vessel was coming which was faster and
had more space, and so all three came scuttling sideways at top
speed over the surface and up on to the *Kon-Tiki*, leaving the
feather to sail on alone. And so the *Kon-Tiki* soon began to swarm
with stowaways. They were small pelagic crabs. As big as a
finger-nail, and now and then a good deal larger, they were
tit-bits for the Goliaths on board if we managed to catch them.
The small crabs were the policemen of the sea's surface, and they
were not slow to look after themselves when they saw anything
eatable. If one day the cook failed to notice a flying fish in between
the logs, next day it was covered with from eight to ten small
crabs, sitting on the fish and helping themselves with their claws.
Most often they were frightened and scurried away and hid when
we came, but aft, in a little hole by the steering block, lived a
crab which was called Johannes and was quite tame. Besides the
parrot, who was everyone's amusing pet, the crab Johannes too
formed one of our community on deck. If the man at the helm,
sitting steering on a sunshiny day with his back to the cabin, had
not Johannes for company, he felt utterly lonely out on the wide
blue sea. While the other small crabs scurried furtively about and
pilfered like cockroaches on an ordinary boat, Johannes sat broad
and round in his doorway with his eyes wide open, waiting for
the change of watch. Every man who came on watch had a scrap
of biscuit or a bit of fish for Johannes, and we only needed to
stoop down over the hole for him to come right out on his
doorstep and stretch out his hands. He took the scraps out of our
fingers with his claws and ran back into the hole, where he sat
down in the doorway and munched like a schoolboy cramming
his food into his mouth.

The crabs clung like flies to the soaked cocoanuts which burst when they fermented, or caught plankton washed on board by the waves. And these, the tiniest organisms in the sea, were good eating too even for us Goliaths on the raft, when we once knew how to catch a number of them at once so that we got a decent mouthful.

It is clear that there must be very nourishing food in these almost invisible plankton which drift about with the current on the oceans in infinite numbers. Fish and sea birds which do not eat plankton themselves live in that case on other fish or sea animals which do, no matter how large they themselves may be. Plankton is a general name for thousands of species of visible and invisible small organisms which drift about near the surface of the sea. Some are plants (*Phyto*-plankton), while others are loose fish ova and tiny living creatures (*Zoo*-plankton). Animal plankton live on vegetable plankton and vegetable plankton live on ammoniac, nitrites and nitrates which are formed from dead animal plankton. And while they reciprocally live on one another they all form food for everything which moves in and over the sea. What they cannot offer in size they can offer in numbers. In good plankton waters there are thousands in a glassful. More than once people have starved to death at sea because they have not found fish large enough to be spitted, netted or hooked. In such cases it has often happened that they have literally been sailing about in strongly diluted raw fish soup. If, in addition to hooks and nets, they had had a utensil for straining the soup they were sitting in, they would have found a nourishing foundation —plankton. Some day in the future, perhaps, men will think of harvesting plankton from the sea to the same extent as once, long ago, they had the idea of harvesting grain on land. A single grain is of no use either, but in large quantities it becomes food.

The marine biologist Dr. A. D. Bajkov gave us the idea and sent with us a fishing net which was suited to the creatures we were to catch. The "net" was a silk net with almost three thousand meshes per square inch. It was sewn in the shape of a funnel with a circular mouth behind an iron ring, 18 inches across, and was towed behind the raft. Just as in other kinds of fishing, the catch varied with time and place. Catches diminished as the sea grew

warmer farther west, and we got the best results at night, because
many species seemed to go deeper down into the water when
the sun was shining.

If we had had no other way of whiling away time on board
the raft, there would have been entertainment enough in lying
with our noses in the plankton net. Not for the sake of the smell,
for that was bad. Nor because the sight was appetising, for it
looked a horrible mess. But because, if we spread the plankton
out on a board and examined each of the little creatures separately
with the naked eye, we had before us fantastic shapes and colours
in unending variety.

Most of them were tiny shrimp-like crustaceans (copepods) or
fish ova floating loose, but there were also larvae of fish and shellfish, curious miniature crabs in all colours, jellyfish, and an endless
variety of small creatures which might have been taken from
Walt Disney's *Fantasia*. Some looked like fringed fluttering spooks
cut out of cellophane paper, while others resembled tiny red-
beaked birds with a hard shell instead of feathers. There was no
end to Nature's extravagant inventions in the plankton world; a
surrealistic artist might well own himself beaten here.

Where the cold Humboldt Current turned west south of the
equator, we could pour several pounds of plankton porridge out of
the bag every few hours. The plankton lay packed together like
cake in coloured layers, brown, red, grey and green according to
the different fields of plankton through which we had passed. At
night, when there was phosphorescence about, it was like hauling
in a bag of sparkling jewels. But when we got hold of it, the
pirates' treasure was turned into millions of tiny glittering shrimps
and phosphorescent fish larvae that glowed in the dark like a
heap of live coals. And when we poured them into a bucket the
squashy mess ran out like a magic gruel composed of glow-worms.
Our night's catch looked as nasty at close quarters as it had been
pretty at long range. And bad as it smelt, it tasted correspondingly
good if one just plucked up courage and put a spoonful of
phosphorus into one's mouth. If this consisted of many dwarf
shrimps, it tasted like shrimp paste, lobster or crab. And if it was
mostly deep sea fish ova, it tasted like caviare and now and then

like oysters. The uneatable vegetable plankton were either so small that they ran away with the water through the meshes of the net, or they were so large that we could pick them up with our fingers. "Snags" in the dish were single jelly-like cœlenterates like glass balloons and jellyfish about half an inch long. These were bitter and had to be thrown away. Otherwise everything could be eaten, either as it was or cooked in fresh water as gruel or soup. Tastes differ. Two men on board thought plankton tasted delicious, two thought they were quite good, and for two the sight of them was more than enough. From a nutrition standpoint they stand on a level with the larger shellfish, and, spiced and properly prepared, they can certainly be a first-class dish for all who like marine food.

That these small organisms contain calories enough has been proved by the blue whale, which is the largest animal in the world and yet lives on plankton. Our own method of capture, with the little net which was often chewed up by hungry fish, seemed to us sadly primitive when we sat on the raft and saw a passing whale send up cascades of water as it simply filtered plankton through its celluloid beard. And one day we lost the whole net in the sea.

"Why don't you plankton-eaters do like him?" Torstein and Bengt said contemptuously to the rest of us, pointing to a blowing whale. "Just fill your mouths and blow out the water through your moustaches!"

I have seen whales in the distance from boats, and I have seen them stuffed in museums, but I have never felt for the gigantic carcase as one usually feels for proper warm-blooded animals, for example a horse or an elephant. Biologically, indeed, I had accepted the whale as a genuine mammal, but in its essence it was to all intents and purposes a large cold fish. We had a different impression when the great whales came rushing towards us, close to the side of the raft. One day when we were sitting as usual on the edge of the raft, having a meal, so close to the water that we just had to lean back to wash out our mugs, we started when suddenly something behind us blew hard like a swimming horse, and a big whale came up and stared at us, so close that we saw a shine like a polished shoe down through its blowhole. It was so unusual to hear real breathing out at sea, where all living creatures wriggle about silently without lungs and quiver their gills, that we really had a warm family feeling for our old distant cousin the whale, who like us had strayed so far out to sea. Instead of the cold, toadlike whale shark, which had not even the sense to stick up its nose for a breath of fresh air, here we had a visit from something which recalled a well-fed jovial hippopotamus in a zoological garden, and which did breathe—that made a most pleasant impression on me—before it sank into the sea again and disappeared.

We were visited by whales many times. Most often they were small porpoises and toothed whales which gambolled about us in large schools on the surface of the water, but now and then there were big cachalots too and other giant whales, which appeared singly or in small schools. Sometimes they passed like ships on the horizon, now and again sending a cascade of water into the air, but sometimes they steered straight for us. We were prepared for a dangerous collision the first time a big whale altered course and came straight towards the raft in a purposeful manner. As it gradually grew nearer we could hear its blowing and puffing, heavy and long-drawn, each time it rolled its head out of the water. It was an enormous, thick-skinned, ungainly land animal that came toiling through the water, as unlike a fish as a bat is unlike a bird. It came straight towards our port side, where we stood gathered on the edge of the raft, while one man sat at the masthead and shouted that he could see seven or eight more making their way towards us.

The big shining black forehead of the first whale was not more than two yards from us when it sank beneath the surface of the water, and then we saw the enormous blue-black whale-back glide quietly just under the raft right beneath our feet. It lay there for a time, dark and motionless, and we held our breath as we looked down on the gigantic curved back of a mammal a good deal longer than the whole raft. Then it sank slowly through the bluish water and disappeared from sight. Meanwhile the whole school were close upon us, but they paid no attention to us.

Whales which have abused their giant strength and sunk whaling boats with their tails have presumably been attacked first. The whole morning we had them puffing and blowing round us in the most unexpected places without their even pushing against the raft or the steering oar. They quite enjoyed themselves gambolling freely among the waves in the sunshine. But about noon the whole school dived as if on a given signal, and disappeared for good.

It was not only whales we could see under the raft. If we lifted up the reed matting we slept on, through the chinks between the logs we saw right down into the crystal-blue water. If we lay thus for a while we saw a breast fin or tail fin waggle past and now and again we saw a whole fish. If the chinks had been a few inches wider, we could have lain comfortably in bed with a line and fished under our mattresses.

The fish which most of all attached themselves to the raft were dolphins and pilot fish. From the moment the first dolphins joined us in the current off Callao, there was not a day on the whole voyage on which we had not large dolphins wriggling round us. What drew them to the raft we do not know, but, either there was a magical attraction in being able to swim in the shade with a moving roof above them, or there was food to be found in our kitchen garden of seaweed and barnacles that hung like garlands from all the logs and from the steering oar. It began with a thin coating of smooth green, but then the green clusters of seaweed grew with astonishing speed, so that the *Kon-Tiki* looked like a bearded sea-god as she tumbled along among the waves. And inside the green seaweed was a favourite resort of tiny small fry and our stowaways, the crabs.

There was a time when ants began to get the upper hand on board. There had been small black ants in some of the logs, and when we had got to sea and the damp began to penetrate into the wood, the ants swarmed out and into the sleeping bags. They were all over the place, and bit and tormented us till we thought they would drive us off the raft. But gradually, as it became wetter out at sea, they realised that this was not their right element, and only a few isolated specimens held out till we reached the other side. What did best on the raft, along with the crabs, were barnacles from an inch to an inch and a half long. They grew in hundreds, especially on the lee side of the raft, and as fast as we put the old ones into the soup kettle new larvae took root and grew up. The barnacles tasted fresh and delicate; we picked the seaweed as salad, and it was eatable, though not so good. We never actually saw the dolphins feeding in the vegetable garden, but they were constantly turning their gleaming bellies upwards and swimming under the logs.

The dolphin (dorado), which is a brilliantly coloured tropical fish, must not be confused with the creature also called dolphin, which is a small toothed whale. The dolphin was ordinarily from 3 feet 3 inches to 4 feet 6 inches long, had much flattened sides with an enormously high head and neck. We jerked on board one which was 4 feet 8 inches long with a head $13\frac{1}{2}$ inches high. The dolphin had a magnificent colour. In the water it shone blue and green like a bluebottle with a glitter of golden-yellow fins. But if we hauled them on board, we sometimes saw a strange sight. As the fish died, it gradually changed colour and became silver grey with black spots, and finally it became a quite uniform silvery white. This lasted for four or five minutes, and then the old colours slowly reappeared. Even in the water the dolphin could occasionally change colour like a chameleon, and often we saw a "new kind" of shining copper-coloured fish, which on a closer acquaintance proved to be our old companion the dolphin.

The high forehead gave the dolphin the appearance of a bull-dog flattened from the side, and the forehead always cut through the surface of the water when the predatory fish shot off like a torpedo after a fleeing shoal of flying fish. When the dolphin was in a good humour it turned over on its flat side, went ahead at a great speed and then sprang high into the air and tumbled down like a flat pancake; it came down on the surface with a regular smack and a column of water rose up. It was no sooner down in the water than it came up in another leap, and yet another, away over the swell. But when it was in a bad temper, for example when we hauled it up on to the raft, then it bit. Torstein limped about for some time with a rag round his big toe because he had let it stray into the mouth of a dolphin which had used the opportunity to close its jaws and chew a little harder than usual. After our return home we heard that dolphins attack and eat people when bathing. This was not very complimentary to us, seeing that we had bathed among them every day without their showing any particular interest. But they were formidable beasts of prey, for we found both squids and whole flying fish in their stomachs.

Flying fish were the dolphins' favourite food. If anything splashed on the surface of the water, they rushed at it blindly in the hope of its being a flying fish. In many a drowsy morning hour, when we crept blinking out of the cabin and, half asleep, dipped a toothbrush in the sea, we became wide awake with a jump when a thirty-pound fish shot out like lightning from under the raft and nosed at the toothbrush in disappointment. And when we were sitting quietly at breakfast on the edge of the raft, a dolphin might jump up and bring off one of its most vigorous sideways splashes, so that the sea water ran down our backs and into our food.

One day when we were sitting at dinner Torstein made a reality of the tallest of fishing stories. He suddenly laid down his fork and put his hand into the sea, and before we knew what was happening the water was boiling and a big dolphin came tumbling in among us. Torstein had caught hold of the home end of a fishing line which came quietly gliding past, and on the other end hung a completely astonished dolphin which had broken Erik's line when he was fishing a few days before.

There was not a day on which we had not six or seven dolphins following us in circles round and under the raft. On bad days there might be only two or three, but on the other hand, as many as thirty or forty might turn up the day after. As a rule it was enough to warn the cook twenty minutes in advance if we wanted fresh fish for dinner. Then he tied a line to a short bamboo stick and put half a flying fish on the hook. A dolphin was there in a flash, ploughing the surface with its head as it chased the hook, with two or three more in its wake. It was a splendid fish to play, and when freshly caught its flesh was firm and delicious

ve—Hesselberg took our position daily
our course was marked on the chart of the
ific.

w—Watzinger taking last wind measure-
t of the day.

Above—The captain at the helm. We each
in turn put in two hours at the steering oar.

Below—Evening outside the cabin door.

PLATE IX

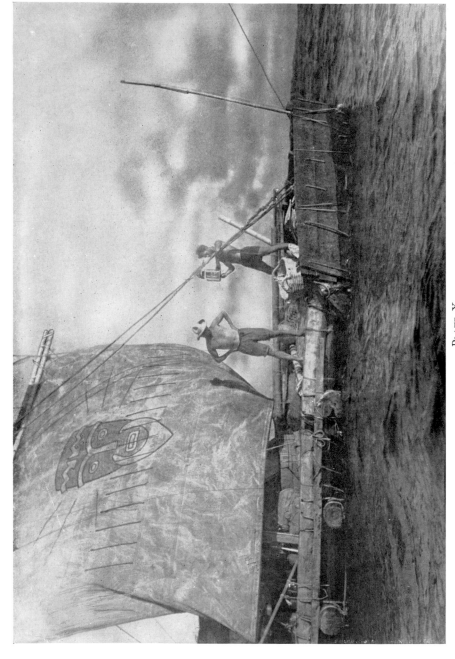

PLATE X

to eat, like a mixture of cod and salmon. It kept for two days, and that was all we needed, for there were fish enough in the sea.

We became acquainted with pilot fish in another way. Sharks brought them and left them to be adopted by us after the sharks' death. We had not been long at sea before the first shark visited us. And sharks soon became an almost daily occurrence. Sometimes the shark just came swimming up to inspect the raft and went on in search of prey after circling round us once or twice. But most often the sharks took up a position in our wake just behind the steering oar, and there they lay without a sound, stealing from starboard to port and very occasionally giving a leisurely wag of their tails to keep pace with the raft's placid advance. The blue-grey body of the shark always looked brownish in the sunlight just below the surface, and it moved up and down with the seas so that the dorsal fin always stuck up menacingly. If there was a high sea the shark might be lifted up by the waves high above our own level, and we had a direct side view of the shark as in a glass case, as it swam towards us in a dignified manner with its fussy retinue of small pilot fish ahead of its jaws. For a few seconds it looked as if both the shark and its striped companions would swim right on board, till the raft leant over gracefully to leeward, rose over the ridge of waves and descended on the other side.

To begin with we had a great respect for sharks on account of their reputation and their alarming appearance. There was an unbridled strength in the streamlined body, consisting just of one great bundle of steel muscles, and a heartless greed in the broad flat head with the small green cat's eyes and the enormous jaws which could swallow footballs. When the man at the helm shouted "shark alongside to starboard" or "shark alongside to port" we used to come out in search of hand harpoons and gaffs and station ourselves along the edge of the raft. The shark usually glided round us with the dorsal fin close up to the logs. And our respect for the shark increased when we saw that the gaffs bent like spaghetti when we struck them against the sandpaper armour on the shark's back, while the spearheads of the hand harpoons were broken in the heat of the battle. All we gained by getting

H

through the shark's skin and into the gristle or muscles was a hectic struggle, in which the water boiled round us till the shark broke loose and was off, while a little oil floated up and spread itself out over the surface.

To save our last harpoon head we fastened together a bunch of our largest fish-hooks and hid them inside the carcase of a whole dolphin. We slung the bait overboard with a precautionary multiplication of steel lines fastened to a piece of our own life-line. Slowly and surely the shark came, and as it lifted its snout above the water it opened its great crescent-shaped jaws with a jerk and let the whole dolphin slip in and down. And there it stuck. There was a struggle in which the shark lashed the water into foam, but we had a good grip of the rope and hauled the big fellow, despite his resistance, as far as the logs aft, where he lay awaiting what might come and only gaped as though to intimidate us with his parallel rows of saw-like teeth. Here we profited by a sea to slide the shark up over the low end logs, slippery with seaweed, and after casting a rope round the tail fin we ran well out of the way till the war dance was over.

In the gristle of the first shark we found our own harpoon head, and we thought at first that this was the reason for the shark's comparatively small fighting spirit. But later we caught shark after shark by the same method, and every time it went just as easily. Even if the shark could jerk and tug, and certainly was fearfully heavy to play, it became quite spiritless and tame and never made full use of its giant strength if we only managed to hold the line tight without letting the shark gain an inch in the tug-of-war. The sharks we got on board were usually from six to ten feet long, and there were blue sharks as well as brown sharks. The last-named had a skin outside the mass of muscles through which we could not drive a sharp knife unless we struck with our whole strength, and often not even then. The skin of the belly was as impenetrable as that of the back, and the five gill-clefts behind the head on each side were the only vulnerable points.

When we hauled in a shark, black slippery remora fish were usually fixed tight to its body. By means of an oval sucking disc

on the top of the flat head, they were fastened so tight that we
could not get them loose by pulling ·their tails. But they themselves could break loose and skip away to take hold at another
place in a second. If they grew tired of hanging tightly to the
shark when their old host gave no sign of returning to the sea,
they leapt off and vanished down between the chinks in the raft
to swim away and find themselves another shark. And if the
remora does not find a shark, it attaches itself to the skin of
another fish for the time being. The remora was generally anything from the length of a finger up to a foot. We tried the
natives' old trick which they sometimes use when they secure a
live remora. They tie a line to its tail and let it swim away. It then
tries to suck itself on to the first fish it sees, and clings so tightly
that a lucky fisherman may haul in the remora's tail and both
fish with it. We had no luck. Every single time we let a remora
go with a line tied to its tail, it simply shot off and sucked itself
fast to one of the logs of the raft, in the belief that it had found
an extra fine big shark. And there it hung, however hard we
tugged on the line. We gradually acquired a number of these small
remoras which hung on and dangled obstinately among the
shells on the side of the raft and travelled with us right across
the Pacific.

But the remora was stupid and ugly and never became such
an agreeable pet as its lively companion the pilot fish. The pilot
fish is a small cigar-shaped fish with zebra stripes, which swims
rapidly in a shoal ahead of the shark's snout. It received its name
because it was thought that it piloted its half-blind friend the
shark about in the sea. In reality it simply goes along with the
shark, and if it acts independently, it is only because it catches
sight of food within its own range of vision. The pilot fish
accompanied its lord and master to the last second. But as it
could not cling fast to the giant's skin, as the remora does, it was
completely bewildered when its old master suddenly disappeared
up into the air and did not come down again. Then the pilot fish
scurried about in a distracted manner, searching, and always came
back and wriggled along astern of the raft, where the shark had
vanished skyward. But as time passed and the shark did not come

down again, they had to look round for a new lord and master. And none was nearer to hand than the *Kon-Tiki* herself.

If we let ourselves down over the side of the raft with our heads down in the brilliantly clear water, we saw the raft as the belly of a sea-monster, with the steering oar as its tail and the centreboards hanging down like blunt fins. And in between them all the adopted pilot fish swam side by side, and took no notice of the bubbling human head except that one or two of them darted swiftly aside and peered right up its nose, only to wriggle back again unperturbed and take their places in the ranks of eager swimmers.

Our pilot fish patrolled in two detachments; most of them swam between the centreboards, the others in a graceful fan formation just ahead of the bows. Now and then they shot away from the raft to snap up some eatable trifle we passed, and after meals, when we washed our crockery in the water alongside, it was as if we had emptied a whole cigar case of striped pilot fish among the scraps. There was not a single scrap they did not examine, and so long as it was not vegetable food, down it went. These queer little fish huddled under our protecting wings with such childlike confidence that we, like the shark, had a fatherly protective feeling towards them. They became the *Kon-Tiki*'s marine pets, and it was tabu on board to lay hand on a pilot fish.

We had in our retinue pilot fish which were certainly in their childhood, for they were hardly an inch long, while most were about six inches. When the whale shark rushed off at lightning speed after Erik's harpoon had entered its skull, some of its old pilot fish strayed over to the victor; they were just two feet long. After a steady continuance of victories the *Kon-Tiki* soon had a following of forty or fifty pilot fish, and many of them so much liked our quiet forward movement, and our daily scraps, that they followed us for thousands of miles over the sea.

But occasionally some were faithless. One day when I was at the steering oar I suddenly noticed that the sea was boiling to southward, and saw an immense shoal of dolphins come shooting across the sea like silver torpedoes. They did not come as usual, splashing along comfortably on their flat sides, but came rushing at frantic speed more through the air than through the water. The blue swell was whipped into white foam in one single turmoil of splashing fugitives, and behind them came a black back dashing along on a zigzag course like a speedboat. The desperate dolphins came shooting through and over the surface right up to the raft; here they dived, while about a hundred crowded together in a tightly packed shoal and swung away to eastward, so that the whole sea astern was a glittering mass of colours. The gleaming back behind them half rose above the surface, dived in a graceful curve under the raft, and shot astern like a torpedo after the shoal of dolphins. It was a devilish big fellow of a blue shark that seemed to be nearly twenty feet long. When it disappeared a number of our pilot fish had gone too. They had found a more exciting sea hero to go campaigning with.

The marine creature against which the experts had begged us to be most on our guard was the octopus, for it could get on board the raft. The National Geographical Society in Washington had shown us reports and dramatic magnesium photographs from an area in the Humboldt Current where monstrous octopuses had their favourite resort and came up on to the surface at night. They were so voracious that if one of them fastened on to a piece of meat and remained on the hook, another came and began to eat its captured kinsman. They had arms which could make an end of a big shark and set ugly marks on great whales, and a devilish beak like an eagle's hidden among their tentacles. We were reminded that they lay floating in the darkness with phos- phorescent eyes, and that their arms were long enough to feel about in every small corner of the raft, if they did not care to come right on board. We did not at all like the prospect of feeling cold arms round our necks, dragging us out of our sleeping-bags at night, and we provided ourselves with sabre-like machete knives, one for each of us, in case we should wake to the embrace of groping tentacles. There was nothing which seemed more disagreeable to us when we started, especially as the marine experts in Peru got on to the same subject and showed us on the chart where the worst area was, right in the Humboldt Current itself.

For a long time we saw no sign of a squid, either on board or in the sea. But then one morning we had the first warning that they must be in those waters. When the sun rose, we found the progeny of an octopus on board, in the form of a little baby the size of a cat. It had come up on deck unaided in the course of the night and lay dead with its arms twined round the bamboo outside the cabin door. A thick black inky liquid was smeared over the bamboo deck and lay in a pool round the squid. We wrote a page or two in the log-book with cuttlefish ink, which was like Indian ink, and then flung the baby overboard for the pleasure of the dolphins.

We saw in this minor incident the harbinger of larger night visitors. If the baby could clamber on board, its hungry progenitor could no doubt do the same. Our forefathers must have felt the same as we when they sat in their Viking ships and thought of the Old Man of the Sea. But the next incident completely bewildered us. One morning we found a single smaller young squid on the top of the roof of palm leaves. This puzzled us very much. It could not have climbed up there, as the only ink marks were smeared in a ring round it in the middle of the roof. Nor had it been dropped by a sea bird, for it was completely intact, with no beak-marks. We came to the conclusion that it had been flung up on to the roof by a sea which had come on board, but none of those on night watch could remember any such sea that night. And as the nights passed, we regularly found more young squids on board, the smallest of them the size of one's middle finger.

It was soon usual to find a small squid or two among the flying fish about the deck in the morning, even if the sea had been calm in the night. And they were young ones of the real devilish kind, with eight long arms covered with sucking discs and two still longer with thorn-like hooks at the end. But large squids never gave a sign of coming on board. We saw the shine of phosphorescent eyes drifting on the surface on dark nights, and on one single occasion we saw the sea boil and bubble while something like a big wheel came up and rotated in the air, while some of our dolphins tried to escape by hurling themselves desperately through space. But why the big ones never came on board, when the small ones were constant night visitors, was a riddle to which we found no answer until two months—two months rich in experience—after we were out of the ill-famed octopus area.

Young squids continued to come aboard. One sunny morning we all saw a glittering shoal of something which shot up out of the water and flew through the air like large rain-drops, while the sea boiled with pursuing dolphins. At first we took it for a shoal of flying fish, for we had already had three different kinds of these on board. But when they came near, and some of them sailed over the raft at a height of four or five feet, one ran straight into Bengt's chest and fell slap on the deck. It was a small squid. Our astonishment was great. When we put it into a sailcloth bucket it kept on taking off and shooting up to the surface, but it did not develop speed enough in the small bucket to get more than half out of the water. It is a known fact that the squid ordinarily swims on the principle of the rocket-propelled aircraft. It pumps sea water with great force through a closed tube along the side of the body, and can thus shoot backwards in jerks at a high speed; and with all its tentacles hanging behind it in a cluster over its head, it becomes streamlined like a fish. It has on its sides two round fleshy folds of skin which are ordinarily used for steering and quiet swimming in the water. But it was thus shown that defenceless young squids, which are a favourite food of many large fish, can escape their pursuers by taking to the air in the same way as flying fish. They had made the principle of the rocket aircraft a reality long before human genius hit upon the idea. They pump sea water through themselves till they get up a terrific speed, and then they steer up at an angle from the surface by unfolding the pieces of skin like wings. Like the flying fish, they make a glider flight over the waves for as far as their speed can carry them. After that, when we had to begin to pay attention, we often saw them sailing along for fifty to sixty yards, singly and in twos and threes. The fact that cuttlefish can "glide" has been a novelty to all the zoologists we have met.

As the guest of natives in the Pacific I have often eaten squid;

it tastes like a mixture of lobster and india rubber. But on board the *Kon-Tiki* squids came last on the menu. If we got them on deck gratis we just exchanged them for something else. We made the exchange by throwing out a hook with the squid on it, and pulling it in again with a big fish kicking at the end of it. Even tunny and bonito liked young squids, and they were food which came at the head of our menu.

But we did not run up against acquaintances only as we lay drifting over the sea's surface. The diary contains many entries of this type:

11/5. To-day a huge marine animal twice came up to the surface alongside us as we sat at supper on the edge of the raft. It made a fearful splashing and disappeared. We have no idea what it was.

6/6. Herman saw a thick dark-coloured fish with a broad white body, thin tail and spikes. It jumped clear of the sea on the starboard side several times.

16/6. Curious fish sighted on port bow. Six feet long, maximum breadth one foot; long brown thin snout, large dorsal fin near head and a smaller one in the middle of the back, heavy sickle-shaped tail fin. Kept near surface and swam at times by wriggling its body like an eel. It dived when Herman and I went out in the rubber dinghy with a hand harpoon. Came up later, but dived and disappeared.

Next day: Erik was sitting at the masthead, 12 noon, when he saw thirty or forty long thin brown fish of the same kind as yesterday. Now they came at a high speed from the port side and disappeared astern like a big brown flat shadow in the sea.

18/6. Knut observed a snake-like creature, two to three feet long and thin, which stood straight up and down in the water below the surface, and dived by wriggling downwards like a snake.

On several occasions we glided past a large dark mass that lay motionless under the surface of the water like a hidden reef, the size of the floor of a room. It was presumably the giant ray of evil repute, but it never moved, and we never went close enough to make out its shape clearly.

With such company in the water time never passed slowly. It was worse when we had to dive down into the sea ourselves and inspect the ropes on the underside of the raft. One day one of the centreboards broke loose and slipped down under the raft, where it was caught up in the ropes without our being able to get hold of it. Herman and Knut were the best divers. Twice Herman swam under the raft and lay there among dolphins and pilot fish, tugging and pulling at the board. He had just come up for the second time and was sitting on the edge of the raft to recover his breath, when an eight-foot shark was detected not more than ten feet from his legs, moving steadily up from the depths towards the tips of his toes. Perhaps we did the shark an injustice, but we suspected it of evil intentions and rammed a harpoon into its skull. The shark felt aggrieved, and a splashy struggle took place, as a consequence of which the shark disappeared leaving a sheet of oil on the surface, while the centreboard remained unsalved, lying caught up under the raft.

Then Erik had the idea of making a diving basket. We had not many raw materials to which we could have recourse, but we had bamboos and ropes and an old chip basket which had contained cocoanuts. We lengthened the basket upwards with bamboos and plaited ropework, and then we were let down in the basket alongside the raft. The enticing legs were then concealed in the basket, and even if the plaited ropework above had only a psychological effect on both us and the fish, in any case we could duck down into the basket in a flash if anything with hostile intentions made a dash at us, and have ourselves pulled up out of the water by the others on deck.

This diving basket was not merely useful, but gradually became a perfect place of entertainment for us on board. It gave us a first-class opportunity to study the floating aquarium we had under the floor.

When the sea was content to run in a calm swell, we crawled into the basket one by one and were let down under water for as long as our breath lasted. There was a curiously transfigured shadowless flow of light down in the water. As soon as we had our eyes under the surface light no longer seemed to have a particular direction, as up in our own above-water world. Re-fraction of light came as much from below as from above; the sun no longer shone, it was present everywhere. If we looked up at the bottom of the raft it was brightly illuminated all over, with the nine big logs and the whole network of rope-lashings bathed in a magic light, and with a flickering wreath of spring-green seaweed all round the sides and along the whole length of the steering oar. The pilot fish swam formally in their ranks like zebras in fishes' skins, while big dolphins circled round with restless, vigilant, jerky movements, eager for prey. Here and there the light fell on the sappy red wood of a centreboard which stuck downwards out of a chink, and on the wood sat peaceful colonies of white barnacles rhythmically beckoning for oxygen and food with their fringed yellow gills. If anyone came too near them they hastily closed their red and yellow-edged shells, and shut the door till they felt the danger was over. The light down here was wonderfully clear and soothing for us who were accustomed to the tropical sun on deck. Even when we looked down into the bottomless depths of the sea where it is eternal black night, the night appeared to us a pleasant light blue on account of the rays of the sun which came back. To our astonish-ment, we saw fish far down in the depths of the clear, clean blue when we ourselves were only just below the surface. They might have been bonitos, and there were other kinds which swam at such a depth that we could not recognise them. Sometimes they were in immense shoals, and we often wondered whether the whole ocean current was full of fish, or whether those down in the depths too had intentionally assembled under the *Kon-Tiki* to keep us company for a few days.

What we liked best was a dip under the surface when the great gold-finned tunnies were paying us a visit. Occasionally they came to the raft in big shoals, but most often just two or three came together and swam round us in quiet circles for several days on end, unless we were able to lure them on to the hook. From the raft they simply looked like big, heavy brown fish without any uncommon adornment, but if we crept down to them in their own element they spontaneously changed both colour and shape. The change was so bewildering that several times we had to come up and take our bearings afresh to see if it was the same fish we had been looking at across the water. The big fellows paid no attention to us whatever; they continued their majestic manoeuvres unperturbed; but now they had acquired a marvellous elegance of form, the equal of which we never saw in any other fish, and their colour had become metallic with a suffusion of pale violet. Powerful torpedoes of shining silver and steel, with perfect proportions and streamlined shape, they had just to move one or two fins slightly to set their 150–180 lbs. gliding about in the water with the most consummate grace.

The closer we came into contact with the sea and what had its home there, the less strange it became, and the more at home we ourselves felt. And we learned to respect the old primitive peoples who lived in close converse with the Pacific and therefore knew it from a standpoint quite different from our own. Maybe we have now estimated its salt content, and given tunnies and dolphins Latin names. They had not done that. But nevertheless I am afraid that the picture the primitive peoples had of the sea was a truer one than ours.

There were not many fixed marks out here at sea. Waves and fish, sun and stars came and went. There was not supposed to be land of any sort in the 4,300 sea miles that separated the South Sea islands from Peru. We were therefore greatly surprised when we approached 100° west and discovered that a reef was marked on the Pacific chart right ahead of us on the course we were following. It was marked as a small circle, and as the chart had been issued the same year we looked up the reference in "Sailing Directions for South America." We read: "Breakers were reported in 1906 and again in 1926 to exist about 600 miles south-westward of Galapagos Islands, in latitude 6° 42′ S., longitude 99° 43′ W. In 1927 a steamer passed one mile westward of this position, but saw no indications of breakers and in 1934 another passed one mile southward and saw no evidence of breakers. The motor vessel Cowrie, in 1935, obtained no bottom at 160 fathoms in this position."

According to the charts the place was clearly still regarded as a doubtful proposition for shipping, and as a deep-draught vessel runs a greater risk by going too near a shoal than we should with a raft, we decided to steer straight for the point marked on the chart and see what we found. The reef was marked a little farther north than the point we seemed to be making for, so we laid the steering oar over to starboard and trimmed the square-sail so that the bow pointed roughly north and we took sea and wind from the starboard side. Now it came about that a little more Pacific splashed into our sleeping-bags than we were accustomed to, especially as at the same time the weather began to freshen considerably. But we saw to our satisfaction that the *Kon-Tiki* could be manoeuvred surely and steadily at a surprising wide angle into the wind, so long as the wind was still on our quarter. Otherwise the sail swung round, and we had the same mad circus business to get the raft under control again. For two days and nights we drove the raft north-north-west. The seas ran high, and became incalculable as the trade wind began to fluctuate between southeast and east, but we were lifted up and down over all the waves that rushed against us. We had a constant look-out at the masthead, and when we rode over the ridges the horizon widened considerably. The crests of the seas reached six feet above the level of the roof of the bamboo cabin, and if two vigorous seas rushed together they rose still higher in combat and flung up a hissing watery tower which might burst in unexpected directions. When night came, we barricaded the doorway with provision boxes, but it was a wet night's rest. We had hardly fallen asleep when the first crash on the bamboo wall came, and while a thousand jets of water sprayed in like a fountain through the bamboo wickerwork, a foaming torrent rushed in over the provisions and in on to us.

"Ring up the plumber," I heard a sleepy voice remark, as we hunched ourselves up to give the water room to run out through the floor. The plumber did not come, and we had a lot of bath-water in our beds that night. A big dolphin actually came on board unintentionally in Herman's watch.

Next day the seas were less confused, as the trade wind had decided that it would now blow for a time from due east. We relieved one another at the masthead, for now we might expect to reach the point we were making for late in the afternoon. We noticed more life than usual in the sea that day. Perhaps it was only because we kept a better look-out than usual.

During the afternoon we saw a big swordfish approaching the raft close to the surface. The two sharp pointed fins which stuck up out of the water were six feet apart, and the sword looked almost as long as the body. The swordfish swept in a curve close by the man at the helm and disappeared behind the wave crests. When we were having a rather wet and salty midday meal, a large sea turtle with carapace, head and sprawling fins was lifted up by a hissing sea right in front of our noses. When that wave gave place to two others, the turtle was gone as suddenly as it had appeared. This time too we saw the gleaming whitish-green of dolphins' bellies tumbling about in the water below the armoured reptile. The area was unusually rich in tiny flying fish an inch long, which sailed along in big shoals and often came on board. We also noted single skuas and were regularly visited by frigate birds which cruised over the raft, with forked tails like giant swallows. Frigate birds are usually regarded as a sign that land is near, and the optimism on board increased.

"Perhaps there is a reef or a sandbank there all the same," some of us thought. And the most optimistic said: "Suppose we find a little green grassy island—one can never know when so few people have been here before. Then we'll have discovered a new land—Kon-Tiki Island!"

From noon onwards Erik was more and more diligent in climbing up on the kitchen box and standing blinking through the sextant. At 6.20 p.m. he reported our position as latitude 6° 42' south by longitude 99° 42' west. We were one sea mile due east of the reef on the chart. The bamboo yard was lowered and the sail rolled up on deck. The wind was due east and would take us slowly right to the place. When the sun went down swiftly into the sea, the full moon in turn shone out in all its brilliance and lit up the surface of the sea which undulated in black and silver from horizon to horizon. Visibility from the masthead was good. We saw breaking seas everywhere, in long

rows, but no regular surf which must indicate a reef or shoal. No
one would turn in; all stood looking out eagerly, and two or
three men were aloft at once. And as we drifted in over the
centre of the marked area we sounded all the time. All the lead
sinkers we had on board were fastened to the end of a 54-thread
silk rope more than 500 fathoms long, and even if the rope hung
rather crooked on account of the raft's leeway, at any rate the
lead hung at a depth of some 400 fathoms. And there was no
bottom, either east of the place, or in the middle of it, or west
of it. We took one last look over the surface of the sea, and when
we had assured ourselves that we could safely call the area
surveyed and free from shallows of any kind, we set sail and laid
the oar over in its usual place, so that wind and sea were again on
our port quarter. And so we went on with the raft on her natural
free course. The waves came and went as before between the
open logs aft. We could now sleep and eat dry, even if the heaving
seas around us took charge in earnest and raged for several days
while the trade wind vacillated from east to south-east.

On this little sailing trip up to the spurious reef we had learnt
quite a lot about the effectiveness of the centreboards as a keel,
and when, later in the voyage, Herman and Knut dived under
the raft together and salved the fifth centreboard, we learned
still more about these curious pieces of board, something which
no one has understood since the Indians themselves gave up this
forgotten sport. That the board did the work of a keel and
allowed the raft to move at an angle to the wind—that was plain
sailing. But when the old Spaniards declared that the Indians to
a large extent "steered" their balsa rafts on the sea with "certain
centreboards which they pushed down into the chinks between
the timbers," this sounded incomprehensible both to us and to
all who had occupied themselves with the problem. As the centreboard was simply held tight in a narrow chink, it could not be
turned sideways and serve as a helm.

We discovered the secret in the following manner. The wind
was steady and the sea had gone down again, so that the *Kon-Tiki*
had kept a steady course for a couple of days without our touching
the lashed steering oar. We pushed the recovered centreboard

down into a chink aft, and in a moment the *Kon-Tiki* altered
course several degrees from west towards north-west, and pro-
ceeded steadily and quietly on her new course. If we pulled this
centreboard up again the raft swung back on to her previous
course. But if we pulled it only halfway up the raft swung only
halfway back on her old course. By simply raising and lowering
the centreboard we could effect changes of course and keep to
them without touching the steering oar. This was the Incas'
ingenious system. They had worked out a simple system of
balances by which the pressure of the wind on the sail made the
mast the fixed point. The two arms were respectively the raft
forward of and the raft aft of the mast. If the aggregate centreboard surface aft was heavier, the stem swung freely round with
the wind, but if the centreboard surface forward was heavier, the
stern swung round with the wind. The centreboards which are
nearest the mast have of course the least effect, on account of the
relation between arm and power. If the wind was due astern the
centreboards ceased to be effective, and then it was impossible to
keep the raft steady without continually working the steering oar.
If the raft lay thus at full length, she was a little too long to ride
the seas freely. And as the cabin door and the place where we had
meals were on the starboard side, we always took the seas on
board on our port quarter.

We could certainly have continued our voyage by making the
steersman stand and pull a centreboard up and down in a chink
instead of hauling sidewise on the ropes of the steering oar, but
we had now grown so accustomed to the steering oar that we
just set a general course with the centreboards and preferred to
steer with the oar.

The next great stage on our voyage was as invisible to the eye
as the shoal which existed only on the map.

It was the forty-fifth day at sea; we had advanced from the
78th degree of longitude to the 108th, and were exactly halfway
to the first islands ahead. There were over 2,000 sea miles between
us and South America in the east, and it was the same distance on
to Polynesia in the west. The nearest land in any direction was
the Galapagos Islands to east-north-east and Easter Island due

south, both more than 500 sea miles away on the boundless ocean.
We had not seen a ship, and we never did see one, because we
were off the routes of all ordinary shipping traffic in the Pacific.

But we did not really feel these enormous distances, for the
horizon glided along with us unnoticed as we moved, and our
own floating world remained always the same, a circle flung up
to the vault of the sky, with the raft itself as centre, while the
same stars rolled on over us night after night.

olphins swam with the raft right
oss the Pacific—splendid eating and
ily caught.

he gold-finned tunny provided excel-
t fishing. There was food enough in
e fish for a whole flotilla of rafts.

Plate XII
Hauling a shark
board.

The shark once on deck, its captor
kept out of the way till it had ceased to snap.

CHAPTER VI

ACROSS THE PACIFIC: II

*A Queer Craft—Out in the Dinghy—Unhindered Progress—
Absence of Sea Marks—At Sea in a Bamboo Hut—On the
Longitude of Easter Island—The Mystery of Easter Island—The
Stone Giants—Red Stone Wigs—The "Long-ears"—Tiki Builds
a Bridge—Suggestive Place-names—Catching Shark with our
Hands—The Parrot—LI 2B Calling—Sailing by the Stars—
Three Seas—A Storm—Blood-bath in the Sea, Blood-bath on
Board—Man Overboard—Another Storm—The Kon-Tiki becomes
Ramshackle—Messengers from Polynesia.*

WHEN the sea was not too rough we were often out in
the little rubber dinghy taking photographs. I shall not
forget the first time the sea was so calm that two men
felt like putting the balloon-like little thing into the water and
going for a row. They had hardly got clear of the raft when they
dropped the little oars and sat roaring with laughter. And as the
swell lifted them away and they disappeared and reappeared among
the seas, they laughed so loud every time they caught a glimpse of
us that their voices rang out over the desolate Pacific. We looked
round us with mixed feelings and saw nothing comic but our
own hirsute bearded faces; but as the two in the dinghy should
be accustomed to those by now, we began to have a lurking
suspicion that they had suddenly gone mad. Sunstroke, perhaps.
The two fellows could hardly scramble back on board the
Kon-Tiki for sheer laughter, and gasping, with tears in their eyes,
beg us just to go and see for ourselves.

Two of us jumped down into the dancing rubber dinghy, and
were caught by a sea which lifted us clear. Immediately we sat
down with a bump and roared with laughter. We had to scramble
back on to the raft as quickly as possible and calm the two last
who had not been out yet, for they thought we had all gone
stark staring mad.

It was ourselves and our proud vessel which made such a

I

completely hopeless, lunatic impression on us the first time we
saw the whole thing at a distance. We had never before had an
outside view of ourselves in the open sea. The logs of timber
disappeared behind the smallest waves, and when we saw anything at all it was the low cabin with the wide doorway and the
bristly roof of leaves that bobbed up from among the seas. The
raft looked exactly like an old Norwegian hay-loft lying helpless,
drifting about in the open sea, a warped hay-loft full of sunburnt
bearded ruffians. If anyone had come paddling after us at sea in a
bath we should have felt the same spontaneous urge to laughter.
Even an ordinary swell rolled halfway up the cabin wall and
looked as if it must pour in unhindered through the wide open
door in which the bearded fellows lay gaping. But then the crazy
craft came up on the surface again and the vagabonds lay there
as dry, shaggy and intact as before. If a higher sea came racing by,
cabin and sail and the whole mast might disappear behind the
mountain of water, but just as certainly the cabin with its vagabonds would be there again next moment.

It looked bad, and we could not realise that things had gone
so well on board the peculiar craft.

Next time we rowed out to have a good laugh at ourselves, we
nearly had a disaster. The wind and sea were higher than we
supposed, and the Kon-Tiki was cleaving a path for herself over
the swell much more quickly than we realised. We in the
dinghy had to row for our lives out in the open sea, in an attempt
to regain the unmanageable raft which could not stop and wait,
and could not possibly turn round and come back. Even when the
boys on board the Kon-Tiki got the sail down, the wind got such a
grip of the bamboo cabin that the balsa raft drifted away to
westward as fast as we could splash after her in the dancing round
rubber dinghy with its tiny toy oars. There was only one thought
in the head of every man—we must not be separated. Those were
horrible minutes we spent out on the sea before we got hold of
the runaway raft and crawled on board to the others, home
again.

From that day it was strictly forbidden to go out in the rubber
dinghy without having a long line made fast to the bows, so that

those who remained on board could haul the dinghy in if necessary. We never went far away from the raft, therefore, except when the wind was light and the Pacific curving itself in a gentle swell. But we had these conditions when the raft was halfway to Polynesia and the ocean, all-dominating, arched itself round the globe towards every point of the compass. Then we could safely leave the *Kon-Tiki* and row away into the blue space between sky and sea. When we saw the silhouette of our craft grow smaller and smaller in the distance, and the big sail at last shrunken to a vague black square on the horizon, a sensation of loneliness sometimes crept over us. The sea curved away under us as blue upon blue as the sky above, and where they met all the blue flowed together and became one. We could almost feel as if we were suspended in space; all our world was empty and blue; there was no fixed point in it but the tropical sun which burned our necks, golden and warm. Then the distant sail of the lonely raft drew us to it like a magnetic point on the horizon. We rowed back and crept on board and felt that we had come home again to our own world, on board and yet on firm, safe ground. And inside the bamboo cabin we found shade, and the scent of bamboos and withered palm leaves. The sunny blue purity outside was now served to us in a suitably large dose through the open cabin wall. So we were accustomed to it, and so it was good, for a time, till the great clean blue tempted us out again.

It was most remarkable what a psychological effect the shaky bamboo cabin had on our minds. It measured eight by fourteen feet, and to diminish the pressure of wind and sea it was built so low that we could not stand upright under the ridge of the roof. Walls and roof were made of strong bamboo canes lashed together and guyed, and covered with a tough wickerwork of split bamboos. The green and yellow bars, with fringes of foliage hanging down from the roof, were restful to the eye as a white cabin wall never could have been, and despite the fact that the bamboo wall on the starboard side was open for one third of its length, and roof and walls let in sun and moon, this primitive lair gave a greater feeling of security than white-painted bulkheads and closed portholes would have given in the same circumstances. We tried to find an explanation for this curious fact, and came to the following result. Our own consciousness was totally unaccustomed to associate a palm-covered bamboo dwelling with sea travel. There was no natural harmony between the great rolling ocean and the draughty palm hut which was floating about among the seas. Therefore, either the hut would seem entirely out of place in among the waves, or the waves would seem entirely out of place round the hut wall. So long as we only kept on board, the bamboo hut and its jungle scent were plain reality and the tossing seas seemed rather visionary. But from the rubber boat, waves and hut exchanged roles. The fact that the balsa logs always rode the seas like a gull, and let the water right through aft if a wave broke on board, gave us an unshakeable confidence in the dry part in the middle of the raft where the cabin was. The longer the voyage lasted the safer we felt in our cosy lair, and we looked at the white-crested waves that danced past outside our doorway as if they were an impressive cinema show conveying no menace to us at all. Even though the gaping wall was only five feet from the unprotected edge of the raft and only a foot and a half above the waterline, yet we felt as if we had travelled many miles away from the sea and occupied a jungle dwelling remote from the sea's perils, once we had crawled inside the door. There we could lie on our backs and look up at the curious roof which twisted about like boughs in the wind, and enjoy the jungle smell of raw wood, bamboos and withered palm leaves.

Sometimes, too, we went out in the rubber boat to look at ourselves by night. Coal-black seas towered up on all sides, and a glittering myriad of tropical stars drew a faint reflection from plankton in the water. The world was simple, stars in the darkness. Whether it was 1947 B.C. or A.D. suddenly became of no significance. We lived, and that we felt with alert intensity. We realised that life had been full for men before the technical age also—indeed, fuller and richer in many ways than the life of modern man. Time and evolution somehow ceased to exist; all that was real and all that mattered were the same to-day as they

had always been and would always be; we were swallowed up
in the absolute common measure of history, endless unbroken
darkness under a swarm of stars. Before us in the night the
Kon-Tiki rose out of the seas to sink down again behind black
masses of water that towered between her and us. In the moonlight there was a singular atmosphere about the raft. Stout shining
wooden logs fringed with seaweed, the square pitch-black outline
of a Viking sail, a bristly bamboo hut with the yellow light of a
paraffin lamp aft—the whole suggested a picture from a fairy tale
rather than the actual reality. Now and then the raft disappeared
completely behind the black seas; then she rose again and stood
out sharp in silhouette against the stars, while glittering water
poured from the logs.

When we saw the atmosphere about the solitary raft, we could
well see in our mind's eye the whole flotilla of such vessels,
spread in fan formation beyond the horizon to increase the chances
of finding land, when the first men made their way across this
sea. The Inca Tupak Yupanqui, who had brought under his rule
both Peru and Ecuador, sailed across the sea with an armada of
many thousand men on balsa rafts, just before the Spaniards came,
to search for islands which rumour had told of out in the Pacific.
He found two islands, which some think were the Galapagos,
and after eight months' absence he and his numerous paddlers
succeeded in toiling their way back to Ecuador. Kon-Tiki and
his followers had certainly sailed in a similar formation several
hundred years before, but having discovered the Polynesian
islands, they had no reason for trying to struggle back.

When we jumped on board the raft again, we often sat down
in a circle round the paraffin lamp on the bamboo deck and
talked of the seafarers from Peru who had had all these same
experiences fifteen hundred years before us. The lamp flung huge
shadows of bearded men on the sail, and we thought of the white
men with beards from Peru, whom we could follow in mythology
and architecture all the way from Mexico to Central America
and into the north-western area of South America as far as Peru;
here this mysterious civilisation disappeared as by the stroke of
a magic wand, before the coming of the Incas and reappeared

just as suddenly out on the solitary islands in the west we were now approaching. Were the wandering teachers men of an early civilised race from across the Atlantic, who in times long past, in the same simple manner, had come over with the westerly ocean current and the trade wind from the Canary Islands to the Gulf of Mexico? That was indeed a far shorter distance than the one we were covering, and we no longer believed in the sea as a completely isolating factor. Many investigators have maintained for weighty reasons, that the great Indian civilisations, from the Aztecs in Mexico to the Incas in Peru, were inspired by sudden impulses from over the seas in the east, while the American Indians in general are Asiatic hunting and fishing peoples who in the course of 20,000 years or more have trickled into America from Siberia. It is certainly striking that there is not a trace of gradual development in the high civilisations which once stretched from Mexico to Peru. The deeper the archaeologists dig, the higher the culture, until a definite point is reached at which the old civilisations have clearly arisen without any foundation in the midst of primitive cultures.

And the civilisations have arisen where the current comes in from the Atlantic, in the midst of the desert and jungle regions of Central and South America, instead of in the more temperate regions where civilisations, in both old and modern times, have had easier conditions for their development.

The same is seen in the South Sea islands. It is the island nearest to Peru, Easter Island, which bears the deepest traces of civilisation, although the insignificant little island is dry and barren, and is the farthest from Asia of all the islands in the Pacific.

When we had completed half our voyage, we had sailed just the distance from Peru to Easter Island, and had the legendary island due south of us. We had left the land at a chance point in the middle of the coast of Peru, to imitate an average raft putting to sea. If we had left the land farther south, nearer Kon-Tiki's ruined city Tiahuanaco, we should have got the same wind, but a weaker current, both of which would have carried us in the direction of Easter Island.

When we passed 110° west we were within the Polynesian

ocean area, inasmuch as the Polynesian Easter Island was now nearer Peru than we were. We were on a level with the first outpost of the South Sea islands, the centre of the oldest island civilisation. And when at night our glowing road guide climbed down from the sky and disappeared beyond the sea in the west with his whole spectrum of colours, the gentle trade wind blew life into the stories of the strange mystery of Easter Island. While the night sky smothered all conception of time, the bearded giants' heads were again thrown upon the sail.

But far down south, on Easter Island, stood yet larger giants' heads cut in stone, with pointed beards and white men's features, brooding over the secret of centuries. Thus they stood when the first Europeans discovered the island in 1722, and thus they stood twenty-two Polynesian generations earlier, when the present inhabitants landed in their canoes and exterminated all the grown men they found among the mysterious civilised people on the island. Since then the giant stone heads on Easter Island have been among the foremost symbols of the insoluble mysteries of antiquity. Here and there on the slopes of the treeless island their huge figures have risen to the sky, stone colossi splendidly carved in the shape of men, and set up as a single block as high as an ordinary house of three or four floors. How had the men of old been able to shape, transport and erect such gigantic stone colossi? As if the problem was not big enough, they had further succeeded in balancing an extra giant block of red stone like a colossal wig on the top of several of the heads, thirty-six feet above the ground. What did it all mean, and what kind of mechanical knowledge had the vanished architects who had mastered problems great enough for the foremost engineers of to-day?

If we put all the pieces together the mystery of Easter Island is perhaps not insoluble after all, seen against a background of raftsmen from Peru. The old civilisation has left on this island traces which the tooth of time has not been able to destroy.

Easter Island is the top of an ancient extinct volcano. Paved roads laid down by the old civilised inhabitants lead to well-preserved landing places on the coast and show that the depth of water round the island was exactly the same as it is to-day. This is no remains of a sunken continent, but a tiny desolate island which was as small and solitary when it was the cultural centre of the Pacific as it is now.

In the middle of this wedge-shaped island lies the extinct crater of the Easter Island volcano, and down in the crater lies the sculptors' amazing quarry and workshop. It lies there exactly as the old artists and architects left it hundreds of years ago, when they fled in haste to the eastern point of the island, where, according to tradition, the newly-arrived island people struck down every single grown man of them. And the sudden interruption of the artists' work gives a clear cross-section of an ordinary working day in the Easter Island crater. The sculptors' stone axes, hard as flint, lie strewn about their working place, and show that this civilised people was as ignorant of iron as Kon-Tiki's sculptors were when they were driven in flight from Peru, leaving similar gigantic stone statues behind them on the Andes plateau. In both places the quarry can be found where the legendary white people with beards hewed blocks of stone thirty or forty feet long right out of the mountain-side with the help of axes of still harder stone. And in both places the gigantic blocks, weighing many tons, were transported for many miles over rough ground before being set up on end as enormous human figures, or raised on top of one another to form mysterious terraces and walls.

Many huge unfinished figures still lie where they were begun in their holes in the crater wall on Easter Island, and show how the work was carried on in the different stages. The largest human figure, which was almost completed when the builders had to flee, was sixty-six feet long; if it had been finished and set up the head of this stone colossus would have been level with the top of an eight-floor building. Every separate figure was hewn out of a single connected block of stone, and the working niches for sculptors round the lying stone figure show that not many men were at work at the same time on each figure. Lying on their backs with their arms bent and their hands placed on their stomachs, exactly like the stone colossi in Peru, the Easter

Island figures were completed in every minute detail before they were removed from the workshop and transported to their destinations round about on the island. In the last stage, inside the quarry the giant was attached to the cliff side only by a narrow ridge under his back; then this too was hewn away, the giant meanwhile being supported by boulders.

Large quantities of these figures were just dragged down to the bottom of the crater and set up on the slope there. But a number of the largest colossi were transported up and over the wall of the crater and for many miles round over difficult country before being set up on a stone platform and having an extra stone colossus of red lava placed on their heads. This transport in itself may appear to be a complete mystery, but we cannot deny that it took place, nor that the architects who disappeared from Peru left in the Andes mountains stone colossi of equal size which show that they were absolute experts in this line. Even if the monoliths are largest and most numerous on Easter Island, and the sculptors there had acquired an individual style, the same vanished civilisation erected similar giant statues in human shape on many of the other Pacific islands nearest to America, and everywhere the monoliths were brought to the temple site from out of the way quarries. In the Marquesas I heard legends of how the gigantic stones were manoeuvred, and as these corresponded exactly to the natives' stories of the transport of the stone pillars to the huge portal on Tongatabu, it can be assumed that the same people employed the same method with the columns on Easter Island.

The sculptors' work in the pit took a long time, but required only a few experts. The work of transport each time a statue was completed was more quickly done, but, on the other hand, required large numbers of men. Little Easter Island was then both rich in fish and thoroughly cultivated, with large plantations of Peruvian sweet potatoes, and experts consider that the island in its great days can have supported a population of seven or eight thousand. About a thousand men were quite enough to haul the huge statues up and over the steep crater wall, while five hundred were sufficient to drag them on farther, across the island.

Wearproof cables were plaited from bast and vegetable fibres, and, using wooden frames, the multitude dragged the stone colossus over logs and small boulders made slippery with taro roots. That old civilised peoples were masters in making ropes and cables is well known from the South Sea islands and still more from Peru, where the first Europeans found suspension bridges a hundred yards long laid across torrents and gorges by means of plaited cables as thick as a man's waist.

When the stone colossus had arrived at its chosen site and was to be set up on end, the next problem arose. The crowd built a temporary inclined plane of stone and sand and pulled the giant up the less steep side, legs first. When the statue reached the top, it shot over a sharp edge and slid straight down so that the foot-piece landed in a ready-dug hole. As the complete inclined plane still stood there, rubbing against the back of the giant's head, they rolled up an extra cylinder of stone and placed it on the top of his head, before the whole inclined plane was removed. Ready-built inclined planes like this stand in several places on Easter Island, waiting for huge figures which have never come. The technique was admirable, but in no way mysterious if we cease to underestimate the intelligence of men in ancient times, and the amount of time and man-power of which they disposed.

But why did they make these statues? And why was it necessary to go right off to another quarry four miles away from the crater workshop to find a special kind of red stone to place on the figure's head? Both in South America and in the Marquesas islands the whole statue was often of this red stone, and they went great distances to get it. Red head-dresses for persons of high rank were an important feature both in Polynesia and in Peru.

Let us see first whom the statues represented. When the first Europeans visited the island, they saw mysterious "white men" on shore, and, in contrast to what is usual among peoples of this kind, they found men with long flowing beards, the descendants of women and children belonging to the first race on the island, who had been spared by the invaders. The natives themselves declared that some of their ancestors had been white, while others had been brown. They calculated precisely that the last-named had immigrated from elsewhere in Polynesia twenty-two generations before, while the first had come from eastward in large vessels as much as fifty-seven generations back (i.e. *c.* A.D. 400–500). The race which came from the east were given the name "long-ears", because they lengthened their ears artificially by hanging weights on the lobes so that they hung down to their shoulders. These were the mysterious "long-ears" who were killed when the "short-ears" came to the island, and all the stone figures on Easter Island had large ears hanging down on to their shoulders, as the sculptors themselves had had them.

Now the Inca legends in Peru say that the sun-king Kon-Tiki ruled over a white people with beards who were called by the Incas "big-ears", because they had their ears artificially lengthened so that they reached down to their shoulders. The Incas emphasised that it was Kon-Tiki's "big-ears" who had erected the abandoned giant statues in the Andes mountains before they were exterminated or driven out by the Incas themselves in the battle on an island in Lake Titicaca.

To sum up: Kon-Tiki's white "big-ears" disappeared from Peru westward with ample experience of working on colossal stone statues, and Tiki's white "long-ears" came to Easter Island from eastward skilled in exactly the same art, which they at once took up in full perfection, so that not the smallest trace can be found on little Easter Island of any development leading up to the masterpieces on the island.

There is often a greater resemblance between the great stone statues in Peru and those on certain South Sea islands than there is between the monoliths on the different South Sea islands compared with one another. In the Marquesas islands and Tahiti such statues were known under the generic name Tiki, and represented ancestors honoured in the islands' history who after their death had been ranked as gods. And therein undoubtedly lies the explanation of the curious red caps on the Easter Island figures. As has been said, there existed on all the islands in Polynesia scattered individuals and whole families with reddish hair and fair skins, and the islanders themselves declared that it was just these who were descended from the first white people on the islands. On certain islands religious festivals were held the participators in which coloured their skins white and their hair red to resemble their earliest ancestors. At annual ceremonies on Easter Island the chief person of the festival had all his hair cut off so that his head might be painted red. And the colossal red stone caps on the giant statues on Easter Island were carved in the shape which was typical of the local hair-styles; they had a round knot on the top, just as the men had their hair tied in a little traditional top-knot in the middle of the head.

The statues on Easter Island had long ears because the sculptors themselves had lengthened ears. They had specially chosen red stones as wigs, because the sculptors themselves had reddish hair. They had their chins carved pointed and projecting, because the sculptors themselves grew beards. They had the typical physiognomy of the white race with a straight and narrow nose and thin sharp lips, because the sculptors themselves did not belong to the Malay race. And when the statues had huge heads and tiny legs, with their hands laid in position on their stomachs, it was because it was just in this way the people were accustomed to make giant statues in Peru. The sole decoration of the Easter Island figures is a belt which was always carved round the figure's stomach. The same symbolic belt is to be found on every single statue in Kon-Tiki's ancient ruins by Lake Titicaca. It is the legendary emblem of the sun-god, the rainbow belt. There was a myth on Mangareva according to which the sun-god had taken off the rainbow which was his magic belt and climbed down it from the sky on to Mangareva to people the island with his white-skinned children. The sun was once regarded as the oldest original ancestor in all these islands, as well as in Peru.

We used to sit on deck under the starry sky and retell Easter Island's strange history, even though our own raft was carrying us straight into the heart of Polynesia, so that we should see nothing of that remote island but its name on the map. But so full is Easter Island of traces from the east that even its name can serve as a pointer.

"Easter Island" appears on the map because some chance

Dutchman "discovered" the island one Easter Sunday. And we have forgotten that the natives themselves, who already lived there, had more instructive and significant names for their home. This island has no less than three names in Polynesian.

One name is Te-Pito-te-Henua, which means "navel of the islands". This poetical name clearly places Easter Island in a special position in regard to the other islands farther westward, and is the oldest designation for Easter Island according to the Polynesians themselves. On the eastern side of the island, near the traditional landing-place of the first "long-ears", is a carefully tooled sphere of stone which is called the "golden navel" and is in turn regarded as the navel of Easter Island itself. When the poetical Polynesian ancestors carved the island's navel on the east coast and selected the island nearest Peru as the navel of their myriad islands farther west, it had a symbolic meaning. And when we know that Polynesian tradition refers to the discovery of the islands as the "birth" of the islands, it is more than suggested that Easter Island of all places was considered to symbolise the islands' birth-mark and to be the connecting link with their original motherland.

Easter Island's second name is Rapa-nui and means "Great Rapa", while Rapa-iti or "Little Rapa" is another island of the same size which lies a very long way west of Easter Island. Now it is the natural practice of all peoples to call their first home, for example, Great Rapa, while the next is called New Rapa or Little Rapa, even if the places are of the same size. And on Little Rapa the natives have quite correctly maintained traditions that the first inhabitants of the island came from Great Rapa, Easter Island, to the eastward, nearest to America. This points directly to an original immigration from the east.

The third and last name of this key island is Mata-Kite-Rani, which means "the eye (which) looks (towards) heaven". At the first glance one may hesitate, for the relatively low Easter Island does not look towards heaven any more than the other lofty mountain islands—for example Tahiti, the Marquesas or Hawaii. But *Rani*, heaven, had a double meaning to the Polynesians. It was also their ancestors' original homeland, the holy land of the sun-god, Tiki's forsaken mountain kingdom. And it is very significant that they should have called just the advanced post Easter Island, of all the thousands of islands in the ocean, the eye which looks towards heaven. It is all the more striking seeing that the kindred name Mata-Rani, which means in Polynesian "the eye of heaven", is an old Peruvian place-name, that of a spot on the Pacific coast of Peru opposite Easter Island, and right underneath Kon-Tiki's old ruined city in the Andes.

Easter Island alone provided us with plenty of subjects of conversation as we sat on deck under the starry sky, feeling ourselves to be participators in the whole prehistoric adventure. We almost felt as if we had done nothing else since Tiki's days but sail about the seas under sun and stars searching for land.

We had no longer the same respect for waves and sea. We knew them and their relationship to us on the raft. Even the shark had become a part of the everyday picture; we knew it and its usual reactions. We no longer thought of the hand harpoon, and we did not even move away from the side of the raft if a shark came up alongside us. On the contrary, we were more likely to try and grasp its back fin as it glided unperturbed along the logs. This finally developed into a quite new form of sport, tug-of-war with shark without a line.

We began quite modestly. We caught all too easily more dolphins than we could eat. To keep a popular form of amusement going without wasting food, we hit on comic fishing without a hook, for the mutual entertainment of the dolphins and ourselves. We fastened unused flying fish to a string and drew them over the surface of the water. The dolphins shot up to the surface and seized the fish, and then we tugged, each in our own direction, and had a fine circus performance, for if one dolphin let go another came in its place. We had fun, and the dolphins got the fish in the end.

Then we started the same game with the sharks. We had either a bit of fish on the end of a rope or often a bag with scraps from dinner which we let out on a line. Instead of turning on his back, the shark pushed his snout above the water and swam forward with jaws wide to swallow the morsel. We could not help pulling on the rope just as the shark was going to close his jaws again, and the cheated shark swam on with an unspeakably foolish, patient expression and opened its jaws again for the offal which jumped out of its mouth every time it tried to swallow it. It ended by the shark coming right up to the logs and jumping up like a begging dog for the food which hung dangling in a bag above its nose. It was just like feeding a gaping hippopotamus in a zoological garden, and one day at the end of July, after three months on board the raft, the following entry was made in the diary:

"We made friends with the shark which followed us to-day. At dinner we fed it with scraps which we poured right down into its open jaws. It has the effect of a half-fierce, half good-natured and friendly dog when it swims alongside us. It cannot be denied that sharks can seem quite pleasant so long as we do not get into their jaws ourselves. At least we find it amusing to have them about us, except when we are bathing."

One day a bamboo stick, with a bag of sharks' food tied to a string, was lying ready for use on the edge of the raft when a sea came and washed it all overboard. The bamboo stick was already lying afloat a couple of hundred yards astern of the raft, when it suddenly rose upright in the water and came rushing after the raft by itself, as if intending to put itself nicely back in its place again. When the fishing-rod came swaying nearer us, we saw a ten-foot shark swimming right under it, while the bamboo stick stuck up out of the waves like a periscope. The shark had swallowed the food-bag without biting off the line. The fishing-rod soon overtook us, passed us quite quietly and vanished ahead.

Even if we gradually came to look upon the shark with quite other eyes, our respect for the five or six rows of razor-sharp teeth which lay in ambush in the huge jaws never disappeared.

One day Knut had an involuntary swim in company with a shark. No one was ever allowed to swim away from the raft, both on account of the raft's drift and because of sharks. But one day it was extra quiet and we had just pulled on board such sharks as had been following us, so permission was given for a quick dip in the sea. Knut plunged in and had gone quite a long way before he came up to the surface to crawl back. At that moment we saw from the mast a shadow bigger than himself coming up behind him, deeper down. We shouted warnings as quietly as we could so as not to create a panic, and Knut heaved himself towards the side of the raft. But the shadow below belonged to a still better swimmer, which shot up from the depths and gained on Knut. They reached the raft at the same time. While Knut was clambering on board, a six-foot shark glided past right under his stomach and stopped beside the raft. We gave it a dainty dolphin's head to thank it for not having snapped.

Generally it is smell more than sight which excites sharks' voracity. We have sat with our legs in the water to test them, and they have swum towards us till they were two or three feet away, only quietly to turn their tails towards us again. But if the water was in the least bloodstained, as it was when we had been cleaning fish, the sharks' fins came to life, and they would suddenly collect like bluebottles from a long way off. If we flung out shark's guts, they simply went mad and dashed about in a blind frenzy. They savagely devoured the liver of their own kind, and then if we put a foot into the sea they came for it like rockets and even dug their teeth into the logs where the foot had been. There are sharks and sharks, because the shark is completely at the mercy of his own emotions.

The last stage in our intercourse with sharks was that we began to pull their tails. Pulling animals' tails is held to be an inferior form of sport, but that may be because no one has tried it on a shark. For it was in truth a lively form of sport.

To get hold of a shark by the tail we first had to give it a real tit-bit. It was ready to stick its head high out of the water to get it. Usually it had its food served dangling in a bag. For if one has fed a shark directly by hand once, it is no longer amusing. If one feeds dogs or tame bears by hand they set their teeth into the meat and tear and worry until they get a bit off, or until they get the whole piece for themselves. But if one holds out a large dolphin at a safe distance from the shark's head, the shark comes

PLATE XIII
Hesselberg singing and playing.

A good catch of tunnies, sharks and bonitos.

PLATE XIV
A meal on deck.

up and smacks his jaws together, and without one having felt
any tug half the dolphin is suddenly gone, and one is left sitting
with a tail in one's hand. We had had a hard job ourselves to cut
the dolphin in two with knives, but in a fraction of a second the
shark, moving its triangular saw-teeth quickly sideways, had
imperceptibly chewed up the backbone and everything else like
a sausage machine. When the shark turned quietly to go under
again, its tail flickered up above the surface and was easy to grasp.
The shark's skin was just like sand-paper to hold on to, and inside
the upper point of its tail there was an indentation which might
have been made to allow of a good grip. If we once got a firm
grasp there, there was no chance of our grip not holding. Then
we had to give a jerk before the shark could collect himself, and
get as much as possible of the tail pulled in tight over the logs.
For a second or two the shark understood nothing, but then it
began to wriggle and struggle in a spiritless manner with the fore
part of its body, for without the help of its tail a shark cannot
get up any speed. The other fins are only apparatus for balancing
and steering. After a few desperate jerks, during which we had
to keep a tight hold of the tail, the surprised shark became quite
crestfallen and apathetic, and as the loose stomach began to sink
down towards the head the shark at last became completely
paralysed. When the shark had become quiet and, as it were,
hung stiff awaiting developments, it was time for us to haul in
with all our might. We seldom got more than half the heavy
fish up out of the water, but then the shark woke up and did
the rest itself. With violent jerks it swung its head round and
up on to the logs, and then we had to tug with all our might and
jump well out of the way, and that pretty quickly if we wanted to
save our legs. For now the shark was in no kindly mood. Jerking
itself round in great leaps, it thrashed at the bamboo wall, using
its tail like a sledge-hammer. Now it no longer spared its iron
muscles. The huge jaws were opened wide, and the rows of teeth
bit and snapped in the air for anything they could reach. It might
happen that the war dance ended in the shark more or less
involuntarily tumbling overboard and disappearing for good
after its shameful humiliation, but most often it flung itself about

K

at random on the same logs aft, till we got a running noose round the root of its tail, or till it had ceased to gnash its devilish teeth for ever.

The parrot was quite thrilled when we had a shark on deck. It came scurrying out of the bamboo cabin and climbed up the wall at frantic speed till it found itself a good safe look-out post on the palm-leaf roof, and there it sat shaking its head, or fluttered to and fro along the ridge, shrieking with excitement. It had at an early date become an excellent sailor, and was always bubbling over with humour and laughter. We reckoned ourselves as seven on board, us six and the green parrot. The crab Johannes had after all to reconcile himself to being regarded as a cold-blooded appendage. At night the parrot crept into its cage under the roof of the bamboo cabin, but in the daytime it strutted about the deck, or hung on to guy-ropes and stays and did the most fascinating acrobatic exercises. To begin with we had turnbuckles on the stays of the mast, but they wore the ropes, so we replaced them by ordinary running knots. When the stays stretched and grew slack from sun and wind, all hands had to turn to and brace up the mast, so that the mangrove-wood masts, as heavy as iron, should not bump against and cut into the ropes till they fell down. And while we were hauling and pulling, at the most critical moment, the parrot began to call out with his cracked voice: "Haul! Haul! ho, ho, ho, ho, ha ha ha!" And if it made us laugh, it laughed till it shook at its own amusingness and swung round and round on the stays.

To begin with the parrot was inimical to our wireless operators. They might be sitting happily absorbed in the wireless corner with their magic earphones on, and perhaps in contact with a wireless fan in Oklahoma. Then their earphones would suddenly go dead, and they could not get a sound however much they coaxed the wires and turned the knobs. The parrot had been busy and bitten off the wire of the aerial. This was specially popular in the early days, when the wire of the aerial stretched upwards attached to a balloon. But one day the parrot became seriously ill. It sat in its cage and moped, and touched no food for two days, while its droppings glittered with golden scraps of aerial. Then the wireless operators repented of their angry words and the parrot its misdeeds, and from that day Torstein and Knut were its chosen friends, and the parrot would never sleep anywhere but in the wireless corner. The parrot's mother tongue was Spanish when it first came on board, and Bengt declared that it took to talking Spanish with a Norwegian accent, long before it began to imitate Torstein's favourite ejaculations in full-blooded Norwegian.

We enjoyed the parrot's humour and brilliant colours for two months, until a big sea came on board from astern while it was on its way down the stay from the masthead. When we discovered that the parrot had gone overboard, it was too late. We did not see it. And the *Kon-Tiki* could not be turned or stopped; if anything went overboard from the raft we had no chance of turning back for it—numerous experiences had shown that.

The loss of the parrot had a depressing effect on our spirits the first evening; we knew that exactly the same thing would happen to ourselves if we fell overboard on a solitary night watch.

We tightened up all the safety regulations, brought into use new life-lines for the night watch, and frightened one another out of believing that we were safe because things had gone well in the first two months. One careless step, one thoughtless movement, could send us where the green parrot had gone, even in broad daylight.

We had several times observed the large white shells of cuttlefish eggs, lying floating like ostrich eggs or white skulls on the blue swell. On one solitary occasion we saw a squid lying wriggling underneath. We observed the snow-white balls floating on a level with ourselves, and thought at first that it would be an easy matter to row out in the dinghy and get them. We thought the same that time when the rope of the plankton net broke so that the cloth net was left behind alone, floating in our wake. We launched the dinghy, with a rope attached, to row back. But we saw to our surprise that the wind and sea held the dinghy off, and that the line from the *Kon-Tiki* had so violent a braking effect in the water that we could never row right back to a point we had already left. We might get within a few yards of what we wanted to pick up, but then the whole line was out and the *Kon-Tiki* was pulling us away westward. "Once overboard always overboard" was a lesson that had gradually burnt itself ineffaceably into our consciousness on board. If we wanted to go with the rest, we must hang on till the *Kon-Tiki* ran her bows against land on the other side.

The parrot left a blank in the wireless corner, but when the tropical sun shone out over the Pacific next day, the mourning was of short duration. We hauled in many sharks in the next few days, and we constantly found black curved parrots' beaks among tunnies' heads and other curiosities in the shark's belly. But the black beaks always proved on closer examination to belong to assimilated cuttlefish.

The two wireless operators had had a tough job in their corner since the first day they came on board. The very first day in the Humboldt Current sea water trickled from the battery cases so that they had to cover the sensitive wireless corner with canvas to save what could be saved in the high seas. And then they had the problem of fitting a long enough aerial on the little raft. They tried to send the aerial up with a kite, but in a gust of wind the kite simply plunged into a wavecrest and disappeared. Then they tried to send it up with a balloon, but the tropical sun burnt holes in the balloon, so that it collapsed and sank into the sea. And then they had the trouble with the parrot. In addition to this, we were a fortnight in the Humboldt Current before we came out of a dead zone of the Andes in which the short wave was as dumb and lifeless as the air in an empty soap-box.

But then one night the short wave suddenly broke through, and Torstein's call sign was heard by a chance wireless fan in Los Angeles who was sitting fiddling with his transmitter to establish contact with another fan in Sweden. The man asked what kind of set we had, and when he got a satisfactory answer to his question he asked Torstein who he was and where he lived. When he heard that Torstein's abode was a bamboo cabin on a raft in the Pacific there were several peculiar clickings until Torstein supplied more details. When the man on the air had pulled himself together, he told us that his name was Hal and his wife's name Anna, and that she was Swedish by birth and would let our families know that we were alive and well.

It was a strange thought for us that evening that a total stranger called Hal, a casual cinema operator far away among the swarming population of Los Angeles, was the only person in the world but ourselves who knew where we were and that we were well. From that night onwards Hal, alias Harold Kempel, and his friend Frank Cuevas took it in turns to sit up every night and listen for signals from the raft, and Herman received grateful telegrams from the head of the U.S. Weather Bureau for his two daily code reports from an area for which there were few reports and no statistics. Later Knut and Torstein established contact with other radio amateurs almost every night, and these passed on greetings to Norway through a wireless fan named Egil Berg at Notodden.

Only for a few days out in mid-ocean there was too much salt water for the wireless corner, and the station stopped working altogether. The operators stood on their heads day and night with screws and soldering irons, and all the distant wireless fans thought the raft's days were ended. But then one night the signal LI 2 B burst out into the ether, and in a moment the wireless corner was buzzing like a wasps' nest as several hundred American operators seized their keys simultaneously and replied to the call. Indeed, one always felt as if one was sitting down on a wasps' nest if one strayed into the wireless operators' domain. It was damp with sea water, which forced its way up along the wood-work everywhere, and even if there was a piece of raw rubber on the balsa log where the operator sat, one got electric shocks both in the hinder parts and in the finger-tips if one touched the Morse key. And if one of us outsiders tried to steal a pencil from the well-equipped wireless corner, either his hair stood straight up on his head, or he drew long sparks from the stump of the pencil. Only Torstein and Knut and the parrot could wriggle their way about in that corner unscathed, and we put up a sheet of cardboard to mark the danger zone for the rest of us.

Late one night Knut was sitting messing about by lamplight in the wireless corner when he suddenly shook me by the leg and said he had been talking to a fellow who lived just outside Oslo and was called Christian Amundsen. This was a bit of an amateur record, for the little short-wave transmitter on board the raft with its 13990 kc. per second did not send out more than 6 watts, about the same strength as a small electric torch. This was August 2, and we had sailed more than 60 degrees round the earth, so that Oslo was at the opposite end of the globe. King Haakon was 75 years old the day after, and we sent him a message of congratulation direct from the raft; and the day after that Christian was again audible and sent us a reply from the King wishing us continued good luck and success on our voyage.

Another episode we remember as a contrast to the whole life on the raft. We had two cameras on board, and Erik had with him a parcel of materials for developing photographs on the voyage, so that we could take fresh snaps of things that had not come out well. After the whale shark's visit he could contain himself no longer, and one evening he mixed the chemicals and water carefully in exact accordance with the instructions, and developed two films. The negatives looked like long distance photographs; nothing but obscure spots and wrinkles. The film was ruined. We telegraphed to our contacts for advice, and our message was picked up by a wireless fan in Hollywood; he rang up a laboratory, and soon afterwards he broke in and told us that our developer was too warm, we must not use water above 60° or the negative would be wrinkled.

We thanked him for his advice and ascertained that the very lowest temperature in our surroundings was that of the ocean current itself, which was nearly 80°. Now Herman was a refrigerating engineer, and I told him by way of a joke to get the temperature of the water down to 60°. He asked to have the use of the little bottle of carbolic acid belonging to the already inflated rubber dinghy, and after some hocus-pocus in a kettle covered with a sleeping-bag and a woollen vest, suddenly there was snow on Herman's stubbly beard, and he came in with a big lump of white ice in the kettle.

Erik developed afresh with splendid results.

But even if the ghost-words carried through the air by short wave were an unknown luxury in Kon-Tiki's early days, the ocean waves beneath us were the same as of old, and carried the balsa raft steadily westward as they did then, fifteen hundred years ago.

The weather became a little more unsettled, with scattered rain squalls, after we had entered the area nearer the South Sea islands, and the trade wind had changed its direction. It had blown steadily and surely from the south-east until we were a good way over in the Equatorial Current; then it had veered round more and more towards due east. We reached our most northerly position on June 10 with latitude 6° 19′ south. We were then so close up to the equator that it looked as if we should sail above even the most northerly islands of the Marquesas group, and disappear completely in the sea without finding land. But then the trade wind swung round farther, from east to north-east, and drove us in a curve down towards the latitude of the world of islands.

It often happened that wind and sea remained unchanged for days on end, and then we clean forgot whose steering watch it was, except at night, when the watch was alone on deck. For if sea and wind were steady, the steering oar was lashed fast and the Kon-Tiki sail remained filled without our attending to it. Then the night watch could sit quietly in the cabin door and look at the stars. For if the constellations changed their position in the sky, it was time for him to go out and see whether it was the steering oar or the wind that had shifted.

It was incredible how easy it was to steer by the stars when we had seen them marching across the vault of the sky for weeks on end. Indeed, there was not much else to look at at night. We knew where we could expect to see the different constellations night after night, and when we came up towards the equator the Great Bear rose so clear of the horizon in the north that we were anxious lest we should catch a glimpse of the Pole Star, which appears when one comes from southward and crosses the equator. But as the north-easterly trade winds set in, the Great Bear sank again.

The old Polynesians were great navigators. They took bearings by the sun by day and the stars by night. Their knowledge of the heavenly bodies was astonishing. They knew that the earth was round, and had names for such abstruse conceptions as the equator and the northern and southern tropics. In Hawaii they cut charts of the ocean on the shells of round bottle gourds, and on certain other islands they made detailed maps of plaited boughs to which shells were attached to mark the islands, while the twigs marked particular currents. The Polynesians knew five planets, which they called wandering stars, and distinguished them from the fixed stars, for which they had nearly two hundred different names. A good navigator in old Polynesia knew well in what part of the sky the different stars would rise, and where they would be at different times of the night, and at different times of the year. They knew which stars culminated over the different islands, and there were cases in which an island was named after the star which culminated over it night after night and year after year.

Apart from the fact that the starry sky lay like a glittering giant compass revolving from east to west, they understood that the different stars right over their heads always showed them how far north or south they were. When the Polynesians had explored and brought under their sway their present domain, which is the whole of the sea nearest to America, they maintained traffic between some of the islands for many generations to come. Historical traditions relate that when the chiefs from Tahiti visited Hawaii, which lay more than 2,000 sea miles farther north and several degrees farther west, the helmsman steered first due north by sun and stars, till the stars right above their heads told them that they were on the latitude of Hawaii. Then they turned at a right angle and steered due west till they came so near that birds and clouds told them where the group of islands lay.

Whence had the Polynesians obtained their vast astronomical knowledge, and their calendar, which was calculated with astonishing thoroughness? Certainly not from Melanesian or Malayan peoples to the westward. But the same old vanished civilised race, the "white and bearded men", who had taught Aztecs, Mayas and Incas their amazing culture in America, had evolved a curiously similar calendar and a similar astronomical knowledge which Europe in those times could not match.

In Polynesia, as in Peru, the calendar year had been so arranged as to begin on the particular day of the year when the constellation of the Pleiades first appeared above the horizon, and in both areas this constellation was considered the patron of agriculture.

In Peru, where the continent slopes down towards the Pacific, there stand to this day in the desert sand the ruins of an astronomical observatory of great antiquity, a relic of the same mysterious civilised people which carved stone colossi, erected pyramids, cultivated sweet potatoes and bottle gourds, and began their year with the rising of the Pleiades. Kon-Tiki knew the stars when he set sail upon the Pacific ocean.

On July 2 the night watch could no longer sit in peace studying the night sky. We had a strong wind and nasty sea after several days of light north-easterly breeze. Late in the night we had brilliant moonlight and a quite fresh sailing wind. We measured our speed by counting the seconds we took to pass a chip flung out ahead on one side of us, and found that we were establishing a speed record. While our average speed was from twelve to eighteen "chips", in the jargon current on board, we were now for a time down to "six chips", and the phosphorescence swirled in a regular wake astern of the raft.

Four men lay snoring in the bamboo cabin while Torstein sat clicking with the Morse key and I was on steering watch. Just before midnight I caught sight of a quite unusual sea which came breaking astern of us right across the whole of my disturbed field of vision, and behind it I could see here and there the foaming crests of two more huge seas like the first following hard on its heels. If we ourselves had not just passed the place, I should have been convinced that what I saw was high surf flung up over a dangerous shoal. I gave a warning shout as the first sea came like a long wall sweeping after us in the moonlight, and wrenched the raft into position to take what was coming.

When the first sea reached us, the raft flung her stern up sideways and rose up over the wave-back which had just broken, so that it hissed and boiled all along the crest. We rode through the welter of boiling foam which poured along both sides of the raft, whilst the heavy sea itself rolled by under us. The bow flung itself up last as the wave passed and we slid stern first down into a broad trough of the waves. Immediately after the next wall of water came on and rose up, while we were again lifted hurriedly into the air and the clear water-masses broke over us aft as we shot over the edge. As a result the raft was flung right broadside on to the seas, and it was impossible to wrench her round quickly enough. The next sea came on and rose out of the stripes of foam like a glittering wall which began to fall along its upper edge just as it reached us. When it plunged down, I saw nothing else for it than to hang on as tight as I could to a projecting bamboo pole of the cabin roof, and there I held my breath while I felt the raft being flung sky-high and everything round me carried away in roaring whirlpools of foam. In a second we and the *Kon-Tiki* were above water again and gliding quietly down a gentle wave-back on the other side. Then the seas were normal again. The three great wave-walls raced on before us, and astern in the moonlight a string of cocoanuts lay bobbing in the water.

The last wave had given the cabin a violent blow, so that Torstein was flung head over heels in the wireless corner and the others woke scared by the noise, while the water gushed up between the logs and in through the wall. On the port side of the foredeck the bamboo wickerwork was blown open like a small crater, and the diving basket had been knocked flat up in the bows, but everything else was as it had been. Where the three big seas came from we have never been able to explain with certainty, unless they were due to disturbances on the sea bottom, which are not so uncommon in those regions.

Two days later we had our first storm. It started by the trade wind dying away completely, and the feathery white trade wind clouds which were drifting over our heads up in the topmost blue being suddenly invaded by a thick black cloud-bank which rolled up over the horizon from southward. Then there came gusts of wind from the most unexpected directions, so that it was impossible for the steering watch to keep control. As quickly as we got our stern turned to the new direction of the wind, so that the sail bellied out stiff and safe, just as quickly the gusts came at us from another quarter, squeezed the proud bulge out of the sail, and made it swing round and thrash about to the peril of both crew and cargo. But then the wind suddenly set in to blow straight from the quarter whence the bad weather came, and as the black clouds rolled over us the breeze increased to a fresh wind which worked itself up into a real storm.

In the course of an incredibly short time the seas round about us were flung up to a height of fifteen feet, while single crests were hissing twenty and twenty-five feet above the trough of the sea, so that we had them on a level with our masthead when we ourselves were down in the trough. All hands had to scramble about on deck bent double, while the wind shook the bamboo wall and whistled and howled in all the rigging.

To protect the wireless corner we stretched canvas over the aftermost wall and port side of the cabin. All loose cargo was lashed securely, and the sail was hauled down and made fast round the bamboo yard. When the sky clouded over the sea grew dark and threatening, and in every direction it was white-crested with breaking waves. Long tracks of dead foam lay like stripes to windward down the backs of the long seas, and everywhere where the wave-ridges had broken and plunged down, green patches, like wounds, lay frothing for a long time in the blue-black sea. The crests blew away as they broke, and the spray stood like salt rain over the sea. When the tropical rain poured over us in horizontal squalls and whipped the surface of the sea, invisible all round us, the water that ran from our hair and beards tasted brackish, while we stumbled about the deck bent double, naked and frozen, seeing that all the gear was in order to weather the storm. When the storm rushed up over the horizon and gathered about us for the first time, strained anticipation and anxiety were discernible in our looks. But when it was upon us in earnest, and the *Kon-Tiki* took everything that came her way with ease and buoyancy, the storm became an exciting form of sport, and we all delighted in the fury round about us which the balsa raft mastered so stylishly, always seeing that she herself lay on the wave-tops like a cork, while all the main weight of the

raging water was always a few inches beneath. The sea had much
in common with the mountains in such weather. It was like
being out in the wilds in a storm, up in the highest mountain
plateaux, naked and grey. Even though we were right in the
heart of the tropics, when the raft glided up and down over the
smoking waste of sea we always thought of racing downhill
among snowdrifts and rock-faces.

The steering watch had to keep its eyes open in such weather.
When the steepest seas passed under the forward half of the raft,
the logs aft rose right out of the water, but the next second they
plunged down again to climb up over the next crest. Each time
the seas came so close upon one another that the hindmost reached
us while the first was still holding the bow in the air; then the
solid sheets of water thundered in over the steering watch in a
terrifying welter, but the next second the stern went up and the
flood disappeared as through the prongs of a fork.

We calculated that in an ordinary calm sea, where there were
usually seven seconds between the highest waves, we took in
about two hundred tons of water astern in twenty-four hours,
which we hardly noticed, because it just flowed in quietly round
the bare legs of the steering watch, and as quietly disappeared
again between the logs. But in a heavy storm more than ten
thousand tons of water poured on board astern in the course of
twenty-four hours, seeing that loads varying from a few gallons
to two or three cubic yards, and occasionally much more, flowed
on board every five seconds. It sometimes broke on board with a
deafening thunder-clap, so that the helmsman stood in water up
to his waist and felt as if he was forcing his way against the current
in a swift river. The raft seemed to stand trembling for a moment,
but then the cruel load that weighed her down astern disappeared
overboard again in great cascades.

Herman was out all the time with his anemometer measuring
the squalls of gale force which lasted for twenty-four hours; then
they gradually dropped to a stiff breeze with scattered rain squalls,
which continued to keep the seas boiling round us as we tumbled
on westward, with a good sailing wind. To obtain accurate wind
measurements down among the towering seas Herman had,

whenever possible, to make his way up to the swaying masthead, where it was all he could do to hold on.

When the weather moderated, it was as though the big fish around us had become completely infuriated. The water round the raft was full of sharks, tunnies, dolphins and a few dazed bonitos, all wriggling about close under the timber of the raft and in the waves nearest to it. It was a ceaseless life and death struggle; the backs of big fishes arched themselves over the water and shot off like rockets, one chasing another in pairs while the water round the raft was repeatedly tinged with thick blood. The combatants were mainly tunnies and dolphins, and the dolphins came in big shoals which moved much more quickly and alertly than usual. The tunnies were the assailants; often a fish of 150–200 lbs. would leap high into the air holding a dolphin's bloody head in its mouth. But even if the individual dolphins dashed off with tunnies hard on their heels, the actual shoal of dolphins did not give ground, although there were always several wriggling round with big gaping wounds in their necks. Now and again the sharks, too, seemed to become blind with rage, and we saw them catch and fight with big tunnies, which met in the shark a superior enemy.

Not one single peaceful little pilot fish was to be seen. Either they had been devoured by the furious tunnies, or they had hidden in the chinks under the raft or fled far away from the battlefield. We dared not put our heads down into the water to see.

I had a nasty shock—and could not help laughing afterwards at my own complete bewilderment—when I was aft obeying a call of nature. We were accustomed to a bit of a swell in the water-closet, but it seemed contrary to all reasonable probabilities when I quite unexpectedly received a violent punch astern from something large and cold and very heavy which came butting up against me like a shark's head in the sea. I was actually on my way up the mast-stay, with a feeling that I had a shark hanging on to my hind-quarters, before I collected myself. Herman, who was hanging over the steering oar doubled up with laughter, was able to tell me that a huge tunny had delivered a sideways smack at my nakedness with his 160 lbs. or so of cold fish. Afterwards, when Herman and then Torstein were on watch, the same fish tried to jump on board with the seas from astern, and twice the big fellow was right up on the end of the logs, but each time it flung itself overboard again before we could get a grip of the slippery body.

After that a stout bewildered bonito came right on board with a sea, and with that, and a tunny caught the day before, we decided to fish, to bring order into the sanguinary chaos that surrounded us.

Our diary says:

"A six-foot shark was hooked first and hauled on board. As soon as the hook was out again it was swallowed by an eight-foot shark, and we hauled that on board. When the hook came out again we got a fresh six-foot shark, and had got it over the edge of the raft when it broke loose and dived. The hook went out again at once, and an eight-foot shark came on to it and gave us a hard tussle. We had its head over the logs when all four steel lines were cut through and the shark dived into the depths. New hook out, and a seven-foot shark was hauled on board. It was now dangerous to stand on the slippery logs aft fishing, because the three sharks kept on throwing up their heads and snapping, long after one would have thought they were dead. We dragged the sharks forward by the tail into a heap on the foredeck, and soon afterwards a big tunny was hooked and gave us more of a fight than any shark before we got it on board. It was so fat and heavy that none of us could lift it by the tail.

"The sea was just as full of furious fish-backs. Another shark was hooked, but broke away when it was just being got on board. But then we got a six-foot shark safely on board. After that a five-foot shark, which also came on board. Then we caught yet another six-foot shark and hauled it up. When the hook came out again, we hauled in a seven-foot shark."

Wherever we walked on deck, there were big sharks lying in the way, beating their tails convulsively on the deck or thrashing against the bamboo cabin as they snapped round them. Tired and worn out already when we began to fish after the nights of the storm, we became completely at sea as to which sharks were quite dead, which were still snapping convulsively if we went near them, and which were quite alive and were lying in ambush for us with their green cat's eyes. When we had nine big sharks lying round us in every direction, we were so weary of hauling on heavy lines and fighting with recalcitrant sharks, that we gave up after five hours' toil.

Next day there were fewer dolphins and tunnies, but just as many sharks. We began to fish and haul them in again, but soon stopped when we perceived that all the fresh shark's blood that ran off the raft only attracted still more sharks. We threw all the dead sharks overboard and washed the whole deck clean of blood. The bamboo mats were torn by shark's teeth and rough shark-skin, and we threw the bloodiest and most torn of them over-board and replaced them with new golden-yellow bamboo mats, several layers of which were lashed fast on the foredeck.

When we turned in on these evenings, in our mind's eye we saw greedy open shark's jaws and blood. And the smell of shark meat stuck in our nostrils. We could eat shark; it tasted like haddock if we just got the ammoniac out of the pieces of fish by putting them in the sea water for twenty-four hours. But bonito and tunny were infinitely better.

That evening, for the first time, I heard one of the fellows say that it would soon be pleasant to be able to stretch oneself out comfortably on the green grass on a palm island; he would be glad to see something else than cold fish and rough sea.

The weather had become quite quiet again, but it was never as constant and dependable as before. Incalculable, violent gusts of wind from time to time brought with them heavy showers, which we were glad to see because a large part of our water supply had begun to go bad and tasted like evil-smelling marsh water. When it was pouring its hardest, we collected water from the cabin roof and stood on deck naked, thoroughly to enjoy the luxury of having the salt washed off with fresh water.

The pilot fish were wriggling along again in their usual places, but whether they were the same old ones which had returned after the blood-bath, or whether they were new followers taken over in the heat of battle, we could not say.

On July 21 the wind suddenly died away again. It was oppressive and absolutely still, and we knew from previous experience what this might mean. And right enough, after a few violent gusts from east and west and south, the wind freshened up to a breeze from southward, where black, threatening clouds had again rushed up over the horizon. Herman was out with his anemometer all the time, measuring already fifty feet and more per second, when suddenly Torstein's sleeping bag went overboard. And what happened in the next few seconds took a much shorter time than it takes to tell it.

Herman tried to catch the bag as it went, took a rash step and fell overboard. We heard a faint cry for help amid the noise of the waves, and saw Herman's head and a waving arm, as well as some vague green object twirling about in the water near him. He was struggling for life to get back to the raft through the high seas which had lifted him out from the port side. Torstein, who was at the steering oar aft, and I myself, up in the bows, were the first to perceive him, and we went cold with fear. We bellowed "man overboard!" at the pitch of our lungs as we rushed to the nearest life-saving gear. The others had not heard Herman's cry at all because of the noise of the sea, but in a trice there was life and bustle on deck. Herman was an excellent swimmer, and though we realised at once that his life was at stake, we had a fair hope that he would manage to crawl back to the edge of the raft before it was too late.

Torstein, who was nearest, seized the bamboo drum round which was the line we used for the lifeboat, for this was within his reach. It was the only time on the whole voyage that this line got caught up. The whole thing happened in a few seconds. Herman was now on a level with the stern of the raft, but a few yards away, and his last hope was to crawl to the blade of the steering oar and hang on to it. As he missed the end of the logs, he reached out for the oar-blade, but it slipped away from him. And there he lay, just where experience had shown we could get nothing back. While Bengt and I launched the dinghy, Knut and

PLATE XVI

A faint breeze and tropical heat—things that troubled us little. On calm days we went for long trips in the rubber dinghy.

Halfway—over 2,000 sea miles from nearest land to east and west. Hesselberg, mounted on a box, taking the sun's altitude.

Erik threw out the lifebelt. Carrying a long line, it hung ready
for use on the corner of the cabin roof, but to-day the wind was
so strong that when they threw the lifebelt it was simply blown
back to the raft. After a few unsuccessful throws Herman was
already far astern of the steering oar, swimming desperately to
keep up with the raft, while the distance increased with each gust
of wind. He realised that henceforth the gap would simply go on
increasing, but he set a faint hope on the dinghy, which we had
now got into the water. Without the line which acted as a brake,
it would perhaps have been practicable to drive the rubber raft
to meet the swimming man, but whether the rubber raft would
ever get back to the *Kon-Tiki* was another matter. Nevertheless,
three men in a rubber dinghy had some chance, one man in the
sea had none.

Then we suddenly saw Knut take off and plunge head first
into the sea. He had the lifebelt in one hand and was heaving
himself along. Every time Herman's head appeared on a wave-
back Knut was gone, and every time Knut came up Herman
was not there. But then we saw both heads at once; they had
swum to meet each other and both were hanging on to the lifebelt. Knut waved his arm, and as the rubber raft had meanwhile
been hauled on board, all four of us took hold of the line of the
lifebelt and hauled for dear life, with our eyes fixed on the great
dark object which was visible just behind the two men. This
same mysterious beast in the water was pushing a big greenish-
black triangle up above the wave-crests; it almost gave Knut a
shock when he was on his way over to Herman. Only Herman
knew then that the triangle did not belong to a shark or any
other sea monster. It was an inflated corner of Torstein's water-
tight sleeping bag. But the sleeping bag did not remain floating
for long after we had hauled the two men safe and sound on
board. Whatever dragged the sleeping bag down into the depths
had just missed a better prey.

"Glad I wasn't in it," said Torstein, and took hold of the
steering oar where he had let it go.

But otherwise there were not many cheery cracks that evening.
We all felt a chill running through nerve and bone for a long

L

time afterwards. But the cold shivers were mingled with a warm thankfulness that there were still six of us on board.

We had a lot of nice things to say to Knut that day, Herman and the rest of us too.

But there was not much time to think about what had happened already, for as the sky grew black over our heads the gusts of wind increased in strength, and before night came a new storm was upon us. At last we got the lifebelt to hang astern of the raft on a long line, so that we had something behind the steering oar towards which to swim if one of us should fall overboard again in a squall. Then it grew pitch dark around us as night fell and hid the raft and the sea, and bouncing wildly up and down in the darkness, we only heard and felt the gale howling in masts and guy-ropes, while the gusts pressed with smashing force against the springy bamboo cabin, till we thought it would fly overboard. But it was covered with canvas and well guyed. And we felt the *Kon-Tiki* tossing with the foaming seas, while the logs moved up and down with the waves' movement like the keys of an instrument. We were just as astonished every time that cascades of water did not gush up through the wide chinks in the floor, but they only acted as a regular bellows through which damp air rushed up and down.

For five whole days the weather varied between full storm and light gale; the sea was dug up into wide valleys filled with the smoke from foaming grey-blue seas which seemed to have their backs pressed out long and flat under the onset of the wind. Then on the fifth day the heavens split to show a glimpse of blue, and the malignant black cloud-cover gave place to the ever victorious blue sky as the storm passed on. We had come through the gale with the steering oar smashed and the sail rent, and the centre-boards hung loose and banged about like crowbars among the logs, because all the ropes which had tightened them up under water were worn through. But we ourselves and the cargo were completely undamaged.

After the two storms the *Kon-Tiki* had become a good deal weaker in the joints. The strain of working over the steep wave-backs had stretched all the ropes, and the continuously working logs had made the ropes eat into the balsa wood. We thanked Providence that we had followed the Incas' prescription and had not used wire ropes, which would simply have sawn the whole raft into match-wood in the gale. And if we had used bone-dry, high-floating balsa at the start, the raft would long ago have sunk into the sea under us, saturated with sea water. It was the sap in the fresh logs which served as an impregnation and hindered the water from filtering in through the porous balsa wood. But now the ropes had become so loose that it was dangerous to let one's foot slip down between two logs, for it could be crushed when they came together violently. Forward and aft, where there was no bamboo deck, we had to give at the knees when we stood with our feet wide apart on two logs at the same time. The logs aft were as slippery as banana leaves with wet seaweed, and even though we had made a regular path through the greenery where we usually walked, and had laid down a broad plank for the steering watch to stand on, it was not easy to keep one's foothold when a sea struck the raft. And on the port side one of the nine giants bumped and banged against the cross-beams with dull, wet thuds both by night and by day. There came also new and fearful creakings from the ropes which held the two sloping masts together at the masthead, for the steps of the masts worked about independently of each other, because they rested on two different logs.

We got the steering oar spliced and lashed with long billets of mangrove wood, as hard as iron, and with Erik and Bengt as sailmakers Kon-Tiki soon raised his head again and swelled his breast in a stiff bulge towards Polynesia, while the steering oar danced behind in seas which the fine weather had made soft and gentle. But the centreboards never again became quite what they had been; they did not meet the pressure of the water with their full strength, because they gave way and hung dangling loose and unguyed under the raft. It was useless to try to inspect the ropes on the underside, for they were completely overgrown with seaweed. On taking up the whole bamboo deck we found only three of the main ropes broken; they had been lying crooked and pressed against the cargo, which had worn them away. It was evident that the logs had absorbed a great weight of water, but the cargo had been lightened, so this was roughly cancelled out. Most of our provisions and drinking water was already used up, likewise the wireless operators' dry batteries.

Nevertheless, after the last storm it was clear enough that we should both float and hold together for the short distance that separated us from the islands ahead. Now quite another problem came into the foreground—how would the voyage end?

The *Kon-Tiki* would slog on inexorably westward until she ran her bows into a solid rock or some other fixed object which would stop her drifting. The voyage would not be ended until all hands had landed safe and sound on one of the numerous Polynesian islands ahead.

When we came through the last storm, it was quite uncertain where the raft would end up. We were at an equal distance from the Marquesas Islands and the Tuamotu group, and in a position which meant that we could perfectly easily pass right between the two groups of islands without having a glimpse of one of them. The nearest island in the Marquesas group lay 300 sea miles north-west, and the nearest island in the Tuamotu group lay 300 sea miles south-west, while wind and current were uncertain, with their general direction westerly and towards the wide ocean gap between the two island groups.

The island which lay nearest to the north-west was no other than Fatuhiva, the little jungle-clad mountainous island where I had lived in a hut built on piles on the beach and heard the old man's vivid stories of the ancestral hero Tiki. If the *Kon-Tiki* stood in to that same beach I should meet many acquaintances, but hardly the old man himself. He must have departed long ago, with a fair hope of meeting the real Tiki again. If she headed in towards these mountain ranges of the Marquesas group, the few islands in this group were a long way apart, and the sea thundered in unchecked against perpendicular cliffs where we should have to keep our eyes open while steering for the mouths of the few valleys, which always ended in a narrow strip of beach.

If, on the contrary, she headed down towards the coral reefs of the Tuamotu group, there the numerous islands lay close together and covered a wide space of sea. But this group of islands is also known as the Low or Dangerous Archipelago, because the whole formation has been entirely built up by coral polyps and consists of treacherous submerged reefs and palm-clad atolls which rise only six or ten feet above the surface of the sea. Dangerous ring-shaped reefs fling themselves protectingly round every single atoll, and are a menace to shipping traffic throughout the area. But even if coral polyps built the Tuamotu atolls, while the Marquesas Islands are remains of extinct volcanoes, both groups are inhabited by the same Polynesian race, and the royal families in both regard Tiki as their primeval ancestor.

As early as July 3, when we were still 1,000 sea miles from Polynesia, Nature herself was able to tell us, as she was able in their time to tell the primitive raftsmen from Peru, that there really was land ahead somewhere out in the sea. Until we were a good thousand sea miles out from the coast of Peru we noted small flocks of frigate birds. They disappeared at about 100° west, and after that we saw only small petrels which have their home on the sea. But on July 3 the frigate birds reappeared, at 125° west, and from now onwards small flocks of frigate birds were often to be seen, either high up in the sky or shooting down over the wave-crests, where they snapped up flying fish which had taken to the air to escape from dolphins. As these birds did not come from America astern of us, they must have their homes in another country ahead.

On July 16 Nature betrayed herself still more obviously. On that day we hauled up a nine-foot shark which threw up from its stomach a large undigested starfish which it had recently brought from some coast out here in the ocean.

And the very next day we had the first definite visit straight from the islands of Polynesia.

It was a great moment on board when two large boobies were spotted above the horizon to westward and soon afterwards came sailing in over our mast, flying low. With a wingspread of five feet they circled round us many times, then folded their wings and settled on the sea alongside us. Dolphins rushed to the spot at once and wriggled inquisitively round the great swimming

birds, but neither party touched the other. These were the first
living messengers that came to bid us welcome to Polynesia.
They did not go back in the evening, but rested on the sea, and
after midnight we still heard them flying in circles round the
mast uttering hoarse cries.

The flying fish which now came on board were now of another
and much larger species; I recognised it from fishing trips with
the natives along the coast of Fatuhiva.

For three days and nights we made straight towards Fatuhiva,
but then a strong north-east wind came on and sent us down in
the direction of the Tuamotu atolls. We were now blown out of
the real South Equatorial Current, and the ocean currents were
no longer behaving dependably. One day they were there,
another day they were gone. The currents could run like invisible
rivers branching out all over the sea. If the current was swift
there was usually more swell, and the temperature of the water
usually fell one degree. The direction and strength of the
current were shown every day by the difference between Erik's
calculated and his measured position.

On the threshold of Polynesia the wind said "pass", having
handed us over to a weak branch of the current which, to our
alarm, had its course in the direction of the Antarctic. It did not
become absolutely still—we never experienced that throughout
the voyage—and if the wind was feeble we hoisted every rag we
had to collect what little there was. There was not one day on
which we moved backwards towards America, and our smallest
distance in twenty-four hours was 9 sea miles, while our average
run for the voyage as a whole was 42½ sea miles in twenty-four
hours.

The trade wind, after all, had not the heart to fail us right
in the last lap. It reported for duty again, and pushed and shoved
at the ramshackle craft which was preparing her entry into a
new and strange part of the world.

With each day that passed larger flocks of sea-birds came and
circled over us aimlessly in all directions. One evening, when the
sun was about to sink into the sea, we perceived clearly that the
birds had received a violent impetus. They were flying away in

a westerly direction without paying any attention to us or the flying fish beneath them. And from the masthead we could see that as they came over they all flew straight on on exactly the same course. Perhaps they saw something from up above which we did not see. Perhaps they were flying by instinct. In any case they were flying with a plan, straight home to the nearest island, their breeding-place.

We twisted the steering oar and set our course exactly in the direction in which the birds had disappeared. Even after it was dark we heard the cries of stragglers flying over us against the starry sky on exactly the same course as that which we were now following. It was a wonderful night; the moon was nearly full for the third time in the course of the *Kon-Tiki*'s voyage.

Next day there were still more birds over us, but we did not need to wait for them to show us our way again in the evening. This time we had detected a curious stationary cloud above the horizon. The other clouds were small feathery wisps of wool which came up in the south and passed across the vault of the sky with the trade wind till they disappeared over the horizon in the west. So I had once come to know the drifting trade-wind clouds on Fatuhiva, and so we had seen them over us night and day on board the *Kon-Tiki*. But the lonely cloud on the horizon to the south-west did not move; it just rose like a motionless column of smoke while the trade wind clouds drifted by. *Cumulunimbus* is the Latin name for such clouds. The Polynesians did not know this, but they did know that under such clouds land lay. For when the tropical sun bakes the hot sand a stream of warm air is created which rises up and causes its vapour content to condense up in the colder strata of air.

We steered on the cloud till it disappeared after sunset. The wind was steady, and with the steering oar lashed tight the *Kon-Tiki* kept to her course unaided, as so often in fine weather at sea. The steering watch's job was now to sit as much as possible on the plank at the masthead, shiny with wear, and keep a look-out for anything that indicated land.

There was a deafening screaming of birds over us all that night. And the moon was nearly full.

CHAPTER VII

TO THE SOUTH SEA ISLANDS

First Sight of Land—We Drift Away from Puka-puka—A Festal Day along the Angatau Reef—On the Threshold of Heaven—The First Natives—The Kon-Tiki *gets a New Crew—Knut on Shore Leave—A Losing Battle—We Drift out to Sea Again—In Dangerous Waters—From Takume to Raroia—Drifting Towards the Witches' Cauldron—At the Mercy of the Breakers—A Shipwreck—Cast Ashore on the Coral Reef—We Find a Desert Island.*

ON the night before July 30 there was a new and strange atmosphere about the *Kon-Tiki*. Perhaps it was the deafening clamour from all the sea birds over us which showed that something fresh was brewing. The screaming of birds with many voices was so hectic and so earthly, after the dead creaking of lifeless ropes which was all we had heard above the noise of the sea in the three months we had behind us. And the moon seemed larger and rounder than ever as it swum round over the look-out at the masthead. In our fancy it reflected palm-tops and warm-blooded romance; it did not shine with such a yellow light over the cold fishes out in the sea.

At six o'clock Bengt came down from the masthead, woke Herman, and turned in. When Herman clambered up the creaking, swaying mast the day had begun to break. Ten minutes later he was down the rope-ladder again and was shaking me by the leg.

"Come out and have a look at your island!"

His face was radiant, and I jumped up, followed by Bengt, who had not quite gone to sleep yet. Hard on each other's heels, we huddled together as high as we could climb, at the point where the masts crossed. There were many birds around us, and a faint violet-blue veil over the sky was reflected in the sea as a last relic of the departing night. But over the whole horizon away to the east a ruddy glow had begun to spread, and far down to the south-east it gradually formed a blood-red background for a faint shadow, like a blue pencil line, drawn for a short way along the edge of the sea.

Land! An island! We devoured it greedily with our eyes, and woke the others, who tumbled out drowsily and stared in all directions as if they thought our bows were just going to run on to a beach. Screaming sea birds formed a bridge across the sky in the direction of the distant island, which stood out sharper against the horizon as the red background widened and turned gold with the approach of the sun and the full daylight.

Our first thought was that the island did not lie where it ought to. And as the island could not have drifted, the raft must have been caught up in a northward current in the course of the night. We had only to cast one glance over the sea to perceive at once, from the direction of the waves, that we had lost our chance in the darkness. Where we now lay, the wind no longer allowed us to press the raft on a course towards the island. The region round the Tuamotu archipelago was full of strong local ocean currents which twisted in all directions as they ran up against land, and many of them varied in direction as they met powerful tidal currents flowing in and out over reefs and lagoons.

We laid the steering oar over, but we knew quite well that it was useless. At half-past six the sun rose out of the sea and climbed straight up as it does in the tropics. The island lay some few sea miles away and had the appearance of a quite low strip of forest creeping along the horizon. The trees were crowded close together behind a narrow light-coloured beach which lay so low that it was hidden behind the seas at regular intervals. According to Erik's positions this was Puka-puka, the first outpost of the Tuamotu group. "Sailing Directions for Pacific Islands 1940", our two different charts, and Erik's observations gave in all four quite different positions for this island, but as there were no other islands in all that neighbourhood there could be no doubt that the island we saw was Puka-puka.

No extravagant outbursts were to be heard on board. After the sail had been trimmed and the oar laid over, we all formed a silent group at the masthead or stood on deck staring towards the land which had suddenly cropped up out in the middle of the endless, all-dominating sea. At last we had a visible proof that we had really been moving in all these months; we had not just been lying tumbling about in the centre of the same eternal circular horizon. To us it seemed as if the island were mobile and had suddenly entered the circle of blue, empty sea in the centre of which we had our permanent abode, as if the island were drifting slowly across our own domain, heading for the eastern horizon. We were all filled with a warm, quiet satisfaction at having actually reached Polynesia, mingled with a faint momentary disappointment at having to submit helplessly to seeing the island lie there like a mirage while we continued our eternal drift across the sea westward.

Just after sunrise a thick black column of smoke rose above the tree-tops to the left of the middle of the island. We followed it with our eyes and thought to ourselves that the natives were rising and getting their breakfast. We had no idea then that native look-out posts had seen us and were sending up smoke signals to invite us to land. About seven o'clock we scented a faint breath of burnt borao wood which tickled our salted nostrils. It awoke in me at once slumbering memories of the fire on the beach on Fatuhiva. Half an hour later we caught the smell of newly cut wood and of forest. The island had now begun to shrink and lay astern of us so that we received flickering wafts of breeze from it. For a quarter of an hour Herman and I clung to the masthead and let the warm smell of leaves and greenery filter in through our nostrils. This was Polynesia—a beautiful, rich smell of dry land after ninety-three salty days down among the waves. Bengt already lay snoring in his sleeping bag again. Erik and Torstein lay on their backs in the cabin meditating, and Knut ran in and out and sniffed the smell of leaves and wrote in his diary.

At half-past eight Puka-puka sank into the sea astern of us, but right on till eleven o'clock we could see, on climbing to the masthead, that there was a faint blue streak above the horizon in the east. Then that too was gone, and a high cumulunimbus cloud, rising motionless skyward, was all that showed where Puka-puka lay. The birds disappeared. They kept by preference to windward of the islands, so that they had the wind with them when they returned home in the evening with full bellies. The dolphins also had become noticeably scarcer, and there were again only a few pilot fish under the raft.

That night Bengt said he longed for a table and chair, for it was so tiring to lie and turn from back to stomach while reading. Otherwise he was glad we had missed our landing, for he had still three books to read. Torstein suddenly had a desire for an apple, and I myself woke up in the night because I definitely smelt a delicious odour of steak and onions. But it turned out to be only a dirty shirt.

The very next morning we detected two new clouds rising up like the steam from two locomotives below the horizon. The map was able to tell us that the names of the coral islands they came from were Fangahina and Angatau. The cloud over Angatau lay the most favourably for us as the wind was blowing, so we set our course for that, lashed the oar fast and enjoyed the wonderful peace and freedom of the Pacific. So lovely was life on a fine day on the bamboo deck of the *Kon-Tiki*, that we drank in all the impressions in the certainty that the journey would soon be over now, whatever might await us.

For three days and nights we steered on the cloud over Angatau; the weather was brilliant, the oar alone held us on our course, and the current played us no tricks. On the fourth morning Torstein relieved Herman after the 4-6 watch, and was told that Herman thought he had seen the outlines of a low island in the moonlight. When the sun rose just afterwards, Torstein stuck his head in at the cabin door and shouted:

"Land ahead!"

We all plunged out on deck, and what we saw made us hoist all our flags. First the Norwegian aft, then the French at the masthead because we were heading for a French colony. Soon the raft's entire collection of flags was fluttering in the fresh trade wind—the American, British, Peruvian and Swedish flags, besides the flag of the Explorers Club, so there was no doubt on board that now the *Kon-Tiki* was dressed. The island was ideally placed this time, right in our own course, and a little farther away from us than Puka-puka had been when it cropped up at sunrise four days before. As the sun rose straight up over the sky astern of us, we could see a clear green glimmer high up towards the misty sky over the island. It was the reflection of the still green lagoon on the inside of the surrounding reef. Some of the low atolls throw up mirages of this kind for many thousand feet into the air, so that they show their position to primitive seafarers many days before the island itself is visible above the horizon.

About ten o'clock we took charge of the steering oar ourselves; we must now decide towards which part of the island we should steer. We could already distinguish individual tree-tops from the others, and could see rows of tree-trunks, shining in the sun, which stood out against the background of dense shadowy foliage.

We knew that somewhere between us and the island there was a dangerous submerged shoal, lying in ambush for anything that approached the innocent island. This reef lay right under the deep, free roll of the swell from the east, and as the huge masses of water lost their balance above the shoal, they wavered skyward and plunged down, thundering and foaming, over the sharp coral reef. Many vessels have been caught in the terrible suction against the submerged reefs in the Tuamotu group and have been smashed to pieces against the coral.

From the sea we saw nothing of this insidious trap. We sailed in following the direction of the waves, and saw only the curved shining back of sea after sea disappearing towards the island. Both the reef and the whole frothing witches' dance over it were hidden behind rising rows of broad wave-backs ahead of us. But along both ends of the island, where we saw the beach in profile, both north and south, we saw that a few hundred yards from land the sea was one white boiling mass flinging itself high into the air.

We laid our course so as to graze the outside of the witches' kitchen off the southern point of the island, and hoped, when we got there, to be able to steer along the atoll till we either came round the point on the lee side or in any case till we touched, before we drifted past, a place where it was so shallow that we could stop our drift with a makeshift anchor and wait till the wind changed and placed us under the lee of the island.

About noon we could see through the glass that the vegetation on shore consisted of young green cocoanut palms which stood with their tops close together over a waving hedge of luxuriant undergrowth in the foreground. On the beach in front of them a number of large coral blocks lay strewn about on the bright sand. Otherwise there was no sign of life, apart from white birds sailing over the palm-tufts.

At two o'clock we had come so close that we began to sail along the island, just outside the baffling reef. As we gradually approached we heard the roar of the breakers, like a steady water-fall, against the reef, and soon they sounded like an endless express train running parallel with us a few hundred yards from our starboard side. Now too we could see the white spray which was occasionally flung high into the air behind the curly breaking wave-backs just inside us, where the "train" was roaring along.

Two men at the same time stood turning the steering oar; they were aft of the bamboo cabin and so had no view ahead whatever. Erik as navigator stood on the top of the kitchen box and gave directions to the two men at the heavy steering oar. Our plan was to keep as close in to the dangerous reef as was safe. We kept a continuous look-out from the masthead for a gap or opening in the reef, where we could try to slip the raft through. The current was now driving us along the whole length of the reef and played us no tricks. The loose centreboards allowed us to steer at an angle of about 20° to the wind on both sides, and the wind was blowing along the reef.

While Erik directed our zigzag course and took his loops as near the reef as was advisable in view of the suction, Herman and I went out in the rubber dinghy at the end of a rope. When the raft was on the inward tack, we swung after her on the rope and came so close to the thundering reef that we caught a glimpse of the glass-green wall of water that was rolling away from us, and saw how, when the seas sucked themselves back, the naked reef exposed itself, resembling a torn-up barricade of rusty iron ore. As far as we could see along the coast there was no gap or passage. So Erik trimmed the sail by tightening the port and loosening the starboard sheets, and the helmsmen followed with the steering oar, so that the *Kon-Tiki* turned her nose out again and tumbled away from the danger zone till her next drive inward.

Each time the *Kon-Tiki* stood in towards the reef and swung out again, we two who were in tow in the dinghy sat with our hearts in our mouths, for each time we came so close in that we felt the beat of the seas becoming nervous as it rose higher and fiercer. And each time we were convinced that this time Erik had gone too far, that this time there was no hope of getting the *Kon-Tiki* out again, clear of the breakers which drew us in towards the devilish red reef. But each time Erik got clear with a smart manoeuvre, and the *Kon-Tiki* ran safely out into the open sea again, well out of the clutch of the suction. And all the time we were gliding along the island, so close that we saw every detail on shore, and yet the heavenly beauty there was inaccessible to us because of the frothing moat that lay between.

About three o'clock the forest of palms ashore opened, and through a wide gap we saw right in to a blue glassy lagoon. But the surrounding reef lay as compact as ever, gnashing its blood-red teeth ominously in the foam. There was no passage, and the palm forest closed again as we plodded on along the island with the wind at our backs. Later the palm forest became thinner and thinner and gave us a view into the interior of the coral island. This consisted of the prettiest, brightest salt water lagoon, like a great silent tarn, surrounded by swaying cocoanut palms and shining bathing beaches. The seductive green palm island itself formed a broad, soft ring of sand round the hospitable lagoon, and a second ring ran round the whole island—the rust-red sword which defended the gates of heaven.

All day we zigzagged along Angatau, and had its beauty at close quarters, just outside the cabin door. The sun beat down on all the palms, and all was Paradise and joy on the island within. As our manoeuvres gradually became a matter of routine, Erik got out his guitar and stood on deck in a huge Peruvian sun-hat playing and singing sentimental South Sea songs, while Bengt served an excellent dinner on the edge of the raft. We opened an old cocoanut from Peru, and drank to the young fresh nuts which hung on the trees inside. The whole atmosphere—the peace over the bright green palm forest which stood deep-rooted and shone towards us, the peace over the white birds that sailed round the palm-tops, the peace over the glassy lagoon and the soft sand beach, and the viciousness of the red reef, the cannonading and roll of drums in the air—the whole made an overwhelming impression on the six of us who had come in from the sea. An impression which can never be effaced from our memories. There was no doubt that now we had reached the other side; we should never see a more genuine South Sea island. Landing or no landing, we had reached Polynesia anyway; the expanse of sea lay behind us for all time.

It happened that this festal day off Angatau was the ninety-seventh day on board. Strangely enough, it was ninety-seven days that we in New York had estimated as the absolute minimum time in which, in theoretically ideal conditions, we could reach the nearest islands of Polynesia.

About five o'clock we passed two palm-roofed huts which lay among the trees on shore. There was no smoke and no sign of life.

At half-past five we stood in towards the reef again; we were getting near the west end of the island, and must have a last look round in the hope of finding a passage. The sun now stood so low that it blinded us when we looked ahead, but we saw a little rainbow in the air where the sea broke against the reef a few hundred yards beyond the last point of the island. This now lay as a silhouette ahead of us. And on the beach inside we detected a cluster of motionless black spots. Suddenly one of them moved slowly down towards the water, while several of the others made off at full speed up to the edge of the woods. They were people! We steered along the reef as close in as we dared; the wind had died down, so that we felt we were within an ace of getting under the lee of the island. Now we saw a canoe being launched, and two individuals jumped on board and paddled off on the other side of the reef. Farther down they turned the boat's head out, and we saw the canoe lifted high in the air by the seas as it shot through a passage in the reef and came straight out towards us.

The opening in the reef, then, was down there; there was our only hope. Now too we could see the whole village lying in among the palm trunks. But the shadows were growing long already.

The two men in the canoe waved. We waved back eagerly, and they increased their speed. It was a Polynesian outrigger canoe, and two brown figures in singlets sat paddling, facing ahead. Now there would be fresh language difficulties. I alone of those on board remembered a few words of Marquesan from my stay on Fatuhiva, but Polynesian is a difficult language to keep up, for lack of practice in our northern countries.

We felt some relief, therefore, when the canoe bumped against the raft's side and the two men leapt on board, for one of them grinned all over his face and held out a brown hand, exclaiming in English;

"Good night!"

"Good night," I replied in astonishment. "Do you speak English?"

The man grinned again and nodded.

"Good night," he said. "Good night."

This was his entire vocabulary in foreign languages, and thereby he scored heavily over his more modest friend, who just stood in the background and grinned, much impressed, at his experienced comrade.

"Angatau?" I asked, pointing towards the island.

"H'angatau," the man nodded affirmatively.

Erik nodded proudly. He had been right, we were where the sun had told him that we were.

"*Maimai hee iuta*," I tried.

According to my knowledge acquired on Fatuhiva, this should mean approximately "want to go to land."

They both pointed towards the invisible passage in the reef, and we laid the oar over and were going to take our chance.

At that moment fresher gusts of wind came from the interior

PLATE XVII
Chaos on board after the stranding: the mast broken and the cabin knocked flat.

Kon-Tiki stranded on the Raroia coral reef. She lay there for several days, continually washed farther in by the seas.

PLATE XVIII

Above—Planting in Polynesia a cocoanut from Peru.

Below—Teriieroo, the last chief on Tahiti. He had adopted the author as his son ten years before under the name Terai Mateata (Blue Sky).

of the island. A small rain-cloud lay over the lagoon. The wind threatened to force us away from the reef, and we saw that the *Kon-Tiki* was not answering the steering oar at a wide enough angle to be able to reach the mouth of the opening in the reef. We tried to find bottom, but the anchor rope was not long enough. Now we had to have resort to the paddles, and pretty quickly too, before the wind got a fair hold of us. We hauled down the sail at top speed and each of us got out his big paddle. I wanted to give an extra paddle to each of the two natives, who stood enjoying the cigarettes they had been given on board.

The natives only shook their heads vigorously, pointed out the course and looked confused. I made signs that we must all paddle, and repeated the words "want-to-go-to-land!" Then the most advanced of the two bent down, made a cranking motion in the air with his right hand, and said:

"Brrrrrrrrr——!"

There was no doubt whatever that he wanted us to start the engine. They thought they were standing on the deck of a curiously deep loaded boat. We took them aft and made them feel under the logs to show them that we had no propeller or screw. They were dumbfounded, put out their cigarettes and flung themselves down on the side of the raft, where we sat, four men on each outside log, digging our paddles into the water. At the same time the sun sank straight into the sea behind the point and the gusts of wind from the interior of the island freshened. It did not look as if we were moving an inch. The natives looked frightened, jumped back into the canoe and disappeared. It grew dark, and we were alone once more, paddling desperately so as not to drift out to sea again.

As darkness fell over the island four canoes came dancing out from behind the reef, and soon there was a crowd of Polynesians on board, all wanting to shake hands and get cigarettes. With these fellows on board, who had local knowledge, there was no danger; they would not let us go out to sea again and out of sight; so we should be ashore that evening!

We quickly had ropes made fast from the stern of all the canoes to the bows of the *Kon-Tiki*, and the four sturdy outrigger

M

canoes spread out in fan formation, like a dog team, ahead of the wooden raft. Knut jumped into the dinghy and found a place as draught dog in among the canoes, and we others, with paddles, posted ourselves on the two outside logs of the *Kon-Tiki*. And so began, for the first time, a struggle against the east wind, which had been at our back for so long.

It was now pitch dark until the moon rose, and there was a fresh wind. On land, the inhabitants of the village had collected brushwood and lighted a big fire to show us the direction of the passage through the reef. The thundering from the reef surrounded us in the darkness like a ceaselessly roaring waterfall, and at first the noise grew louder and louder.

We could not see the team that was pulling us in the canoes ahead, but we heard them singing exhilarating war-songs in Polynesian at the pitch of their lungs. We could hear that Knut was with them, for every time the Polynesian music died away we heard Knut's solitary voice singing Norwegian folk-songs in the midst of the Polynesians' chorus. To complete the chaos we on board the raft chimed in with "Tom Brown's baby had a pimple on his nose", and both white and brown men heaved at their paddles with laughter and song.

We were overflowing with high spirits. Ninety-seven days. Arrived in Polynesia. There would be a feast in the village that evening. The natives cheered and bellowed and shouted. There was a landing on Angatau only once a year, when the copra schooner came from Tahiti to fetch cocoanut kernels. So there would indeed be a feast round the fire on land that evening.

But the angry wind blew stubbornly. We toiled till every limb ached. We held our ground, but the fire did not come any nearer, and the thunder from the reef was just the same as before. Gradually the singing died away. All grew still. It was all and more the men could do to row. The fire did not move, it only danced up and down as we fell and rose with the seas. Three hours passed, and it was now nine o'clock. Gradually we began to lose ground. We were tired.

We made the natives understand that we needed more help from land. They explained to us that there were plenty of people ashore, but they had only these four sea-going canoes in the whole island.

Then Knut appeared out of the darkness with the dinghy. He had an idea; he could row in in the rubber dinghy and fetch more natives. Five or six men could sit crowded together in the dinghy at a pinch.

This was too risky. Knut had no local knowledge; he would never be able to feel his way forward to the opening in the coral reef in that pitch-black darkness. He then proposed to take with him the leader of the natives, who could show him the way. I did not think this plan a safe one either, for the native had no experience in manoeuvring a clumsy rubber dinghy through the narrow and dangerous passage. But I asked Knut to fetch the leader, who was sitting paddling in the darkness ahead of us, so that we might hear what he thought of the situation. It was clear enough that we were no longer able to prevent ourselves from drifting astern.

Knut disappeared into the darkness to find the leader. When some time had passed, and Knut had not returned with the leader, we shouted for them, but received no answer except from a cackling chorus of Polynesians ahead. Knut had vanished into the darkness. At that moment we understood what had happened. In all the bustle, noise and turmoil Knut had misunderstood his instructions and rowed shoreward with the leader. All our shouting was useless, for where Knut now was all other sounds were drowned by the thunder all along the barrier.

We quickly got hold of a Morse lamp, and a man climbed up to the masthead and signalled "Come back. Come back."

But no one came back.

With two men away and one continuously signalling at the masthead, our drift astern increased, and the rest of us had begun to grow really tired. We threw marks overboard, and saw that we were moving slowly but surely the wrong way. The fire grew smaller, and the noise from the breakers less. And the farther we emerged from under the lee of the palm forest, the firmer hold of us the eternal east wind took. We knew it again now; now it was almost as it had been out at sea. We gradually realised that all hope had gone. We were drifting out to sea. But we must not slacken our paddling. We must put the brake on the drift astern with all our might till Knut was safe on board again.

Five minutes went. Ten minutes. Half an hour. The fire grew smaller; now and then it disappeared altogether when we ourselves slid down into the trough of the sea. The breakers became a distant murmur. Now the moon rose; we could just see the glimmer of its disc behind the palm-tops on land, but the sky seemed misty and half clouded over.

We heard the natives beginning to murmur and exchange views. Suddenly we noticed that one of the canoes had cast off its rope into the sea and disappeared. The men in the other three canoes were tired and frightened and were no longer pulling their full weight. The Kon-Tiki went on drifting out over the open sea.

Soon the three remaining ropes slackened and the three canoes bumped against the side of the raft. One of the natives came on board and said quietly with a jerk of his head:

"Iuta". (To land).

He looked anxiously at the fire, which now disappeared for long periods at a time, and only flashed out now and again like a spark. We were drifting fast. The breakers were silent; only the sea roared as it used to, and all the ropes on board the Kon-Tiki creaked and groaned.

We plied the natives with cigarettes, and I hurriedly scrawled a note which they were to take with them and give to Knut if they found him. It ran:

"Take two natives with you in a canoe with the dinghy in tow. Do not come back in the dinghy alone."

We counted on the helpful islanders being willing to take Knut with them in a canoe—assuming that they thought it advisable to put to sea at all—and if they did not think it advisable, it would be madness for Knut to venture out on to the ocean in the dinghy in the hope of overtaking the runaway raft.

The natives took the scrap of paper, jumped into the canoes and disappeared into the night. The last we heard was the shrill voice of our first friend out in the darkness calling politely:

"Good night!"

There was a murmur of appreciation from the less accomplished linguists, and then all was as silent, as free from sounds from without, as when we were two thousand sea miles from the nearest land.

It was useless for us four to do anything more with the paddles out here in the open sea, under the full pressure of the wind, but we continued the light signals from the masthead. We dared not send "Come back" any longer; we now sent out only regular flashes. It was pitch dark. The moon appeared only through occasional rifts in the bank of clouds. It must be Angatau's cumulunimbus cloud which was hanging over us.

At ten o'clock we gave up the last faint hope of seeing Knut again. We sat down in silence on the edge of the raft and munched a few biscuits, while we took turns to flash signals from the masthead, which seemed just a naked projection without the broad Kon-Tiki sail.

We decided to keep the lamp signalling going all night, so long as we did not know where Knut was. We refused to believe that he had been caught by the breakers. Knut always landed on his feet, whether it was heavy water or breakers; he was alive all right. Only it was so damnable to have him stuck down among Polynesians on an out of the way island in the Pacific. An accursed business! After all that long voyage, all we could do was to nip in and land a man on a remote South Sea island and sail off again. No sooner had the first Polynesians come smiling on board than they had to clear out headlong to escape being themselves caught up in the Kon-Tiki's wild, incontinent rush westward. It was the devil of a situation. And the ropes were creaking so horribly that night. Not one of us showed a sign of wanting to sleep.

It was half-past ten. Bengt was coming down to be relieved at the swaying masthead. Then we all started. We had heard voices clearly, out on the sea in the darkness. There it was again. It was Polynesians talking. We shouted into the black night with all the strength of our lungs. They shouted back, and—there was Knut's voice among the rest! We were mad with excitement;

our tiredness had gone; the whole thunder-cloud had lifted. What did it matter if we drifted away from Angatau? There were other islands in the sea. Now the nine balsa logs, so fond of travel, could drift where they liked, so long as all six of us were assembled on board again.

Three outrigger canoes emerged from the darkness, riding over the swell, and Knut was the first man to jump across to the dear old *Kon-Tiki*, followed by six brown men. There was little time for explanations; the natives must have presents and be off on their adventurous journey back to the island. Without seeing light or land, and with hardly any stars, they had to find their course by paddling against wind and sea till they saw the light from the fire. We rewarded them amply with provisions, cigarettes and other gifts, and each of them shook us by the hand heartily in a last farewell.

They were clearly anxious on our account; they pointed westward, indicating that we were heading towards dangerous reefs. The leader had tears in his eyes and kissed me tenderly on the chin, which made me thank Providence for my beard. Then they crept into the canoes, and we six comrades were left on the raft, together and alone.

We left the raft to her own devices and listened to Knut's story.

Knut had in good faith made for land in the dinghy with the native leader on board. The native himself was sitting at the little oars and rowing towards the opening in the reef, when Knut to his surprise saw the light signals from the *Kon-Tiki* asking him to come back. He made signs to the rower to turn, but the native refused to obey. Then Knut took hold of the oars himself, but the native tore his hands away, and with the reef thundering round them it was no use starting a fight. They had bounded right in through the opening in the reef, and gone on inside it until they were lifted right up on to a solid coral block on the island itself. A crowd of natives caught hold of the dinghy and dragged it high up on the shore, and Knut stood alone under the palm trees surrounded by a huge crowd of natives chattering away in an unknown lingo. Brown, bare-legged men, women and children of all ages flocked round him and felt the material of his shirt and trousers. They themselves wore ragged old European clothes, but there were no white men on the island.

Knut got hold of some of the smartest fellows and made signs to them that they should go out in the dinghy with him. Then a big fat man came waddling up whom Knut presumed must be the chief, for he had an old uniform cap on his head and talked in a loud, authoritative voice. All made way for him. Knut explained both in Norwegian and in English that he needed men and must get back to the raft before we others drifted away. The chief beamed and understood nothing, and Knut, despite his most vehement protests, was pushed over to the village by the whole shouting crowd. There he was received by dogs and pigs and pretty South Sea girls who came along carrying fresh fruit. It was clear that the natives were prepared to make Knut's stay as agreeable as possible, but Knut was not to be enticed; he thought sadly of the raft which was vanishing westward. The natives' intention was obvious. They badly wanted our company, and they knew that there was a lot of good things on board white men's ships. If they could keep Knut ashore, the rest of us and the queer boat would certainly come in also. No vessel would leave a white man behind on such an out of the way island as Angatau.

After some curious experiences Knut got away and hurried down to the dinghy, surrounded by admirers of both sexes. His international speech and gesticulations could no longer be mis-understood; they realised that he must and would return to the odd craft out in the night which was in such a hurry that she had to go on at once.

Then the natives tried a trick; they indicated by signs that the rest of us were coming ashore on the other side of the point. Knut was puzzled for a few minutes, but then loud voices were heard down on the beach, where women and children were tending the flickering fire. The three canoes had come back, and the men brought Knut the note. He was in a desperate situation. Here were instructions not to row out on the sea alone, and all the natives absolutely refused to go with him.

There was a high-pitched, noisy argument among all the natives. Those who had been out and seen the raft understood perfectly well that it was of little use to keep Knut back in the hope of getting the rest of us ashore. The end of it was that Knut's promises and threats in international accents induced three canoes' crews to accompany him out to sea in pursuit of the *Kon-Tiki*. And they put out to sea in the tropical night with the dinghy dancing along in tow, while the natives stood motionless by the dying fire and watched their new blonde friend disappear as quickly as he had come.

Knut and his companions could see the faint light signals from the raft far out to sea when the swell lifted the canoes. The long, slim Polynesian canoes, stiffened by pointed side-floats, cut through the water like knives, but it seemed an eternity to Knut before he felt the thick round logs of the *Kon-Tiki* under his feet again.

"Have a good time ashore?" Torstein asked enviously.

"Oho, you should just have seen the hula girls!" Knut teased him.

We left the sail down and the oar inboard, and we all six crept into the bamboo cabin and slept like boulders on the beach at Angatau.

For three days we drifted across the sea without a sight of land.

We were drifting straight towards the ominous Takume and Raroia reefs, which together blocked up 40–50 miles of the sea ahead of us. We made desperate efforts to steer clear, to the north of these dangerous reefs, and things seemed to be going well till one night the watch came hurrying in and called us all out.

The wind had changed. We were heading straight for the Takume reef. It had begun to rain, and there was no visibility at all. The reef could not be far off.

In the middle of night we held a council of war. It was a question of saving our lives now. To get past on the north side was now hopeless, we must try to get through on the south side instead. We trimmed the sail, laid the oar over, and began a dangerous piece of sailing with the uncertain north wind behind us. If the east wind came back before we had passed the whole façade of the fifty-mile long reefs, we should be hurled in among the breakers, at their mercy.

We agreed on all that should be done if shipwreck was imminent. We would stay on board the *Kon-Tiki* at all costs. We would not climb up the mast, from which we should be shaken down like rotten fruit, but would cling tight to the stays of the mast when the seas poured over us. We laid the rubber raft loose on the deck, and made fast to it a small water-tight wireless transmitter, a small quantity of provisions, water-bottles and medical stores. This would be washed ashore independently of us if we ourselves should get over the reef safe but empty-handed. In the stern of the *Kon-Tiki* we made fast a long rope with a float which also would be washed ashore, so that we could try to pull in the whole timber raft if she were stranded out on the reef. And so we crept into bed and left the watch to the helmsman out in the rain.

As long as the north wind held, we glided slowly but surely down along the façade of the coral reefs which lay in ambush below the horizon. But then one afternoon the wind died away, and when it returned it had gone round into the east. According to Erik's position we were already so far down that we now had some hope of steering clear of the southernmost point of the Raroia reef. We would try to get round it and into shelter before going on to other reefs beyond it.

When night came, we had been a hundred days at sea.

Late in the night I woke feeling restless and uneasy. There was something unusual in the movement of the waves. The *Kon-Tiki*'s motion was rather different from what it usually was in such conditions. We had become sensitive to changes in the rhythm of the logs. I thought at once of suction from a coast which was drawing near, and was continually out on deck and up the mast. Nothing but sea was visible. But I could get no quiet sleep. Time passed.

At dawn, just before six, Torstein came hurrying down from the masthead. He could see a whole line of small palm-clad islands far ahead. Before doing anything else we laid the' oar over to southward as far as we could. What Torstein had seen must be the small coral islands which lay strewn like pearls on a string behind the Raroia reef. A northward current must have caught us.

At 7.30 palm-clad islets had appeared in a row all along the horizon to westward. The southernmost lay roughly ahead of our bows, and thence there were islands and clumps of palms all along the horizon on our starboard side till they disappeared as dots away to northward. The nearest were four or five sea miles away.

One survey from the masthead showed that even if our bows pointed towards the bottom island in the chain, our drift sideways was so great that we were not advancing in the direction in which our bows pointed. We were drifting diagonally right in towards the reef. With fixed centreboards we should still have had some hope of steering clear. But sharks were following close astern, so that it was impossible to dive under the raft and tighten up the loose centreboards with fresh guy-ropes.

We saw that we had now only a few hours more on board the *Kon-Tiki*. They must be used in preparation for our inevitable wreck on the coral reef. Every man learned what he had to do when the moment came; each one of us knew where his own limited sphere of responsibility lay, so that we should not fly round treading on each other's toes when the time came and seconds counted. The *Kon-Tiki* pitched up and down, up and down, as the wind forced us in. There was no doubt that here was the turmoil of waves created by the reef—some waves advancing while others were hurled back after beating vainly against the surrounding wall.

We were still under full sail in the hope of even now being able to steer clear. As we gradually drifted nearer, half sideways, we saw from the mast how the whole string of palm-clad islets was connected with a coral reef, part above and part under water, which lay like a mole where the sea was white with foam and leapt high into the air. The Raroia atoll is oval in shape and has a diameter of twenty-five miles, not counting the adjoining reefs of Takume. The whole of its longer side faces the sea to eastward, where we came pitching in. The reef itself, which runs in one line from horizon to horizon, is only a few hundred yards clear, and behind it idyllic islets lie in a string round the still lagoon inside.

It was with mixed feelings we saw the blue Pacific being ruthlessly torn up and hurled into the air all along the horizon ahead of us. I knew what awaited us; I had visited the Tuamotu group before, and had stood safe on land looking out over the immense spectacle in the east, where the surf from the open Pacific broke in over the reef. New reefs and islands kept on gradually appearing to southward. We must be lying off the middle of the façade of the coral wall.

On board the *Kon-Tiki* all preparations for the end of the voyage were being made. Everything of value was carried into the cabin and lashed fast. Documents and papers were packed into water-tight bags, along with films and other things which would not stand a dip in the sea. The whole bamboo cabin was covered with canvas, and specially strong ropes were lashed across it. When we saw that all hope was gone, we opened up the bamboo deck and cut off with machete knives all the ropes which held the centreboards down. It was a hard job to get the centreboards drawn up, because they were all thickly covered with stout barnacles. With the centreboards up the draught of our vessel was no deeper than to the bottom of the timber logs, and we would therefore be more easily washed in over the reef. With no centreboards and with the sail down the raft lay completely sideways on and was entirely at the mercy of wind and sea.

We tied the longest rope we had to the home-made anchor, and made it fast to the step of the port mast, so that the *Kon-Tiki* would go into the surf stern first when the anchor was thrown overboard. The anchor itself consisted of empty water cans filled with used wireless batteries and heavy scrap, and solid mangrove-wood sticks projected from it, set crosswise.

Order number one, which came first and last, was: Hold on to the raft! Whatever happened we must hang on tight on board and let the nine great logs take the pressure from the reef. We ourselves had more than enough to do to withstand the weight of the water. If we jumped overboard we should become helpless victims of the suction which would fling us in and out over the sharp corals. The rubber raft would capsize in the steep seas or, heavily loaded with us in it, it would be torn to ribbons against the reef. But the wooden logs would sooner or later be cast ashore, and we with them, if only we managed to hold fast.

Next, all hands were told to put on their shoes for the first time in a hundred days, and to have their lifebelts ready. The last-named, however, were not of much value, for if a man fell overboard he would be battered to death, not drowned. We had time too to put our passports, and such few dollars as we had left, into our pockets. But it was not lack of time that was troubling us.

Those were anxious hours in which we lay drifting helplessly sideways, step after step, in towards the reef. It was noticeably quiet on board; we all crept in and out from cabin to bamboo deck, silent or laconic, and carried on with our jobs. Our serious faces showed that no one was in doubt as to what awaited us, and the absence of nervousness showed that we had all gradually acquired an unshakeable confidence in the raft. If it had got across the sea, it would also manage to bring us ashore alive.

Inside the cabin there was a complete chaos of provision cartons and cargo lashed fast. Torstein had barely found room for himself in the wireless corner, where he had got the short wave transmitter working. We were now over 4,000 sea miles from our old base at Callao, where the Peruvian Naval War School had maintained regular contact with us, and still farther from Hal and Frank and the other radio amateurs in the United States. But as chance willed, we had on the previous day got into touch with a capable wireless fan who had a set on Rarotonga in the Cook Islands, and the operators, quite contrary to all our usual practice, had arranged for an extra contact with him early in the morning. And all the time we were drifting closer and closer in to the reef, Torstein was sitting tapping his key and calling Rarotonga.

Entries in the *Kon-Tiki*'s log ran:

8.15: We are slowly approaching land. We can now make out with the naked eye the separate palm trees inside on the starboard side.

8.45: The wind has veered into a still more unfavourable quarter for us, so we have no hope of getting clear. No nervousness on board, but hectic preparations on deck. There is something lying on the reef ahead of us which looks like the wreck of a sailing vessel, but it may be only a heap of drift-wood.

9.45: The wind is taking us straight towards the last island but one we see behind the reef. We can now see the whole coral reef clearly; here it is built up like a white and red speckled wall which just sticks up out of the water in a belt in front of all the islands. All along the reef white foaming surf is flung up towards the sky. Bengt is just serving up a good hot meal, the last before the great action! It is a wreck lying in there on the reef. We are so close now that we can see right across the shining lagoon behind the reef, and see the outlines of other islands on the other side of the lagoon.

As this was written the dull drone of the surf came near again; it came from the whole reef inside us and filled the air like thrilling rolls of the drum, heralding the exciting last act of the *Kon-Tiki*.

9.50: Very close now. Drifting along the reef. Only a hundred yards or so away. Torstein is talking to the man on Rarotonga. All clear. Must pack up log now. All in good spirits; it looks bad, but *we shall make it!*

A few minutes later the anchor rushed overboard and caught hold of the bottom, so that the *Kon-Tiki* swung round and turned her stern inwards towards the breakers. It held us for a few valuable minutes, while Torstein sat hammering like mad on the key. He had got Rarotonga now. The breakers thundered in the air and the sea rose and fell furiously. All hands were at work on deck, and now Torstein got his message through. He said we were drifting towards the Raroia reef. He asked Rarotonga to listen in on the same wave-length every hour. If we were silent for more than thirty-six hours Rarotonga must let the Norwegian Embassy in Washington know. Torstein's last words were: "O.K. 50 yards left. Here we go. Good-bye." Then he closed down the station, Knut sealed up the papers, and both crawled out on deck as fast as they could to join the rest of us, for it was clear now that the anchor was giving way.

The swell grew heavier and heavier, with deep troughs between the waves, and we felt the raft being swung up and down, up and down, higher and higher.

Again the order was shouted: "Hold on, never mind about the cargo, hold on!"

We were now so near the waterfall inside that we no longer heard the steady continuous roar from all along the reef. We now heard only a separate boom each time the nearest breaker crashed down on the rocks.

All hands stood in readiness, each clinging fast to the rope he thought the most secure. Only Erik crept into the cabin at the last moment; there was one part of the programme he had not yet carried out—he had not found his shoes!

No one stood aft, for it was there the shock from the reef would come. Nor were the two firm stays which ran from the masthead down to the stern safe. For if the mast fell they would be left hanging overboard, over the reef. Herman, Bengt and Torstein had climbed up on some boxes which were lashed fast forward of the cabin wall, and while Herman clung on to the guy-ropes from the ridge of the roof, the other two held on to the ropes from the masthead by which the sail at other times was hauled up. Knut and I chose the stay running from the bows up to the masthead, for if mast and cabin and everything else went overboard, we thought the rope from the bows would nevertheless remain lying inboard, as we were now head on to the seas.

When we realised that the seas had got hold of us, the anchor rope was cut, and we were off. A sea rose straight up under us, and we felt the *Kon-Tiki* being lifted up in the air. The great moment had come; we were riding on the wave-back at breath-less speed, our ramshackle craft creaking and groaning as she quivered under us. The excitement made one's blood boil. I remember that, having no other inspiration, I waved my arm and bellowed "hurrah!" at the pitch of my lungs; it afforded a certain relief and could do no harm anyway. The others certainly thought I had gone mad, but they all beamed and grinned enthusiastically. On we ran with the seas rushing in behind us; this was the *Kon-Tiki*'s baptism of fire; all must and would go well.

But our elation was soon damped. A new sea rose high up astern of us like a glittering green glass wall; as we sank down it came rolling after us, and in the same second in which I saw it high above me I felt a violent blow and was submerged under floods of water. I felt the suction through my whole body, with such great strength that I had to strain every single muscle in my frame and think of one thing only—hold on, hold on! I think that in such a desperate situation the arms will be torn off before the brain consents to let go, evident as the outcome is. Then I felt that the mountain of water was passing on and relaxing its devilish grip of my body. When the whole mountain had rushed on, with an earsplitting roaring and crashing, I saw Knut again hanging on beside me, doubled up into a ball. Seen from behind the great sea was almost flat and grey; as it rushed on it swept just over the ridge of the cabin roof which projected from the water, and there hung the three others, pressed against the cabin roof as the water passed over them.

We were still afloat.

In an instant I renewed my hold, with arms and legs bent round the strong rope. Knut let himself down and with a tiger's leap joined the others on the boxes, where the cabin took the strain. I heard reassuring exclamations from them, but at the same time I saw a new green wall rise up and come towering towards us. I shouted a warning and made myself as small and hard as I could where I hung. And in an instant hell was over us again, and the *Kon-Tiki* disappeared completely under the masses of water. The sea tugged and pulled with all the force it could bring to bear at the poor little bundle of a human body. The second sea rushed over us, and a third like it.

Then I heard a triumphant shout from Knut, who was now hanging on to the rope-ladder:

"Look at the raft, she's holding!"

After three seas only the double mast and the cabin had been knocked a bit crooked. Again we had a feeling of triumph over the elements, and the elation of victory gave us new strength.

Then I saw the next sea come towering up, higher than all the rest, and again I bellowed a warning aft to the others as I climbed up the stay as high as I could get in a hurry and hung on fast. Then I myself disappeared sideways into the midst of the green wall which towered high over us; the others, who were farther aft and saw me disappear first, estimated the height of the wall of water at twenty-five feet, while the foaming crest passed by fifteen feet above the part of the glassy wall into which I had vanished. Then the great wave reached them, and we had all one single thought—hold on, hold on, hold, hold, hold!

We must have hit the reef that time. I myself felt only the strain on the stay, which seemed to bend and slacken jerkily. But whether the bumps came from above or below I could not tell, hanging there. The whole submersion lasted only seconds, but it demanded more strength than we usually have in our bodies. There is greater strength in the human mechanism than that of the muscles alone. I determined that if I was to die, I would die in this position, like a knot on the stay. The sea thundered on, over and past, and as it roared by it revealed a hideous sight. The *Kon-Tiki* was wholly changed, as by the stroke of a magic wand. The vessel we knew from weeks and months at sea was no more; in a few seconds our pleasant world had become a shattered wreck.

I saw only one man on board besides myself. He lay pressed flat across the ridge of the cabin roof, face downwards, with his arms stretched out on both sides, while the cabin itself was crushed in like a house of cards, towards the stern and towards the starboard side. The motionless figure was Herman. There was no other sign of life, while the hill of water thundered by, in across the reef. The hardwood mast on the starboard side was broken like a match, and the upper stump, in its fall, had smashed right through the cabin roof, so that the mast and all its gear slanted at a low angle over the reef on the starboard side. Astern, the steering block was twisted round lengthways and the cross-beam broken, while the steering oar was smashed to splinters.

The splashboards at the bows were broken like cigar boxes, and the whole deck was torn up and pasted like wet paper against the forward wall of the cabin, along with boxes, cans, canvas and other cargo. Bamboo sticks and rope-ends stuck up everywhere, and the general impression was of complete chaos.

I felt cold fear run through my whole body. What was the good of my holding on? If I lost one single man here, in the run in, the whole thing would be ruined, and for the moment there was only one human figure to be seen after the last buffet. In that second Torstein's hunched up form appeared outside the raft. He was hanging like a monkey in the ropes from the mast-head, and managed to get on to the logs again, where he crawled up on to the debris forward of the cabin. Herman too now turned his head and gave me a forced grin of encouragement, but did not move. I bellowed in the faint hope of locating the others, and heard Bengt's calm voice call out that all hands were aboard. They were lying holding on to the ropes behind the tangled barricade which the tough plaiting from the bamboo deck had built up.

All this happened in the course of a few seconds, while the *Kon-Tiki* was being drawn out of the witches' kitchen by the backwash, and a fresh sea came rolling over her. For the last time I bellowed "hang on!" at the pitch of my lungs amid the uproar, and that was all I myself did; I hung on and disappeared in the masses of water which rushed over and past in those endless two or three seconds. That was enough for me. I saw the ends of the logs knocking and bumping against a sharp step in the coral reef without going over it. Then we were sucked out again. I also saw the two men who lay stretched out across the ridge of the cabin roof, but none of us smiled any longer. Behind the chaos of bamboo I heard a calm voice call out:

"This won't do."

And I myself felt equally discouraged. As the masthead sank farther and farther out over the starboard side I found myself hanging on to a slack line outside the raft. The next sea came. When it had gone by I was dead tired, and my only thought was to get up on to the logs and lie behind the barricade. When the

N

backwash retreated, I saw for the first time the rugged red reef
naked beneath us, and perceived Torstein standing bent double
on gleaming red corals, holding on to a bunch of ropes' ends
from the mast. Knut, standing aft, was about to jump. I shouted
that we must all keep on the logs, and Torstein, who had been
washed overboard by the pressure of water, sprang up again like
a cat.

Two or three more seas rolled over us with diminishing force,
and what happened then I do not remember, except that water
foamed in and out, and I myself sank lower and lower towards
the red reef over which we were being lifted in. Then only crests
of foam full of salt spray came whirling in, and I was able to
work my way in on to the raft, where we all made for the after
end of the logs, which was highest up on the reef.

At the same moment Knut crouched down and sprang up on
to the reef with the line which lay clear astern. While the
backwash was running out, he waded at the double some thirty
yards in and stood safely at the end of the line when the next
sea foamed in towards him, died down, and ran back from the
flat reef like a broad stream.

Then Erik came crawling out of the collapsed cabin, with
his shoes on. If we had all done as he did, we should have got
off cheaply. As the cabin had not been washed overboard, but
had been pressed down pretty flat under the canvas, Erik lay
quietly stretched out among the cargo and heard the peals of
thunder crashing above him while the collapsed bamboo walls
curved downwards. Bengt had had a slight concussion when the
mast fell, but had managed to crawl under the wrecked cabin
alongside Erik. We should all of us have been lying there if we
had realised in advance how indissolubly the countless lashings
and plaited bamboo sheets would hang on to the main logs under
the pressure of the water.

Erik was now standing ready on the logs aft, and when the
sea retired he too jumped up on to the reef. It was Herman's
turn next, and then Bengt's. Each time the raft was pushed a bit
farther in, and when Torstein's turn and my own came, the
raft already lay so far in on the reef that there was no longer any

ground for abandoning her. All hands began the work of salvage.

We were now twenty yards away from that devilish step up on the reef, and it was there and beyond it that the breakers came rolling after one another in long lines. The coral polyps had taken care to build the atoll so high that only the very top of the breakers was able to send a fresh stream of sea water past us and into the lagoon, which abounded in fish. Here inside was the corals' own world, and they disported themselves in the strangest shapes and colours.

A long way in on the reef the others found the rubber raft, lying drifting and quite waterlogged. They emptied it and dragged it back to the wreck, and we loaded it to the full with the most important equipment, like the radio set, provisions and water-bottles. We dragged all this across the reef and piled it up on the top of a huge block of coral which lay alone on the inside of the reef like a large meteorite. Then we went back to the wreck for fresh loads. We could never know what the sea would be up to when the tidal currents got to work around us.

In the shallow water inside the reef we saw something bright shining in the sun. When we waded over to pick it up, to our astonishment we saw two empty tins. This was not exactly what we had expected to find there, and we were still more surprised when we saw that the little boxes were quite bright and newly-opened and stamped "pineapple", with the same inscription as that on the new field rations we ourselves were testing for the quartermaster. They were indeed two of our own pineapple tins which we had thrown overboard after our last meal on board the *Kon-Tiki*. We had followed close behind them up on to the reef.

We were standing on sharp, rugged coral blocks, and on the uneven bottom we waded now ankle-deep, now chest-deep, according to the channels and stream-beds in the reef. Anemones and corals gave the whole reef the appearance of a rock garden covered with mosses and cactus and fossilised plants, red and green and yellow and white. There was no colour that was not represented, either in corals or in algae, or in shells and sea slugs and fantastic fish which were wriggling about everywhere. In the deeper channels small sharks about four feet long came sneaking up to us in the crystal-clear water. But we had only to smack the water with the palms of our hands for them to turn about and keep at a distance.

Where we had stranded we had only pools of water and wet patches of coral about us, and farther in lay the calm blue lagoon. The tide was going out, and we continually saw more corals sticking up out of the water round us, while the surf which thundered without interruption along the reef sank down, as it were, a floor lower. What would happen there on the narrow reef when the tide began to flow again was uncertain. We must get away.

The reef stretched like a half-submerged fortress wall up to the north and down to the south. In the extreme south was a long island densely covered with palm forest. And just above us to the north, only 600 or 700 yards away, lay another but considerably smaller palm island. It lay inside the reef, with palm-tops rising into the sky and snow-white sandy beaches running out into the still lagoon. The whole island looked like a bulging green basket of flowers, or a little bit of concentrated paradise.

This island we chose.

Herman stood beside me beaming all over his bearded face. He did not say a word, only stretched out his hand and laughed quietly. The *Kon-Tiki* still lay far out on the reef with the spray flying over her. She was a wreck, but an honourable wreck. Everything above deck was smashed up, but the nine balsa logs from the Quivedo forest in Ecuador were as intact as ever. They had saved our lives. The sea had claimed but little of the cargo, and none of what we had stowed inside the cabin. We ourselves had stripped the raft of everything of real value, which now lay in safety on the top of the great sun-smitten rock inside the reef.

Since I had jumped off the raft, I had genuinely missed the sight of all the pilot fish wriggling in front of our bows. Now the great balsa logs lay right up on the reef in six inches of water, and brown sea slugs lay writhing under the bows. The pilot fish were gone. The dolphins were gone. Only unknown flat fish with peacock patterns and blunt tails wriggled inquisitively in and out between the logs. We had arrived in a new world. Johannes had left his hole. He had doubtless found another lurking-place here.

I took a last look round on board the wreck, and caught sight of a little baby palm in a flattened basket. It projected from an eye in a cocoanut to a length of eighteen inches, and two roots stuck out below. I waded in towards the island with the nut in my hand. A little way ahead I saw Knut wading happily landwards with a model of the raft, which he had made with much labour on the voyage, under his arm. We soon passed Bengt. He was a splendid steward. With a lump on his forehead and sea water dripping from his beard, he was walking bent double pushing a box, which danced along before him every time the breakers outside sent a stream over into the lagoon. He lifted the lid proudly. It was the kitchen box, and in it were the Primus and cooking utensils in good order.

I shall never forget that wade across the reef towards the heavenly palm island that grew larger as it came to meet us. When I reached the sunny sand beach, I slipped off my shoes and thrust my bare toes down into the warm, bone-dry sand. It was as though I enjoyed the sight of every footprint which dug itself into the virgin sand beach that led up to the palm trunks. Soon the palm-tops closed over my head, and I went on, right in towards the centre of the tiny island. Green cocoanuts hung under the palm-tufts, and some luxuriant bushes were thickly covered with snow-white blossoms, which smelt so sweet and seductive that I felt quite faint. In the interior of the island two quite tame terns flew about my shoulders. They were as white and light as wisps of cloud. Small lizards shot away from my feet, and the most important inhabitants of the island were large blood-red hermit crabs, which lumbered along in every direction with stolen snail-shells as large as eggs adhering to their soft hinder-parts.

I was completely overwhelmed. I sank down on my knees and thrust my fingers deep down into the dry warm sand.

The voyage was over. We were all alive. We had run ashore

on a small uninhabited South Sea island. And what an island! Torstein came in, flung away a sack, threw himself flat on his back and looked up at the palm-tops and the white birds, light as down, which circled noiselessly just above us. Soon we were all six lying there. Herman, always energetic, climbed up a small palm and pulled down a cluster of large green cocoanuts. We cut off their soft tops, as if they were eggs, with our machete knives, and poured down our throats the most delicious refreshing drink in the world—sweet, cold milk from young and seedless palm fruit. On the reef outside resounded the monotonous drumbeats from the guard at the gates of paradise.

"Purgatory was a bit damp," said Bengt, "but heaven was more or less as I'd imagined it."

We stretched ourselves luxuriously on the ground and smiled up at the white trade wind clouds drifting by westward up above the palm-tops. Now we were no longer following them helplessly; now we lay on a fixed, motionless island, really in Polynesia.

And as we lay and stretched ourselves, the breakers outside us rumbled like a train, to and fro, to and fro all along the horizon.

Bengt was right; this was heaven.

CHAPTER VIII

AMONG POLYNESIANS

A Robinson Touch—Fear of Relief—All Well, Kon-Tiki!—
Other Wrecks—Uninhabited Islands—Fight with Marine Eels—
Natives Find Us—Ghosts on the Reef—Envoy to the Chief—The
Chief Visits us—The Kon-Tiki *is Recognised—A High Tide—*
Our Craft's Overland Cruise—Only Four on the Island—Natives
Fetch Us—Reception in the Village—Forefathers from the Sunrise—
Hula Feast—Medicine Men on the Air—We Become Royalty—
Another Shipwreck—The Tamara *Salves the* Maoae—To Tahiti
—Meeting on the Quay—A Royal Stay—Six Wreaths.

OUR little island was uninhabited. We soon got to know every palm clump and every beach, for the island was barely two hundred yards across. The highest point was less than six feet above the lagoon.

Over our heads, in the palm-tops, there hung great clusters of green cocoanut husks, which insulated their contents of cold cocoanut milk from the tropical sun, so we should not be thirsty in the first weeks. There were also ripe cocoanuts, a swarm of hermit crabs and all sorts of fish in the lagoon; so we should be well off.

On the north side of the island we found the remnants of an old unpainted wooden cross, half buried in the coral sand. Here there was a view northward along the reef to the stripped wreck which we had first seen closer in as we drifted by on the way to our stranding. Still farther northward we saw in a bluish haze the palm-tufts of another small island. The island to southward, on which the trees grew thickly, was much closer. We saw no sign of life there either, but for the time we had other matters to think about.

Robinson Hesselberg came limping up in his big straw hat with his arms full of crawling hermit crabs. Knut set light to some dry wood, and soon we had crab and cocoanut milk with coffee for dessert.

"Feels all right being ashore, doesn't it, boys?" Knut asked delightedly.

He had had this experience before on the voyage. As he spoke he stumbled and poured half a kettle of boiling water over Bengt's bare feet. We were all of us a bit unsteady the first day ashore after 101 days on board the raft, and would suddenly begin reeling about among the palm-trunks because we had put out a foot to counter a sea that did not come.

When Bengt handed over to us our respective mess utensils, Erik grinned broadly. I remember that after the last meal on board I had leaned over the side of the raft and washed up as usual, while Erik looked in across the reef, saying: "I don't think I shall bother to wash up to-day." When he found his things in the kitchen box, they were as clean as mine.

After the meal and a good stretch on the ground we set about putting together the soaked wireless apparatus; we must do it quickly so that Torstein and Knut might get onto the air before the man on Rarotonga sent out a report of our sad end.

Most of the wireless equipment had already been brought ashore, and among the things which lay drifting on the reef Bengt found a box, on which he laid hands. He jumped high into the air from an electric shock; there was no doubt that the contents belonged to the wireless section. And while the operators unscrewed, coupled and put together, we others set about pitching camp.

Out on the wreck we found the heavy waterlogged sail, and dragged it ashore. We stretched it between two big palms in a little opening looking on to the lagoon, and supported two other corners with bamboo sticks which came drifting in from the wreck. A thick hedge of wild flowering bushes forced the sail together so that we got a roof and three walls and, moreover, a clear view of the shining lagoon, while our nostrils were filled with an insinuating scent of blossoms. It was good to be here. We all laughed quietly and enjoyed our ease; we each made our beds of fresh palm leaves, pulling up loose branches of coral which stuck up inconveniently out of the sand. Before night fell we had a very pleasant rest, and over our heads we saw the big

bearded face of good old Kon-Tiki. No longer did he swell out
his breast with the east wind behind him. He now lay motionless
on his back looking up at the stars which came twinkling out
over Polynesia.

On the bushes round us hung wet flags and sleeping bags,
and soaked articles lay on the sand to dry. Another day on this
island of sunshine and everything would be nicely dry. Even the
wireless boys had to give it up until the sun had a chance of
drying the inside of their apparatus next day. We took the
sleeping bags down from the trees and turned in, disputing
boastfully as to who had the driest bag. Bengt won, for his did
not squelch when he turned over. Heavens, how good it was to
be able to sleep.

When we woke next morning at sunrise, the sail was bent
down and full of rain-water as pure as crystal. Bengt took charge
of this asset, and then pottered down to the lagoon and jerked
ashore some curious breakfast fish which he decoyed into
channels in the sand.

That night Herman had had pains in the neck and back where
he had damaged himself before the start from Lima, and Erik
had a return of his vanished lumbago. Otherwise we had come
out of the trip over the reef astonishingly lightly, with scratches
and small wounds, except for Bengt, who had had a blow on
the forehead when the mast fell and had a slight concussion. I
myself looked most peculiar, with my arms and legs bruised
blue-black all over by the pressure against the rope.

But none of us was in such a bad state that the sparkling clear
lagoon did not entice him to a brisk swim before breakfast. It
was an immense lagoon. Far out it was blue and rippled by the
trade wind, and it was so wide that we could only just see the
tops of a row of misty blue palm islands which marked the
curve of the atoll on the other side. But here, in the lee of the
islands, the trade wind rustled peacefully in the fringed palm-tops
and made them stir and sway, while the lagoon lay like a motionless mirror below and reflected all their beauty. The bitter salt
water was so pure and clear that gaily-coloured corals in nine
feet of water seemed so near the surface that we should cut our

toes on them in swimming. And the water abounded in beautiful varieties of colourful fish. It was a marvellous world in which to disport oneself. The water was just cold enough to be refreshing, and the air was pleasantly warm and dry from the sun. But we must get ashore again quickly to-day; Rarotonga would broadcast alarming news if nothing had been heard from the raft at the end of the day.

Coils and wireless parts lay drying in the tropical sun on bone-dry slabs of coral, and Torstein and Knut coupled and screwed. The whole day passed, and the atmosphere grew more and more hectic. We abandoned all other jobs and crowded round the wireless boys in the hope of being able to give assistance. We must be on the air before 10 p.m. Then the thirty-six hours time limit would be up, and the radio amateur on Raratonga would send out appeals for aircraft and relief expeditions.

Noon came, afternoon came, and the sun set. If only the man on Rarotonga would contain himself! Seven o'clock, eight, nine. The tension was at breaking-point. Not a sign of life in the transmitter, but the receiver, an NC-173, began to liven up somewhere right at the bottom of the scale, where we heard faint music. But not on the amateur wave-length. It was eating its way up, however; perhaps it was a wet coil which was drying inwards from one end. The transmitter was still stone dead—short-circuits and sparks everywhere.

There was less than an hour left. This would never do. The transmitter was given up, and a little sabotage transmitter from war-time was tried again. We had tested it several times before in the course of the day, but without result. Now perhaps it had become a little drier. All the batteries were completely ruined, and we got power by cranking a tiny hand accumulator. It was heavy, and we four who were laymen in wireless matters took turns all day long to sit and turn the infernal thing.

The thirty-six hours would soon be up. I remember someone whispering "seven minutes more", "five minutes more", and then no one would look at his watch again. The transmitter was as dumb as ever, but the receiver was sputtering upwards towards the right wave-length. Suddenly it crackled on the Rarotonga man's frequency, and we gathered that he was in full contact with the telegraph station in Tahiti. Soon afterwards we picked up the following fragment of a message sent out from Rarotonga:

"—no plane this side of Samoa. I am quite sure——"

Then it died away again. The tension was unbearable. What was brewing out there? Had they already begun to send out aircraft and rescue expeditions? Now, no doubt, messages concerning us were going over the air in every direction.

The two operators worked feverishly. The sweat trickled from their faces as freely as it did from ours, who sat turning the handle. Power began slowly to come into the transmitter's aerial, and Torstein pointed ecstatically to an arrow which swung slowly up over a scale when he held the Morse key down. Now it was coming!

We turned the handle madly while Torstein called Rarotonga. No one heard us. Once more. Now the receiver had woken up again, but Rarotonga did not hear us. We called Hal and Frank at Los Angeles and the Naval School at Lima, but no one heard us.

Then Torstein sent out a CQ-message: that is to say, he called all the stations in the world which could hear us on our special amateur wave-length.

That was of some use. Now a faint voice out in the ether began to call us slowly. We called again and said that we heard him. Then the slow voice out in the ether said:

"My name is Paul, I live in Colorado; what is your name and where do you live?"

This was a wireless fan. Torstein seized the key, while we turned the handle, and replied:

"This is the *Kon-Tiki;* we are stranded on a desert island in the Pacific."

Paul did not believe this information at all. He thought it was a wireless fan in the next street pulling his leg, and he did not come on the air again once. We tore our hair in desperation. Here were we, sitting under the palm-tops on a starry night on a desert island, and no one even believed what we said.

Torstein did not give up; he was at the key again sending "all well, all well, all well" unceasingly. We must at all costs stop all this rescue machinery from starting out across the Pacific.

Then we heard, rather faintly, in the receiver:

"If all's well, why worry?"

Then all was quiet in the ether. That was all.

We could have leapt into the air and shaken down all the cocoanuts for sheer desperation, and heaven knows what we should have done if both Rarotonga and good old Hal had not suddenly heard us. Hal wept for delight, he said, at hearing LI2B again. All the racket stopped immediately; we were once more alone and undisturbed on our South Sea island, and turned in, worn out, on our beds of palm leaves.

Next day we took it easy and enjoyed life to the full. Some bathed, others fished, or went out exploring on the reef in search of curious marine creatures, while the most energetic cleared up in camp and made our surroundings pleasant. Out on the point which looked towards the *Kon-Tiki* we dug a hole on the edge of the trees, lined it with leaves, and planted in it a sprouting cocoanut from Peru. A cairn of corals was erected beside it, right opposite the place where the *Kon-Tiki* had run ashore.

The *Kon-Tiki* had been washed still farther in during the night and lay almost dry in a few pools of water, squeezed in among a group of big coral blocks a long way through the reef.

After a thorough baking in the warm sand Erik and Herman were in fine fettle again, and were anxious to go southwards along the reef in the hope of getting over to the large island which lay down there. I warned them more against eels than against sharks, and each of them stuck his long machete knife into his belt. The coral reef is the resort of frightful eels with long poisonous teeth which can easily tear off a man's leg. They wriggle to the attack with lightning rapidity and are the terror of the natives, who are not afraid to swim round a shark.

The two men were able to wade over long stretches of the reef to southward, but there were occasional channels of deeper water running this way and that where they had to jump in and swim. They reached the big island safely and waded ashore. The island, long and narrow and covered with palm forest, ran farther south between sunny beaches under the shelter of the reef.

The two continued right along the island till they came to the southern point. Hence the reef, covered with white foam, ran on southward to other distant islands. They found the wreck of a big ship down there; she had four masts and lay on the shore cut in two. She was an old Spanish sailing vessel which had been loaded with rails, and rusty rails lay scattered all along the reef. They returned along the other side of the island, but did not find so much as a track in the sand.

On the way back across the reef they were continually disturbing curious fish, and were trying to catch some of these when they were suddenly attacked by no fewer than eight large eels. They saw them coming in the clear water and jumped up on to a large coral block, round and under which the eels writhed. The slimy brutes were as thick as a man's calf and speckled green and black like poisonous snakes, with small heads, malignant snake's eyes and teeth an inch long and as sharp as an awl. The men hacked with their machete knives at the little swaying heads which came writhing towards them; they cut the head off one and another was injured. The blood in the sea attracted a whole flock of young blue sharks which attacked the dead and injured eels, while Erik and Herman were able to jump over to another block of coral and get away.

On the same day I was wading in towards the island when something, with a lightning movement, caught hold of my ankle on both sides and held on tight. It was a cuttle-fish. It was not large, but it was a horrible feeling to have the cold griping arms about one's limb and to exchange looks with the evil little eyes in the bluish red, beaked sack which constituted the body. I jerked in my foot as hard as I could, and the squid, which was barely three feet long, followed it without letting go. It must have been the bandage on my foot which attracted it. I dragged myself in jerks towards the beach with the disgusting carcase hanging on to my foot. Only when I reached the edge of the dry sand did it let go and retreat slowly through the shallow water, with arms outstretched and eyes directed shoreward, as though ready for a new attack if I wanted one. When I threw a few lumps of coral at it it darted away.

Our various experiences out on the reef only added a spice to our heavenly existence on the island within. But we could not spend all our lives there, and we must begin to think about how we should get back to the outer world. After a week the *Kon-Tiki* had bumped her way in to the middle of the reef, where she lay stuck fast on dry land. The great logs had pushed away and broken off large slabs of coral in the effort to force their way forward to the lagoon, but now the wooden raft lay immovable, and all our pulling and all our pushing were equally unavailing. If we could only get the wreck into the lagoon we could always splice the mast and rig her sufficiently to be able to sail with the wind across the friendly lagoon and see what we found on the other side. If any of the islands were inhabited, it must be that which lay along the horizon away in the west, where the atoll turned its façade towards the lee side.

The days passed.

Then one morning some of the fellows came tearing up and said they had seen a white sail on the lagoon. From up among the palm-trunks we could see a tiny speck which was curiously white against the opal-blue lagoon. It was evidently a sail close to land on the other side. We could see that it was tacking. Soon another appeared.

They grew in size as the morning went on, and came nearer. They came straight towards us. We hoisted the French flag on a palm tree and waved our own Norwegian flag on a pole. One of the sails was now so near that we could see that it belonged to a Polynesian outrigger canoe. The rig was of more recent type. Two brown figures stood on board gazing at us. We waved. They waved back and sailed straight in on to the shallows.

"*Ia ora na,*" we greeted them in Polynesian.

"*Ia ora na,*" they shouted back in chorus, and one jumped out and dragged his canoe after him as he came wading over the sandy shallows straight towards us.

The two men had white men's clothes, but brown men's bodies. They were bare-legged, well-built, and wore home-made straw hats to protect them from the sun. They landed and approached us rather uncertainly, but when we smiled and shook hands with them in turn, they beamed on us with rows of pearly teeth which said more than words.

Our Polynesian greeting had astonished and encouraged the two canoers in exactly the same way as we ourselves had been deceived when their kinsman off Angatau had called out "good night", and they reeled off a long rhapsody in Polynesian before they realised that their outpourings were going wide of the mark. Then they had nothing more to say, but giggled amiably and pointed to the other canoe which was approaching.

There were three men in this, and when they waded ashore and greeted us, it appeared that one of them could talk a little French. We learned that there was a native village on one of the islands across the lagoon, and from it the Polynesians had seen our fire several nights earlier. Now there was only one single passage leading in through the Raroia reef to the circle of islands round the lagoon, and as this passage ran right past the village, no one could approach these islands inside the reef without being seen by the inhabitants of the village. The old people in the village, therefore, had come to the conclusion that the light they saw on the reef to eastward could not be the work of men, but must be something supernatural. This had quenched in them all desire to go across and see for themselves. But then part of a box had come drifting across the lagoon, and on it some signs were painted. Two of the natives, who had been in Tahiti and learnt the alphabet, had deciphered the inscription and read TIKI in big black letters on the slab of wood. Then there was no longer any doubt that there were ghosts on the reef, for Tiki was the long dead founder of their own race, they all knew that. But then tinned bread, cigarettes, cocoa, and a box with an old shoe in it, came drifting across the lagoon. Now they all realised that there had been a shipwreck on the eastern side of the reef, and the chief sent out two canoes to search for the survivors whose fire they had seen on the island.

Urged on by the others, the brown man who spoke French asked why the slab of wood that drifted across the lagoon had "Tiki" on it. We explained that "Kon-Tiki" was on all our equipment, and that it was the name of the vessel in which we had come.

Our new friends were loud in their astonishment when they heard that all on board had been saved when the vessel stranded, and that the flattened wreck out on the reef was actually the craft in which we had come. They wanted to put us all into the canoes at once and take us across to the village. We thanked them and refused, as we wanted to stay till we had got the *Kon-Tiki* off the reef. They looked aghast at the flat contraption out on the reef; surely we could not dream of getting that collapsed hull afloat again! Finally the spokesman said emphatically that we must go with them; the chief had given them strict orders not to return without us.

We then decided that one of us should go with the natives as envoy to the chief, and should then come back and report to us on the conditions on the other island. We would not let the raft remain on the reef, and could not abandon all the equipment on our little island. Bengt went with the natives. The two canoes were pushed off from the sand and soon disappeared westward with a fair wind.

Next day the horizon swarmed with white sails. Now, it seemed, the natives were coming to fetch us with all the craft they had.

The whole convoy tacked across towards us, and when they came near we saw our good friend Bengt waving his hat in the first canoe, surrounded by brown figures. He shouted to us that the chief himself was with him, and we formed up respectfully down on the beach where they were wading ashore.

Bengt presented us to the chief with great ceremony. The chief's name, Bengt said, was Tepiuraiarii Teriifaatau, but he would understand whom we meant if we called him Teka. We did call him Teka.

The chief Teka was a tall slender Polynesian with uncommonly intelligent eyes. He was an important person, a descendant of the old royal line in Tahiti, and was chief of both the Raroia and the Takume islands. He had been to school in Tahiti, so that he spoke French and could both read and write. He told me that the capital of Norway was called Christiania, and asked if I knew Bing Crosby. He also told us that only three foreign vessels had called at Raroia in the last ten years, but that the village was visited several times a year by the native copra schooner from Tahiti, which brought merchandise and took away cocoanut kernels. They had been expecting the schooner for some weeks now, so she might come at any time.

Bengt's report, summarised, was that there was neither school, wireless nor any white men on Raroia, but that the 120 Polynesians in the village had done all they could to make us comfortable there, and had prepared a great reception for us when we came over.

The chief's first request was to see the boat which had brought us ashore on the reef alive. We waded out towards the *Kon-Tiki* with a string of natives after us. When we drew near, the natives suddenly stopped and uttered loud exclamations, all talking at once. We could now see the logs of the *Kon-Tiki* plainly, and one of the natives burst out:

"That's not a boat, it's a *pae-pae!*"

"*Pae-pae!*" they all repeated in chorus.

They splashed out across the reef at a gallop and clambered up on to the *Kon-Tiki*. They scrambled about everywhere like excited children, felt the logs, the bamboo plaiting and the ropes. The chief was in as high spirits as the others; he came back and repeated with an inquiring expression:

"The *Tiki* isn't a boat, she's a *pae-pae*."

Pae-pae is the Polynesian word for "raft" and "platform", and on Easter Island it is also the word used for the natives' canoes. The chief told us that such pae-paes no longer existed, but that the oldest men in the village could relate old traditions of pae-paes. They all outshouted one another in admiration for the great balsa logs, but they turned up their noses at the ropes. Ropes like that did not last many months, in salt water and sun. They showed us with pride the lashings on their own outriggers; they had plaited them themselves of cocoanut hemp, and such ropes remained just as good for five years at sea.

When we waded back to our little island, it was named Fenua

o

Kon-Tiki, or Kon-Tiki Island. This was a name we could all pronounce, but our brown friends had a hard job trying to pronounce our short Nordic Christian names. They were delighted when I said they could call me Terai Mateata, for the great chief in Tahiti had given me that name when adopting me as his "son" the first time I was in those parts.

The natives brought out fowls and eggs and breadfruit from the canoes, while others speared big fish in the lagoon with three-pronged spears, and we had a feast round the camp fire. We had to narrate all our experiences with the *pae-pae* at sea, and they wanted to hear about the whale shark again and again. And every time we came to the point at which Erik rammed the harpoon into its skull, they uttered the same cries of excitement. They recognised at once every single fish of which we showed them sketches, and promptly gave us the names in Polynesian. But they had never seen or heard of the whale shark or the *Gempylus*.

When the evening came, we turned on the wireless, to the great delight of the whole assemblage. Church music was most to their taste until, to our astonishment, we picked up real hula music from America. Then the liveliest of them began to wriggle with their arms curved over their heads, and soon the whole company sprang up on their haunches and danced the hula-hula in time with the music. When night came, all camped round a fire on the beach. It was as much of an adventure to the natives as it was to us.

When we awoke next morning, they were already up and frying newly caught fish, while six freshly opened cocoanut shells stood ready for us to quench our morning thirst.

The reef was thundering more than usual that day; the wind had increased in strength, and the surf was whipping high into the air out there behind the wreck.

"The *Tiki*'ll come in to-day," said the chief, pointing to the wreck. "There'll be a high tide."

About eleven o'clock the water began to flow past us into the lagoon. The lagoon began to fill like a big basin, and the water rose all round the island. Later in the day the real inflow from the sea came. The water came rolling in terrace after terrace, and more and more of the reef sank below the surface of the sea. The masses of water rolled forward along both sides of the island. They tore away large coral blocks and dug up great sandbanks which disappeared like flour before the wind, while others were built up. Loose bamboos from the wreck came sailing past us, and the *Kon-Tiki* began to move. Everything that was lying along the beach had to be carried up into the interior of the island so that it might not be caught by the tide. Soon only the highest stones on the reef were visible, and all the beaches round our island had gone, while the water flowed up towards the herbage of the pancake island. This was creepy. It looked as if the whole sea was invading us. The *Kon-Tiki* swung right round and drifted until she was caught by some other coral blocks.

The natives flung themselves into the water and swam and waded through the eddies till, moving from bank to bank, they reached the raft. Knut and Erik followed. Ropes lay ready on board the raft, and when she rolled the last coral blocks over and broke loose from the reef, the natives jumped overboard and tried to hold her. They did not know the *Kon-Tiki* and her ungovernable urge to push on westward; so they were towed along helplessly with her, and she was soon moving at a good speed right across the reef and into the lagoon. She became slightly at a loss when she reached quieter water, and seemed to be looking round as though to obtain a survey of further possibilities. Before she began to move again, and discovered the exit across the lagoon, the natives had already succeeded in getting the end of the rope round a palm on land. And there the *Kon-Tiki* hung, tied up fast in the lagoon. The craft that went over land and water had made her way across the barricade and into the lagoon in the interior of Raroia.

With inspiring war-cries, to which *"ke-ke-te-huru-huru"* formed an animating refrain, we hauled the *Kon-Tiki* by our combined efforts in to the shore of the island of her own name. The tide reached a point four feet above normal high water. We had thought the whole island was going to disappear.

The wind-whipped waves were breaking all over the lagoon, and we could not get much of our equipment into the narrow, wet canoes. The natives had to get back to the village in a hurry, and Bengt and Herman went with them to see to a small boy who lay dying in a hut in the village. The boy had an abscess on his head, and we had penicillin.

Next day we four were alone on Kon-Tiki Island. The east wind was now so strong that the natives could not come across the lagoon, which was studded with sharp coral formations and shoals. The tide, which had somewhat receded, flowed in again fiercely, in long rushing step formations.

Next day it was quieter again. We were now able to dive under the *Kon-Tiki* and ascertain that the nine logs were intact, even if the reef had planed an inch or two off the bottom. The cordage lay so deep in its grooves that only four of the numerous ropes had been cut across by the corals. We set about clearing up on board. Our proud vessel looked better when the mess had been removed from the deck, the cabin pulled out again like a concertina, and the mast spliced and set upright.

In the course of the day the sails appeared on the horizon again; the natives were coming to fetch us and the rest of the cargo. Herman and Bengt were with them, and they told us that the natives had prepared great festivities in the village. When we got over to the other island, we must not leave the canoes till the chief himself had indicated that we might do so.

We ran across the lagoon, which here was seven miles wide, before a fresh breeze. It was with real sorrow that we saw the familiar palms on Kon-Tiki Island waving us good-bye, as they changed into a clump and shrank into one small undefinable island like all the others along the eastern reef. But ahead of us larger islands were broadening out. And on one of them we saw a jetty, and smoke rising from huts among the palm-trunks.

The village looked quite dead; not a soul was to be seen. What was brewing now? Down on the beach, behind a jetty of coral blocks, stood two solitary figures, one tall and thin and one big and stout as a barrel. As we came in, we saluted them both. They were the chief Teka and the vice-chief Tupuhoe.

We all fell for Tupuhoe's broad hearty smile. Teka was a clear brain and a diplomat, but Tupuhoe was a pure child of nature and a sterling fellow, with a humour and primitive force the like of which one meets but rarely. With his powerful body and kingly features, he was exactly what one expects a Polynesian chief to be. Tupuhoe was, indeed, the real chief on the island, but Teka had gradually acquired the supreme position because he could speak French and count and write, so that the village was not cheated when the schooner came from Tahiti to fetch copra.

Teka explained that we were to march together up to the meeting-house in the village, and when all the boys had come ashore we set off thither in ceremonial procession, Herman first with the flag waving on a harpoon shaft, and then I myself between the two chiefs.

The village bore obvious marks of the copra trade with Tahiti; both planks and corrugated iron had been imported in the schooner. While some huts were built in a picturesque old-fashioned style, with twigs and plaited palm leaves, others were knocked together with nails and planks as small tropical bungalows. A large house built of planks, standing alone among the palms, was the new village meeting-house; there we six whites were to stay. We marched in with the flag by a small back door and out on to a broad flight of steps before the façade. Before us in the square stood everyone in the village who could walk or crawl—women and children, old and young. All were intensely serious; even our cheerful friends from Kon-Tiki Island stood drawn up among the others and did not give us a sign of recognition.

When we had all come out on to the steps, the whole assembly opened their mouths simultaneously and joined in singing—the Marseillaise! Teka, who knew the words, led the singing, and it went fairly well in spite of a few old women getting stuck up on the high notes. They had been training hard for this. The French and Norwegian flags were hoisted in front of the steps, and this ended the official reception by the chief Teka; he retired quietly into the background, and now stout Tupuhoe sprang forward and became master of the ceremonies. Tupuhoe gave a quick sign, on which the whole assembly burst into a new song. This time it went better, for the tune was composed by themselves and the words too, in their own language, and sing their own hula they could. The melody was so fascinating, in all its touching simplicity, that we felt a tingling down our backs as the South Sea came roaring towards us. A few individuals led the singing and the whole choir joined in regularly; there were variations in the melody, though the words were always the same:

"Good day, Terai Mateata and your men, who have come across the sea on a *pae-pae* to us on Raroia; yes, good day, may you remain long among us and share memories with us so that we can always be together, even when you go away to a far land. Good day."

We had to ask them to sing the song over again, and more and more life came into the whole assembly as they began to feel less constrained. Then Tupuhoe asked me to say a few words to the people as to why we had come across the sea on a *pae-pae*; they had all been counting on this. I was to speak in French, and Teka would translate bit by bit.

It was an uneducated, but highly intelligent gathering of brown people that stood waiting for me to speak. I told them that I had been among their kinsmen out here in the South Sea islands before, and that I had heard of their first chief, Tiki, who had brought their forefathers out to the islands from a mysterious country whose whereabouts no one knew any longer. But in a distant land called Peru, I said, a mighty chief had once ruled whose name was Tiki. The people called him Kon-Tiki, or Sun-Tiki, because he said he was descended from the sun. Tiki and a number of followers had at last disappeared from their country on big pae-paes; therefore we six thought that he was the same Tiki who had come to those islands. As nobody would believe that a *pae-pae* could make the voyage across the sea, we ourselves had set out from Peru on a *pae-pae*, and here we were, so it could be done.

When the little speech was translated by Teka, Tupuhoe was all fire and flame, and sprang forward in front of the assembly in a kind of ecstasy. He rumbled away in Polynesian, flung out his arms, pointed to heaven and us, and in his flood of speech constantly repeated the word Tiki. He talked so fast that it was impossible to follow the thread of what he said, but the whole assembly swallowed every word and was visibly excited. Teka, on the contrary, looked quite embarrassed when he had to translate.

Tupuhoe had said that his father and grandfather, and his fathers before him, had told of Tiki, and had said that Tiki was their first chief who was now in heaven. But then the white men came and said that the traditions of their ancestors were lies. Tiki had never existed. He was not in heaven at all, for Jehovah was there. Tiki was a heathen god, and they must not believe in him any longer. But now we six had come to them across the sea on a *pae-pae*. We were the first whites who had admitted that their fathers had spoken the truth. Tiki had lived, he had been real, but now he was dead and in heaven.

Horrified at the thought of upsetting the missionaries' work, I had to hurry forward and explain that Tiki had lived, that was sure and certain, and now he was dead. But whether he was in heaven or in hell to-day only Jehovah knew, for Jehovah was in heaven, while Tiki himself had been a mortal man, a great chief like Teka and Tupuhoe, perhaps still greater.

This produced both cheerfulness and contentment among the brown men, and the nodding and mumbling among them showed clearly that the explanation had fallen on good soil. Tiki had lived, that was the main thing. If he was in hell now no one was any the worse for it but himself; on the contrary, Tupuhoe suggested, perhaps it increased the chances of seeing him again.

Three old men pushed forward and wanted to shake hands with us. There was no doubt that it was they who had kept the memories of Tiki alive among the population, and the chief told us that one of the old men knew an immense number of traditions and historical ballads from his forefathers' time. I asked the old man if there was in the traditions any hint of the direction from which Tiki had come. No, none of the old men could remember having heard that. But after long and careful reflection the oldest of the three said that Tiki had with him a near relation who was called Maui, and in the ballad of Maui it was said that he came to the islands from Pura, and *pura* was the word for the part of the sky where the sun rose. If Maui had come from Pura, the old man said, Tiki had no doubt come from the same place, and we six on the *pae-pae* had also come from *pura,* that was sure enough.

I told the brown men that on a lonely island nearer to Easter Island, called Mangareva, the population had never learnt the use of canoes, and had continued to use big *pae-paes* at sea right down to our own time. This the old men did not know, but they knew that their forefathers also had used big *pae-paes*, but these had gradually gone quite out of use, and now they had nothing but the name and traditions left. In really ancient times they had been called *rongo-rongo*, the oldest man said, but that was a word which no longer existed in the language. But *rongo-rongo* are mentioned in the most ancient legends.

This name was interesting, for Rongo—on certain islands pronounced Lono—was the name of one of the Polynesians' best known legendary ancestors. He was expressly described as white and fair-haired. When Captain Cook first came to Hawaii he was received with open arms by the islanders, because they thought he was their white kinsman Rongo, who, after an absence of generations, had come back from their ancestors' homeland in his big sailing ship. And on Easter Island the word *rongo-rongo* was the designation for the mysterious hieroglyphs whose secret was lost with the last "long-ears" who could write!

While the old men wanted to discuss Tiki and *rongo-rongo*, the young ones wanted to hear about the whale shark and the voyage across the sea. But the food was waiting, and Teka was tired of interpreting.

Now the whole village was allowed to come up and shake hands with each of us. The men mumbled "*ia-ora-na*" and almost shook our hands out of joint, while the girls squirmed forward and greeted us coquettishly and shyly, and the old women babbled and cackled and pointed to our beards and the colour of our skins. Friendliness beamed from every single face, so it was quite immaterial that there was a mighty linguistic confusion. If they said something incomprehensible to us in Polynesian we gave them tit for tat in Norwegian, and we had the greatest fun together. The first native word we all learned was the word for "like", and when, moreover, one could point to what one liked and count on getting it at once, it was all very simple. If one wrinkled one's nose when "like" was said, it meant "don't like", and on this basis we could get along pretty well.

As soon as we had become acquainted with the 127 inhabitants of the village, a long table was laid for the two chiefs and us six, and the village girls came round bearing the most delicious dishes. While some arranged the table, others came and hung plaited wreaths of flowers round our necks, and smaller wreaths were placed round our heads. These exhaled a languishing scent and were cool and refreshing in the heat. And so a feast of welcome began which did not end till we left the island weeks after. Our eyes opened wide and our mouths watered, for the tables were loaded with roast sucking pigs, chickens, roast ducks, fresh lobsters, Polynesian fish dishes, breadfruit, papaya and cocoanut milk. And while we attacked the dishes we were entertained by the crowd singing hula songs, while young girls danced round the table.

The boys laughed and thoroughly enjoyed themselves, each of us looking more absurd than the next as we sat and gorged like starving men, with flowing beards and wreaths of flowers in our hair. The two chiefs were enjoying life as unconcealedly as ourselves.

After the meal there was hula dancing on a grand scale. The village wanted to show us the local folk dances. While we six and Teka and Tupuhoe were each given a stool in the stalls, two guitar players advanced, squatted down and began to strum real South Sea melodies. Two ranks of dancing men and women, with rustling skirts of palm leaves round their hips, came gliding and wriggling forward through the ring of spectators who squatted and sang. They had a lively and spirited leading singer in a luxuriantly fat *vahine* who had had one arm bitten off by a shark. To begin with the dancers seemed a little theatrical and nervous, but when they saw that the white men from the *pae-pae* did not turn up their noses at their grandparents' folk dances, the dancing became more and more animated. Some of the older people joined in; they had a splendid rhythm and could dance dances which were certainly no longer in ordinary use. And as the sun sank into the Pacific, the dancing under the palm trees became livelier and livelier, and the applause of the spectators more and more spontaneous. They had forgotten that we who sat watching them were six strangers; we were now six of their own people, enjoying ourselves with them.

The repertory was endless; one fascinating display followed another. Finally a crowd of young men squatted down in a close ring just in front of us, and at a sign from Tupuhoe began to beat time rhythmically on the ground with the palms of their hands. First slowly, then more quickly, and the rhythm grew more and more perfect when a drummer suddenly joined in and accompanied them, beating at a furious pace with two sticks on a bone-dry hollowed block of wood which emitted a sharp, intense sound. When the rhythm reached the desired degree of animation, the singing began, and suddenly a hula girl with a wreath of flowers round her neck and flowers behind one ear leapt into the ring. She kept time to the music with bare feet and bent knees, swaying rhythmically at the hips and curving her arms above her head in true Polynesian style. She danced splendidly, and soon the whole assembly were beating time with their hands. Another girl leapt into the ring, and after her another. They moved with incredible suppleness in perfect rhythm, gliding round one another in the dance like graceful shadows. The dull beating of hands on the ground, the singing and the cheerful wooden drum increased their tempo in time, faster and faster, and the dance grew wilder and wilder while the spectators howled and clapped in perfect rhythm.

This was the South Seas life as the old days had known it. The stars twinkled and the palms waved. The night was mild and long and full of the scent of flowers and the song of crickets. Tupuhoe beamed and slapped me on the shoulder.

"*Maitai?*" he asked.

"Yes, *maitai*," I replied.

"*Maitai?*" he asked all the others.

"*Maitai*," they all replied emphatically, and they all really meant it.

"*Maitai*," Tupuhoe nodded, pointing to himself; he too was enjoying himself now.

Even Teka thought it was a very good feast; it was the first time white men had been present at their dances on Raroia, he said. Faster and faster, faster and faster went the rolls of the drums, the clapping, singing, and dancing. Now one of the girl dancers ceased to move round the ring, and remained on the same spot, performing a wriggling dance at a terrific tempo with her arms stretched out towards Herman. Herman sniggered behind his beard; he did not quite know how to take it.

"Be a good sport," I whispered; "you're a good dancer."

And to the boundless delight of the crowd, Herman sprang into the ring and, half crouching, tackled all the difficult wriggling movements of the hula. The jubilation was unbounded. Soon Bengt and Torstein leapt into the dance, working till the perspiration streamed down their faces to keep up with the tempo, which rose and rose to a furious pace, till the drum alone was beating in one prolonged drone and the three real hula dancers quivering in time like aspen leaves till they sank down in the finale and the drum-beats ceased abruptly.

Now the evening was ours. There was no end to the enthusiasm.

The next item on the programme was the bird dance, which was one of the oldest ceremonies on Raroia. Men and women in two ranks jumped forward in a rhythmic dance, imitating flocks of birds being led by a dance leader. The dance leader had the title of chief of the birds and performed curious manoeuvres without actually joining in the dance. When the dance was over, Tupuhoe explained that it had been performed in honour of the raft, and would now be repeated, but the dance leader would be relieved by myself. As the dance leader's main task appeared to me to consist in uttering wild howls and hopping round on his haunches, wriggling his backside and waving his hands over his head, I pulled the wreath of flowers well down over my head

and marched out into the arena. While I was curving myself in
the dance I saw old Tupuhoe laughing till he nearly fell off his
stool, and the music grew feeble because the singers and players
followed Tupuhoe's example.

Now everyone wanted to dance, old and young alike, and soon
the drummer and earth-beaters were there again, giving the lead
to a fiery hula-hula dance. First the hula girls sprang into the
ring and started the dance at a tempo that grew wilder and wilder,
and then we were invited to dance in turn, while more and more
men and women followed, stamping and writhing along, faster
and faster.

But Erik could not be made to stir. The draughts and damp
on board the raft had revived his vanished lumbago, and he sat
like an old yacht skipper, stiff and bearded, puffing at his pipe.
He would not be moved by the hula girls who tried to lure him
into the arena. He had put on a pair of wide sheepskin trousers
he had worn at nights in the coldest spells in the Humboldt
Current, and sitting under the palms with his big beard, body
bare to the waist, and sheepskin breeches he was a faithful copy
of Robinson Crusoe. One pretty girl after another tried to
ingratiate herself, but in vain. He only sat gravely puffing his
pipe, with the wreath of flowers in his bushy hair.

Then a well-developed matron with powerful muscles entered
the arena, executed a few more or less graceful hula steps, and
then marched determinedly towards Erik. He looked alarmed,
but the amazon smiled as ingratiatingly as a pat of butter, caught
him resolutely by the arm and pulled him off his stool. Erik's
comic pair of breeches had the sheep's wool inside and the skin
outside, and it had a rent behind so that a white spot of wool
stuck out like a rabbit's scut. Erik followed most reluctantly,
and limped into the ring with his pipe in one hand and the other
pressed against the spot where his lumbago hurt him. When he
tried to jump round he had to let go of his trousers to save his
wreath which was threatening to fall off, and then, with the
wreath on one side, he had to catch hold of his trousers again,
which were coming down of their own weight. The stout dame
who was hobbling round in the hula in front of him was just as

funny, and tears of laughter trickled down our beards. Soon all
the others who were in the ring stopped, and salvoes of laughter
rang through the palm grove as Hula-Erik and the female heavy-
weight circled gracefully round. At last even they had to stop,
because both singers and musicians had more than they could do
to hold their sides for laughter.

The feast went on till broad daylight, when we were allowed
to have a little pause, after again shaking hands with every one
of the 127. We shook hands with every one of them every
morning and every evening throughout our stay on the island.
Six beds were scraped together from all the huts in the village
and placed side by side along the wall in the meeting-house, and
in these we slept in a row like the seven little dwarfs in the fairy
story with sweet-smelling wreaths of flowers hanging above
our heads.

Next day the boy of six who had an abscess on his head seemed
to be in a bad way. He had a temperature of nearly 106° and the
abscess on the top of his head was as large as a man's fist and
throbbed painfully.

Teka declared that they had lost a number of children in this
way, and that if none of us could do any doctoring the boy had
not many days to live. We had bottles of penicillin in a new
tablet form, but we did not know what dose a small child could
stand. If the boy died under our treatment it might have serious
consequences for all of us.

Knut and Torstein got the wireless out again and slung up an
aerial between the tallest cocoanut palms. When evening came
they got into touch again with our unseen friends Hal and Frank,
sitting in their rooms at home in Los Angeles. Frank got a doctor
on the telephone, and we signalled with the Morse key all the
boy's symptoms and a list of what we had available in our medical
chest. Frank passed on the doctor's reply, and that night we went
off to the hut where little Haumata lay tossing in a fever with
half the village weeping and making a noise about him.

Herman and Knut were to do the doctoring, while the others had
more than enough to do to keep the villagers outside. The mother
became hysterical when we came with a sharp knife and asked

for boiling water. All the hair was shaved off the boy's head and the abscess was opened. The pus squirted up almost to the roof, and several of the natives forced their way in in a state of fury and had to be turned out. It was no joke. When the abscess was evacuated and sterilised, the whole head was bound up and we began the penicillin cure. For two days and nights the boy was treated every four hours while the fever was at its maximum, and the abscess was kept open. And each evening the doctor in Los Angeles was consulted. Then the boy's temperature fell suddenly, the pus was replaced by plasma which was to be allowed to heal up, and the boy was beaming and wanting to look at pictures from the white man's strange world where there were motor-cars and cows and houses with several floors.

A week later Haumata was playing on the beach with the other children, his head bound up in a big bandage, which he was soon allowed to take off.

When this had gone well, there was no end to the maladies which cropped up in the village. Toothache and gastric trouble were everywhere, and both old and young had boils in one place or another. We referred the patients to Dr. Knut and Dr. Herman, who ordered diets and emptied the medicine chest of pills and ointments. Some were cured and none became worse, and when the medicine chest was empty, we made cocoa and oatmeal porridge, which were admirably efficacious with hysterical women.

We had not been among our brown admirers for many days before the festivities culminated in a fresh ceremony. We were to be adopted as citizens of Raroia and receive Polynesian names. I myself might no longer be Terai Mateata; I could be called that in Tahiti, but not here, among them.

Six stools were placed for us in the middle of the square, and the whole village was out early to get good places in the circle round. Teka sat solemnly among them; he was chief all right, but not where old local ceremonies were concerned. Then Tupuhoe took over.

All sat waiting, silent and profoundly serious, while big fat Tupuhoe approached solemnly and slowly with his stout knotted stick. He was conscious of the solemnity of the moment, and the eyes of all were upon him as he came up, deep in thought, and took up his position in front of us six. He was the born chief, a brilliant speaker and actor.

He turned to the chief singers, drummers and dance leaders, pointed at them in turn with his knotted stick, and gave them curt orders in low, measured tones. Then he turned to us again, and suddenly opened his great eyes wide, so that the large white eyeballs shone as bright as the teeth in his expressive copper-brown face. He raised the knotted stick and, the words streaming from his lips like peas from a bag, he recited ancient rituals which none but the oldest people understood, because they were in an old forgotten dialect.

Then he told us, with Teka as interpreter, that Tikaroa was the name of the first king who had established himself on the island, and that he had reigned over this same atoll from north to south, from east to west, and up into the sky above men's heads.

While the whole choir joined in the old ballad about King Tikaroa, Tupuhoe laid his great hand on my chest and, turning to the audience, said that he was naming me Varoa Tikaroa, or Tikaroa's Spirit.

When the song died away, it was the turn of Herman and Bengt. They had the big brown hand laid upon their chests in turn, and received the names Tupuhoe-Itetahua and Topakino. These were the names of the two old-time heroes who had fought a sea monster and killed it at the entrance to the Raroia reef.

The drummer delivered a few vigorous rolls, and two robust men sprang forward with knotted up loin-cloths, and a long spear in each hand. They broke into a march in double quick time, with their knees raised to their chests and their spears pointing upwards, and turning their heads from side to side. At a fresh beat of the drum they leapt into the air and, in perfect rhythm, began a ceremonial battle in the purest ballet style. The whole thing was short and swift, and represented the heroes' fight with the sea monster. Then Torstein was named with song and ceremony; he was called Maroake, after a former king in the present village, and Erik and Knut received the names of Tane-Matarau and Tefaunui, after two navigators and sea heroes of the past. The long monotonous recitation which accompanied their naming was delivered at breakneck speed and with a continuous flow of words whose incredible rapidity was calculated both to impress and amuse.

The ceremony was over. Once more there were white and bearded chiefs among the Polynesian people on Raroia. Two ranks of male and female dancers came forward in plaited straw skirts with swaying bast crowns on their heads. They danced forward to us and transferred the crowns from their own heads to ours; we had rustling straw skirts put round our waists; and the festivities continued.

One night the flower-clad wireless operators got into touch with the radio amateur on Rarotonga, who passed on a message to us from Tahiti. It was a cordial welcome from the governor of the French Pacific colonies.

On instructions from Paris he had sent the Government schooner *Tamara* to fetch us to Tahiti, so we should not have to wait for the uncertain arrival of the copra schooner. Tahiti was the central point of the French colonies, and the only island which had contact with the world in general. We should have to go via Tahiti to get the regular boat home to our own world.

The festivities continued on Raroia. One night some queer howls were heard from out at sea, and look-out men came down from the palm-tops and reported that a vessel was lying at the entrance to the lagoon. We ran through the palm forest and down to the beach on the lee side. Here we looked out over the sea in the opposite direction to that from which we had come. There were much smaller breakers on this side, which lay under the shelter of the entire atoll and the reef.

Just outside the entrance to the lagoon we saw the lights of a vessel. It was clear and starry, and we saw the outlines of a broad-beamed schooner with two masts. Was this the governor's ship which was coming for us? Why did she not come in?

The natives grew more and more fidgety. Now we too saw.

The vessel had a heavy list and threatened to capsize. She was aground on an invisible coral reef under the surface.

Torstein got hold of a light and signalled:

"*Quel bateau?*"

"*Maoae*", it was flashed back.

The *Maoae* was the copra schooner which ran between the islands. She was on her way to Raroia to fetch copra. There was a Polynesian captain and crew on board, and they knew the reefs inside out. But the current was treacherous in darkness. It was lucky that the schooner lay under the lee of the island and that the weather was quiet, but the current out of the lagoon was rather dangerous. The list of the *Maoae* became heavier and heavier, and the crew took to the boat. Strong ropes were made fast to her mastheads and rowed in to the land, where the natives fastened them round cocoanut palms to prevent the schooner from capsizing. The crew, with other ropes, stationed themselves off the opening in the reef in their boat, in the hope of rowing the *Maoae* off when the tidal current ran out of the lagoon. The population of the village launched all their canoes and set out to salve the cargo of copra. There were ninety tons of valuable copra on board. Load after load of sacks of copra was transferred from the rolling schooner and brought on to dry land.

At high water the *Maoae* was still aground, bumping and rolling against the corals until she sprang a leak. When day broke she was lying in a worse position on the reef than ever. The crew could do nothing; it was useless to try to haul the heavy 150-tons schooner off the reef with her own boat and the canoes. If she continued to lie bumping where she was, she would knock herself to pieces, and if the weather changed she would be lifted in by the suction and be a total loss in the surf which beat against the atoll.

The *Maoae* had no wireless, but we had. At the same time, it was impossible to get a salvage vessel from Tahiti until the *Maoae* would have had ample time to roll herself into wreckage. But for the second time that month the Raroia reef was baulked of its prey.

About noon the same day the schooner *Tamara* came in sight

P

on the horizon to westward. She had been sent to fetch us from Raroia, and those on board were not a little astonished when they saw, instead of a raft, the two masts of a large schooner lying and rolling helplessly on the reef.

On board the *Tamara* were the French administrator of the Tuamotu and Tubuai groups, M. Frédéric Ahnne, whom the Governor had sent with the vessel from Tahiti to meet us. There were also a French cinema photographer and a French telegraphist on board, but the captain and crew were Polynesian. M. Ahnne himself had been born in Tahiti of French parents, and was a splendid seaman. He took over the command of the vessel with the consent of the Tahitian captain, who was delighted to be freed from the responsibility in those dangerous waters. While the *Tamara* was avoiding a myriad of submerged reefs and eddies, stout hawsers were stretched between the two schooners, and M. Ahnne began his skilful and dangerous evolutions, while the tide threatened to drag both vessels on to the same coral bank.

At high tide the *Maoae* came off the reef, and the *Tamara* towed her out into deep water. But now water poured through the hull of the *Maoae*, and she had to be hauled with all speed on to the shallows in the lagoon. For three days the *Maoae* lay off the village in a sinking condition, with all pumps going day and night. The best pearl divers among our friends on the island went down with lead plates and nails and stopped the worst leaks, so that the *Maoae* could be escorted by the *Tamara* to the dockyard in Tahiti, with her pumps working.

When the *Maoae* was ready to be escorted, M. Ahnne manoeuvred the *Tamara* between the coral shallows in the lagoons and across to Kon-Tiki Island. The raft was taken in tow, and then he set his course back to the opening with the *Kon-Tiki* in tow and the *Maoae* so close behind that the crew could be taken off if the leaks got the upper hand out at sea.

Our farewell to Raroia was more than sad. Everyone who could walk and crawl was down on the jetty, playing and singing our favourite tunes as the ship's boat took us out to the *Tamara*.

Tupuhoe bulked large in the centre, holding little Haumata by the hand. Haumata was crying, and tears trickled down the cheeks of the potent chief. There was not a dry eye on the jetty, but they kept the singing and music going long, long after the breakers from the reef drowned all other sounds in our ears.

Those faithful souls who stood on the jetty singing were losing six friends. We who stood mute at the *Tamara*'s rail, till the jetty was hidden by the palms and the palms sank into the sea, were losing 127. We still heard the strange music with the inner ear:

"—and share memories with us so that we can always be together, even when you go away to a far land. Good day."

Four days later Tahiti rose out of the sea. Not like a string of pearls with palm-tufts. As wild jagged blue mountains flung skyward, with wisps of cloud like wreaths round the peaks.

As we gradually approached, the blue mountains showed green slopes. Green upon green, the lush vegetation of the South rolled down over rust-red hills and cliffs, till they plunged down into deep ravines and valleys running out towards the sea. And when the coast came near, we saw slender palms standing close-packed up all the valleys and all along the coast behind a golden beach. Tahiti was built by old volcanoes. They were dead now, and the coral polyps had slung their protecting reef about the island so that the sea could not erode it.

Early one morning we headed through an opening in the reef into the harbour of Papeete. Before us lay church spires and red roofs half hidden by the foliage of giant trees and palm-tops. Papeete was the capital of Tahiti, the only town in French Oceania. It was a city of pleasure, the seat of government and the centre of all traffic in the eastern Pacific.

When we came into the harbour the population of Tahiti stood waiting, packed tight like a gaily-coloured living wall. News spreads like the wind in Tahiti, and the *pae-pae* which had come from America was something everyone wanted to see.

The *Kon-Tiki* was given the place of honour alongside the shore promenade; the Mayor of Papeete welcomed us, and a little Polynesian girl presented us with an enormous wheel of

Tahitian wild flowers on behalf of the Polynesian Society. Then young girls came forward and hung sweet-smelling white wreaths of flowers round our necks as a welcome to Tahiti, the pearl of the South Seas.

There was one particular face I was looking for in the multitude, that of my old adoptive father in Tahiti, the chief Teriieroo, head of the seventeen native chiefs on the island. He was not missing. Big and bulky, and as bright and alive as in old days, he emerged from the crowd calling "Terai Mateata!" and beaming all over his broad face. He had become an old man, but he was the same impressive chieftainly figure.

"You come late," he said smiling, "but you come with good news. Your *pae-pae* has in truth brought blue sky (*terai mateata*) to Tahiti, for now we know where our fathers came from."

There was a reception at the governor's palace and a party at the Town Hall, and invitations poured in from every corner of the hospitable island.

As in former days, a great feast was given by the chief Teriieroo at his house in the Papeno valley which I knew so well, and as Raroia was not Tahiti, there was a new ceremony at which Tahitian names were given to those who had none before.

Those were carefree days under sun and drifting clouds. We bathed in the lagoon, climbed in the mountains, and danced the hula on the grass under the palms. The days passed and became weeks. It seemed as if the weeks would become months before a ship came which could take us home to the duties that awaited us.

Then came a message from Norway saying that Lars Christensen had ordered the 4,000-tonner *Thor I* to proceed from Samoa to Tahiti to pick up the expedition and take it to America.

Early one morning the big Norwegian steamer glided into Papeete harbour, and the *Kon-Tiki* was towed out by a French naval craft to the side of her large compatriot, which swung out a huge iron arm and lifted her small kinsman up on to her deck. Loud blasts of the siren echoed over the palm-clad island. Brown and white people thronged the quay of Papeete and poured on board with farewell gifts and wreaths of flowers. We stood at the rail stretching out our necks like giraffes to get our chins free from the ever-growing load of flowers.

"If you wish yourselves back at Tahiti," the chief Teriieroo cried as the whistle sounded over the island for the last time, "you must throw a wreath out into the lagoon when the boat goes!"

The ropes were cast off, the engines roared, and the propeller whipped the water green as we slid sideways away from the quay.

Soon the red roofs disappeared behind the palms, and the palms were swallowed up in the blue of the mountains which sank like shadows into the Pacific.

Waves were breaking out on the blue sea. We could no longer reach down to them. White trade wind clouds drifted across the blue sky. We were no longer travelling the same way. We were defying Nature now. We were on our way to the twentieth century which lay so far, far away.

But the six of us on deck, standing beside our nine great balsa logs, were all alive. And in the lagoon at Tahiti six white wreaths lay alone, washing in and out, in and out with the wavelets on the beach.

THE END

APPENDIX

My migration theory as such was not proved by the successful outcome of the Kon-Tiki expedition. What we *did* prove was, that the South American balsa raft possesses qualities not previously known to scientists of our time, and that the Pacific islands are located well inside the range of prehistoric craft from Peru. Primitive people are capable of undertaking immense voyages over the open ocean. The distance is not the determining factor in the case of oceanic migrations, but whether the wind and the current have the same general course, day and night—all the year round. The trade winds and the Equatorial Currents are turned westwards by the rotation of the earth, and this rotation has never changed, in the history of mankind.

INDEX

A

Agurto, *see* Alvarez
Ahnne, M. Frédéric, 226
Air Force laboratory, 36
Air Material Command, 29, 32, 37
Alvarez, Captain Agurto Alexis, 48–54
Amazon expedition, 61
Ambjörg, Wilhelm, 26–8
American Military Attaché in Ecuador, 48
Amundsen, Christian, 150
Andes, 41, 45, 48–50, 71, 136–7, 139, 142, 148
Angatau, 171–84, 207
Angelo, 52–3
Antarctic, 31, 77, 166
Ants, 110
Arabia, 16
Army Supply Department, 36
Asia, 18, 134
Atlantis, 16
Australia, 18
Aztecs, 134, 152

B

Bahr, Consul-General, 59, 70
Bajkov, Dr. A. D., 106
Balsa rafts, 23–8, 35, 41, 52–3, 64, 66, 77, 79, 104, 127, 133
Balsa trees, wood, logs : 41–5, 52–7, 64 : then *see Kon-Tiki*
Bamboos, giant, 100
Bandidos, 48–9
Bank of Norway, 25
Barnacles, 110–1, 122
Behre, Professor, 39
Bengt, *see* Danielsson
Berg, Egil, 149
" Big-Ears ", 139
Bird dance, 219
Björn Rörholt, 36, 63
Blue Shark, 87–8, 114, 117, 205
Blue whale, 108–9
Bonito, 88, 101, 120, 122, 157–9
Boobies, 165–6
Bottle gourd, 100, 103–4
British Columbia, 21
British Military Mission in Washington, 39
Brooklyn, 25
Brown shark, 114
Bryhn, Consul-General, 48–9
Buchwald, Don Frederico von, 44, 52–5 ; Don Gustavo von, 44

Bustamante y Rivero, Don Jose (President of Peru), 42, 59–61, 71

C

Cachalot, 109
Callao, 12, 58, 64, 71, 73, 77–8, 110, 188
Canary Islands, 134
Cari, 20
Carl, 23–5
Caucasus, 16
Central America, 84, 104, 133, 134
Centreboards, 66, 98, 120–1, 126–7, 162–3, 173, 186–7
Chicago, university at, 24, 26
Chile, 42
China, 16
Christensen, Lars, 228
Christian Amundsen, 150
Coca plant, 102
Cocoanut, cocoanut palm, 104–5, 173–6, 178–80, 188, 196–9, 201, 218, 221
Cœlenterates, 108
Cohen, Dr. Benjamin, 42
Colossi on Easter Island, 135–40
Columbia University, 39
Columbus, 45, 85, 104
Cook, Captain, 216
Cook Islands, 188
Copepods, 107
Copra, 178, 209, 213, 225
Coquimbo valley, 20
Cuevas, Frank, 149, 188, 203, 221
Currents : Humboldt, 68, 77, 80, 84–5, 100, 107, 117, 148, 221 : South Equatorial, 95, 100, 151, 166 ; cross-currents off Peruvian coast, 78 ; towards Central America, 84 ; round Galapagos Islands, 85, 96
Cuttlefish (squid), 11, 91, 112, 117–20, 147–8, 205

D

Dangerous Archipelago, 165
Danielsson, Bengt, 11–12 ; joins expedition at Lima, 61–2 ; 64, 68–9 ; takes 73 books with him on raft, 70 ; 71, 75, 77–8, 88, 90 ; pursues sea turtle, 96 ; as steward is responsible for rations, 98 ; restricted to special provisions by way of experiment, 99 ; 108, 119, 147, 164, 168, 170–1, 175, 181, 189–90, 193 ; concussion in stranding of raft, 194 ; salves kitchen utensils, 197 ; 198, 200–1 ; goes as envoy to chief on

Raroia, 208–9 ; 211–2 ; dances the hula, 219 ; receives Polynesian name, 223
Diving basket, 121, 154
Dolphin (dorado), 88, 92–4, 96, 110–2, 116–9, 121–5, 142, 144–5, 157–9, 165, 196
Dolphin (toothed whale), 111

E

Easter Island, 16–17, 19–20, 103, 127, 134–42, 216
Ecuador, 41–58, 66, 79, 85, 133, 196
Eels, 204–5
Egypt, 16
Erik, see Hesselberg
Eskimos, 29–30
Explorers' Club, 28–32, 171
" Eye of Heaven ", 142
" Eye which looks toward Heaven ", 141

F

Fangahina, 171
Fatuhiva, 13–15, 164, 166–7, 170, 176
Fehmer, 34
Fenua Kon-Tiki, 209–10
Finmark, 21, 34–6
Fire-Tiki, 20
Flying fish, 11, 88–9, 99, 101, 105, 111–2, 119, 125, 166
Foreign liaison section of War Department, 36–7
Frank Cuevas, 149, 188, 203, 221
Fred Olsen Line, 26
Freuchen, Peter, 29, 31–2
Frigate birds, 125, 165

G

Galapagos Islands, 84–5, 90, 95, 123, 127, 133
Gempylus, 89–91, 210
Gerd Vold, 63, 71, 85
Germans invade Norway, 21
Germany, 16
Gestapo, 34
Giant bamboos, 100
Giant ray, 92
Glover, Admiral, 39
" Golden navel ", 141
Great Bear, 151
Great Rapa, 141
Greenland, 29, 31
Greenwich Village, 23
Guardian Rios, 73–7
Guayaquil, 43–4, 53, 57
Guayas, river, 57

H

Haakon, King, 150
Hal (Harold Kempel), 148–9, 188, 203–4, 221
Harpoon, 88, 95, 113–4, 116, 121, 142, 211
Haskin, Colonel, 29–30
Haugland, Knut, 12 ; war experiences, 34 ; agrees to join expedition, 35 ; arrives in New York, 62 ; at Lima, 64 ; 70, 83 ; experiments with wireless aerials, 84 ; 89 ; sights whale shark, 93 ; wireless under difficulties, 98 ; 120–1 ; has a swim with a shark, 143–4 ; 147 ; establishes wireless contacts, 149–50 ; rescues Watzinger, 160–2 ; 170, 178 ; goes ashore on Angatau, 179–82 ; 191, 194, 197, 200, 211 ; he and Watzinger treat sick boy with penicillin, 221–2 ; receives Polynesian name, 224
Haumata, 212, 221–2, 227
Hawaii, 17, 21, 103, 141, 152, 216
Head-hunters, 46–8
Heavy water sabotage, 34
Herman, see Watzinger
Hermit crabs, 197, 199
Hesselberg, Erik, 12 ; agrees to join expedition, 35 ; coming by sea from Oslo to Panama, 62 ; arrives at Lima, 64 ; 70–1, 75, 77–8, 81 ; takes position of raft, 84 ; harpoons whale shark, 95 ; occupations on board, 98 ; 112, 120 ; has idea of diving basket, 121 ; develops photographs, 150 ; 164, 169–71 ; navigates raft along Angatau reef, 173–5 ; 185, 190, 194, 199–201, 204 ; attacked by eels, 205 ; 210–1 ; becomes a hula dancer, 220–1 ; receives Polynesian name, 224
Hiti, 55
Hotu Matua, 20
Hula hula girls, 69, 184, 210, 217–21, 228
Humboldt Current, 68, 77, 80, 84–5, 100, 107, 117, 148, 221

I

Iguanas, 56
Illa-Tiki, 20
Ilo, 55
Incas, 18–20, 27, 84, 102, 134, 152, 163
India, 16
Indians (South American), 49–50, 104, 126, see also Incas
Indonesia, 18
Ipomœa batatas, 103

J

Japan, 16
Jelly-fish, 76

Johannes, 105, 146, 197
Jorge, 46–7
Jungle orchestra, 57

K

Kama, 55
Kane, 20, 55
Kayak, 29
Kempel, Harold, 148–9, 188, 203–4, 221
Kimi, 104
Kirkenes, 34
Knut, see Haugland
Kon-Tiki, 20–1, 64, 68, 71, 78, 80, 100,
  133–4, 136, 139–40, 142, 151, 153, 201,
  214
Kon-Tiki (raft), construction, 65–6 ;
  pessimism of foreign observers, 67–8,
  and Norwegian seamen, 68 ; trial trip
  in harbour, 70 ; christened, 71 ; towed
  out to sea, 75–7 ; performance in heavy
  sea, 79–84 ; logs' absorption of water,
  86 ; strain on ropes, 87 ; course
  changes, 87 ; daily life on raft, 97–8 ;
  tropical garden on board, 103–4 ; invaded by small crabs, 105–6 ; floating
  aquarium under raft, 121–2 ; comic
  appearance at sea, 129–30 ; masters
  heavy storm, 155–6 ; weaker in joints
  after storm, 162–4 ; stranding on
  Raroia reef, 192–3 ; brought into
  lagoon, 211 ; towed to Tahiti, 226–7 ;
  shipped on board Thor I, 228
Kon-Tiki Island, 209–10, 212–3, 226
Kongo, 55
Ku, 54–5
Kukara, 55
Kumara potato, 35 ; see sweet potato
Kura, 55

L

Lagenaria vulgaris, 103–4
Lakatunga, 49
Lamour, Dorothy, 69
Lewis, Colonel, 37–9
LI 2 B, 149, 204
Lie, Trygve, 42
Lima, 57–64, 68, 71, 73, 85, 201, 203
Little Rapa, 141
Liv, 13–15
" Long-Ears ", 139–41, 216
Lono, 216
Los Angeles, 148–9, 203, 221–2
Low (or Dangerous) Archipelago, 165
Lumsden, Colonel, 39

M

Machete knives, 64, 117, 187, 204–5
Malay race, 140, 152

Malaya, 16
Mangareva, 140, 216
Maoae, 225–6
Maroake, 224
Marquesas Islands, 12, 19, 29, 137–9, 141,
  151, 164–5
Mata-Kite-Rani, 141
Mata-Rani, 142
Maui, 216
Mauri, 55
Mayas, 152
Melanesia, 18, 152
Mexico, 133–4
Military Mission in Washington, British,
  39
Monoliths, 15 ; see Easter Island
Munthe af Morgenstierne, Wilhelm von,
  42
Munthe-Kaas, Colonel Otto, 36, 41
Murmansk, 21

N

National Geographical Society, 117
Naval Hydrographic Institute, 39
Naval War School (Peru) 188, 203
" Navel of the islands ", 141
" Navel, golden ", 141
New York, 12, 22–42, 62, 175
New Zealand, 17, 103
Nieto, Manuel, 58, 61, 66
Nordmark, 34
North-West Indians, 21
Norway, 16, 21, 149
Norwegian Ambassador (Embassy) in
  Washington, 42, 189
Norwegian Consul-General in Ecuador,
  48–9 ; in Peru, 59, 70
Norwegian Military Attaché in Washing-
  ton, 36, 41 ; assistant, 36
Norwegian Sailors' Home, 25–6, 28, 30, 32
Notodden, 149

O

Octopus, 117–9
Oslo, 34, 62, 150
Ossining, 26, 28
Ouia valley, 13
Oviedo, 104

P

Pae-pae, 209–10, 214–6, 218, 227–8
Palenque river, 51–2, 57, 79
Palms, see cocoanut
Panama, 62
Pani, 103
Papa, 55

Papeete, 227–8
Papeno valley, 228
Parrots, 56 ; Kon-Tiki parrot, 11–12, 73–4, 78, 146–9
Paul, 203
Penicillin, 212, 221–2
Pentagon building, 36–7
Peru, 12, 19–20, 25, 27–8, 31, 33, 35, 39, 41–2, 57–78, 80, 84, 100, 103–4, 117, 123, 133–42, 153, 165, 204, 214
Peruvian Air Minister, 60–1 ; Foreign Ministry, 59, 61 ; Minister of Marine, 58, 61, 66 ; Naval Attaché in Washington, 58 ; President, 42, 59–61, 71
Petrels, 104, 165
Phyto-plankton, 106
Pilot-fish, 93–5, 113, 115–7, 121–2, 157, 159, 196
Pitcairn Island, 19
Pizarro, 77
Plankton, 91, 106–8, 132
Pleiades, 153
Pole Star, 151
Polynesia, Polynesians, 13–14, 16–21, 23, 35, 54–5, 58, 71, 98, 102–4, 127, 131, 133–5, 138–9, 141, 151–3, 164–7, 170, 175–84, 201, 206–28
" Polynesia and America ", 23
Polynesian Society, 228
Porpoises, 88, 109
Potatoes, 35, 100, 103–4, 137
President of Peru, 42, 59–61, 71
Primus stove, 78, 99, 197
Puka-puka, 169–70, 172
Pura, 216

Q

Quartermaster-General's laboratory, 37–8
Quito, 45–9
Quivedo, 45–6, 48, 64, 196

R

Ra, 55
Raaby, Torstein, 11–12 ; war experiences, 34–5 ; agrees to join expedition, 35 ; arrives in New York, 62 ; sent by air to Lima, 63 ; 70–1, 77–8 ; experiments with wireless aerials, 84 ; fish in sleeping bag, 89–90 ; pursues sea turtle, 96 ; wireless under difficulties, 98 ; restricted to special provisions by way of experiment, 99 ; 108 ; adventures with dolphins, 111–2 ; 147 ; establishes wireless contacts, 148–9 ; 153–4, 158 ; sleeping bag goes overboard, 160–1 ; 170–1, 185 ; sends out wireless messages just before stranding, 188–9 ; 190, 193–4, 198, 200, 203 ; dances the hula,

219 ; 221 ; receives Polynesian name, 223–4
Radio Amateur League of America, 63
Rainbow belt, 140
Rangi, 55
Rani, 141
Rapa-iti, 141
Rapa-nui, 141
Raroia, 184–6, 189, 207–28
Rarotonga, 188–9, 200, 202–4
Rations, 38, 69, 98–9
Ray, giant, 92
Remora, 93, 114–5
Reveredo, General, 60–1
Rjukan, 34
Roggeween, 20
Rongo, 216
Rongo-rongo, 216
Rörholt, Björn, 36, 63
Rubber boat, 29 ; Kon-Tiki's dinghy, 77, 96, 98, 120, 129–31, 147–8, 160–1, 173–4, 179–80, 184–5, 188, 195
Russians in Norway, 34

S

Sailing Directions for Pacific Islands, 169 ; for South America, 123
Sailors' Home, Norwegian, 25–6, 28 30, 32
Samoa, 17, 19, 203, 228
Sardines, 87, 89
Scorpions, 53–4
Sea slugs, 195–6
Sea turtles, 96, 124
Sharks, 87–8, 93–5, 113–7, 121, 142–6, 148, 157–9, 165, 186, 196, 204–5 ; blue, 87–8, 114, 117, 205 ; brown, 114 ; whale, 93–5, 109, 116, 210, 216
Shark powder, 40
" Short-ears ", 139
Siberia, 32, 134
Skua, 125
Slugs, sea, 195–6
Snakes, 53
Snake mackerel, 89–91, 210
South Equatorial Current, 95, 100, 151, 166
South Sea Islands, 12, 35, 102–3, 123, 134–5, 138–9, 151, 214
Spaniards, 19, 70, 77, 79, 104, 127, 133
Squid (cuttlefish), 11, 91, 112, 117–20, 147–8, 205
Starfish, 165
Steering of raft on river, 56 ; of Kon-Tiki, 78–85, 98, 126–7, 156
Stone Age, 18, 21, 71
Sun-Tiki, 20, 214
Sweden, 35, 148
Swedish-Finnish Amazon expedition, 61
Sweet potato, 100, 103–4, 137
Swordfish, 124

T

Tahiti, 12, 139, 152, 178, 203 208–10, 213, 224–9
Takume, 184, 186, 208
Tamara, 224–7
Tane-Mataran, 224
Tangaroa, 20
Taranga, 55
Te-Pito-te-Henua, 141
Tefaunui, 224
Tei Tetua, 14–15, 164
Teka, 208–9, 212–7, 219, 221–3
Tepiuraiarii Teriifaatau, 208
Terai Mateata, 210, 214, 222, 228
Teriieroo, 228–9
Thor I, 228–9
Tiahuanaco, 71, 134
Tikaroa, 223
Tiki, 14–15, 17, 20, 55, 103, 139, 142, 164, 207, 214–6
Tirpitz, 35
Titicaca, Lake, 20, 100, 140
Tongatabu, 137
Topakino, 223
Torstein, see Raaby
Trade wind, 78–80, 98, 100, 166, 198
Tromsö, 34
Trondheim, 30
Trygve Lie, 42
Tuamotu group, 12, 28, 164–6, 169, 172, 186
Tunny, 88, 120, 122–3, 157–9
Tupac Yupanqui, 85, 133
Tupuhoe, 212–5, 217–20, 222–3, 227
Tupuhoe-Itetahua, 223
Turtles, sea, 96, 124

U

United Nations, 41–2
Uppsala University, 61
Urukehu, 19

V

Varoa, Tikaroa, 223
Viking ships, 21, 117

Vinces, 57
Virakocha, 20
Vold, Gerd, 63, 71, 85

W

War Department, American; foreign liaison section, 36–7; geographical research committee, 39
Washington, 36–42, 62–4, 98, 189
Water Street, 26
Water supply, 100–2, 159
Watzinger, Herman, 12; meets author in New York, helps to organise expedition in U.S. and flies with him to Ecuador, 30–57; waits for timber at Guayaquil, 57, 62; injured at Lima, 63–4; 69, 73, 78, 87; captures *Gempylus*, 89; pursues sea turtle, 96; technical chief on raft, 98; 120–1, 124, 149, 150; measures squalls with anemometer, 156–7; 158; falls overboard and is rescued by Haugland, 160–2; sights land, 168; 170–1, 173–4, 190, 192–4, 198, 201, 204; attacked by eels, 205; 211–2; dances the hula, 219; he and Haugland treat sick boy with penicillin, 221–2; receives Polynesian name, 223
Weather Bureau, U.S., 149
West 72nd Street, 28
Whales, 108–10, 117
Whale shark, 93–5, 109, 116, 211, 216
Wilhelm Ambjörg, 26–8
Wireless, 33–5, 70, 84, 98, 146, 148–50, 185, 188–9, 200–4, 210

Y

Yacht Club, Callao, 70

Z

Zarate, 77
Zoo-plankton, 106

GEORGE ALLEN & UNWIN LTD.
LONDON: 40 MUSEUM STREET, W.C.1
CAPE TOWN: 58–60 LONG STREET
TORONTO: 91 WELLINGTON STREET WEST
BOMBAY: 15 GRAHAM ROAD, BALLARD ESTATE
CALCUTTA: 17 CENTRAL AVENUE, P.O. DHARAMTALA
WELLINGTON, N.Z.: 8 KINGS CRESCENT, LOWER HUTT
SYDNEY, N.S.W.: BRADBURY HOUSE, 55 YORK STREET

ESKIMO DOCTOR

by AAGE GILBERG   Second Impression. Demy 8vo. 15s. net.

'Most vivid and delightful . . . illustrated by magnificent photographs.'
E. O. LORIMER in *John O'London's Weekly*.
'Unusually attractive.' *Country Life*. 'Absorbingly interesting.' *Tribune*. 'He
writes with a humorous grace., *Birmingham Post*.

RED INDIAN EXPERIENCES

by DECOST SMITH   Demy 8vo. 18s. net.

DeCost Smith led a colourful life. Born in 1864, he was familiar as a child with
the Iroquois Indians, and at the age of twenty he and his brother went to the
Western States to get acquainted with the less sophisticated Indians. For a great
part of his life he lived among the Indians.

Smith travelled widely and observed closely. We have therefore unusually
interesting accounts of the Indians. There is much, and authentic, adventure.
It is a remarkable, and exceptional, book, depicting a vanished and colourful
world—the wild west when it was still wild.

DRAGON FANGS

by CLAIRE and WILLIAM BAND   Demy 8vo. 18s. net.

For a dozen years Claire and William Band dwelt in the philosophical atmosphere of a college community in Peiping, romantic centre of ancient Chinese
culture. But when the war with Japan broke out they made a hairbreadth escape
into the desert mountains of the Border Region, living for two years an intensely strenuous life with patriotic Chinese guerillas and the poorest village
peasants.

Dragon Fangs tells of rivers forded in flood, of enemy patrols outwitted, of
night marches through blockade lines with guerilla regiments, of epidemics,
bath-houses, and soldiers' drama clubs, of communist generals, and the Oriental
gestapo: of medical doctors, literary pundits, student 'bandits', landlords,
peasants, soldiers, engineers. Marxist philosophers, and Taoist priests, all
amazingly united in action against a common foe.

UNCLIMBED NEW ZEALAND

by JOHN PASCOE   Second Edition. Small Royal 8vo. 21s. net.

"A well written record of many interesting expeditions into the High Alps
and lesser known ranges of New Zealand and a valuable addition to the litera-
ture of mountaineering. It should prove very useful to all contemplating a visit
to the mountains of New Zealand as it gives much useful information on the
conditions of travel both in the bush and on the high snows, together with notes

on equipment . . . and the organization of rescue parties in the event of accident. The bibliography is proof of the growth of interest in New Zealand mountaineering, whilst numerous excellently reproduced photographs convey a clear idea of the manifold and varied beauties of the New Zealand Alps which are unquestionably one of the loveliest ranges of mountains within the British Empire."—Frank Smythe.

"The author's descriptions of this uniquely beautiful country are very well done, and the climbing narratives, together with some fine photographs and maps, should be of exceptional interest to Alpinists . . . Discursive, amusing and full of history."—*Time and Tide.*

ICELAND YESTERDAY AND TODAY

by HORACE LEAF, F.R.G.S.   Illustrated. Demy 8vo. 15s. net.

Author of *Under the Southern Cross*

Bordering on the arctic circle, Iceland was for many centuries an almost forgotten country, developing in its own way a fascinating and romantic history. Its culture was often of the highest order, developed and maintained in the face of powerful impediments. In some respects it was in the forefront of political progress.

Iceland Yesterday and Today gives a favoured eye-witness's view of this country as it is today and shows its trend towards the future. It presents a brilliant picture of the many historic and picturesque beauty spots such as Thingvellir, Videy, Dettifoss and Gullfoss. It gives short accounts of the Constitution and of such vital matters as Making Fishing Smacks and Afforestation. Altogether it is a full and fascinating description of the haunting beauty and attractive people of "the greatest little country in the world."

WAS IT ALL CRICKET?

by DANIEL REESE   Demy 8vo. 21s. net.

Was it all Cricket? is an interesting story of the eventful life of a well-known New Zealander. It begins with a lad of fifteen being apprenticed to engineering, and a year later, as a cricketer, gaining prominence by performing the hat trick in his first important match. The recounting of the youth's experiences in the foundry and on the cricket field makes delightful reading. There are chapters on world-wide travel in British tramp steamers, and bright stories of life as a marine engineer. The author's cricket career, and his association with W. G. Grace and many other famous players, establish his claim to write on the world's cricket. The book ends with exciting experiences in shipping and sawmilling ventures in New Zealand.

GEORGE ALLEN AND UNWIN LTD.

books that matter